THE NATURE OF THE RELIGIOUS RIGHT

THE NATURE OF THE RELIGIOUS RIGHT

THE STRUGGLE BETWEEN CONSERVATIVE EVANGELICALS AND THE ENVIRONMENTAL MOVEMENT

NEALL W. POGUE

CORNELL UNIVERSITY PRESS

Ithaca and London

First published 2022 by Cornell University Press

Library of Congress Cataloging-in-Publication Data

Names: Pogue, Neall W., 1979– author.
Title: The nature of the religious right : the struggle between conservative evangelicals and the environmental movement / Neall W. Pogue.
Description: Ithaca [New York] : Cornell University Press, 2022. | Includes bibliographical references and index.
Identifiers: LCCN 2021034128 (print) | LCCN 2021034129 (ebook) | ISBN 9781501762000 (hardcover) | ISBN 9781501762024 (pdf) | ISBN 9781501762017 (epub)
Subjects: LCSH: Environmentalism—Religious aspects—Christianity. | Human ecology—Religious aspects—Christianity. | Environmental protection—Religious aspects—Christianity. | Environmental degradation—Religious aspects—Christianity. | Evangelicalism—Political aspects—United States. | Religious right—United States. | Christianity and politics—United States. | Christian conservatism—United States.
Classification: LCC BR115.N3 P64 2022 (print) | LCC BR115.N3 (ebook) | DDC 261.8/8—dc23
LC record available at https://lccn.loc.gov/2021034128
LC ebook record available at https://lccn.loc.gov/20210 34129

To conservative evangelicals and environmentalists

Contents

Acknowledgments

I would like to thank Mark Harvey for initially encouraging me to pursue and develop the topic for this book. Thomas Dunlap, Elizabeth Ellis, Katherine Carté, and Harold Livesay offered important suggestions that expanded the breadth of research and cultivated thematic material. Over the years, conference panel participation allowed for helpful feedback from individuals like Mark Stoll and led Cornell University Press to express an interest in my subject matter. Additionally, peers, family, and friends including Jeffery Crean, Claire Cruickshank, Martha Gregory, and Grant Harward read and reread drafts, which made the prose sharper, ideas more pronounced, and the conclusion a little more optimistic than it initially was.

Thanks also to the friendly staff at the numerous libraries and archives I visited over the years. My research especially benefited from the support of Taffey Hall and Bill Sumners at the Southern Baptist Historical Library & Archives and travel grants offered by Texas A&M University and the American Society for Environmental History.

Finally, thanks to my friends and family for their encouragement and support.

Abbreviations

BJU Press	Bob Jones University Press
CLC	Christian Life Commission
CT	*Christianity Today*
ECI	Evangelical Climate Initiative
EEN	Evangelical Environmental Network
ESA	Evangelicals for Social Action
ICR	Institute for Creation Research
NAE	National Association of Evangelicals
NRPE	National Religious Partnership for the Environment
SBC	Southern Baptist Convention
UEA	*United Evangelical Action*

THE NATURE OF THE RELIGIOUS RIGHT

Introduction

It is no coincidence that both Scott Pruitt, former President Donald Trump's first appointed head of the Environmental Protection Agency (EPA), and former Vice President Mike Pence are conservative evangelical Christians and opponents of the environmental movement, including solutions for human-caused climate change. Despite the existence of socially progressive evangelical groups such as the Evangelical Environmental Network (founded in 1993), the politically conservative evangelicals who make up the religious right have for years openly brandished anti-environmentalist views. The questions that religious and environmental historians, sociologists, and political scientists as well as the general public have yet to agree on are where do such views originate and have they always existed?

I first became fascinated with these questions as a graduate student concentrating in environmental history. While researching attacks against environmentalists waged by groups such as the Sagebrush Rebellion and the Wise Use Movement, I found little information regarding the relationship between the environment and the religious right. I was familiar with an anti-environmentalist formal statement released in 2000 titled "A Faith Community Commitment to the Environment and Our Children's Future," which was signed by religious right heavyweights Jerry Falwell and Patricia Combs, Pat Robertson's Christian Coalition president. This document made the classic conservative argument that a healthy economy trumps that of nature conservation. What was unclear,

economy > environment

however, is when this view originated. Was this the standard politically conservative evangelical view at Earth Day 1970? Why did Falwell help develop this statement as late as 2000? Falwell and Robertson were intensely involved with social issues since the mid-1970s. They could not have been oblivious to the environmental movement until 2000. When Robertson ran for the White House in 1988, what environmental position did he support? These questions, it seemed, did not have answers.

Initially, I approached my investigation with the impression that the stereotypically militant, stubborn, and intolerant conservative evangelicals likely rejected the environmental movement in 1970, just as they had virtually done with women's liberation, gay rights, and pro-choice issues. This supposition proved to be surprisingly incorrect. In 1971 for example, the National Association of Evangelicals (NAE) passed resolutions condemning homosexuality and abortion—two traditional religious right positions. That same year, the NAE pledged to protect the environment. Other period documents from this community beyond the NAE corroborated such nature-friendly sentiments. What happened between 1971 and 2000? Following a decade of research that expanded the investigation from 1967 to 2020, a clearer picture developed between politically conservative evangelicals and the environment proving the relationship to be much more complex than previously supposed.

In fact, conservative evangelicals nearly became active supporters of nature protection efforts not only in 1970, when Earth Day was first observed, but also twenty years later, in 1990, on its twentieth anniversary. Thus, *The Nature of the Religious Right* is a story of missed opportunities, especially at those two key moments, when segments of politically conservative evangelicals tried but failed to excite the whole community into action. Moreover, these two attempts were supported and fueled by underlying eco-friendly philosophies held by the conservative evangelical mainstream from the late 1960s to the early 1990s. In other words, during these years, conservative evangelicals did not support secular environmentalism, but at the same time they did not ignore or oppose environmental protection. Instead, they developed an eco-friendly theologically based philosophy, termed here as Christian environmental stewardship, which almost gave rise to action on two separate occasions. However, for a variety of reasons, in the early 1990s, the community shifted to strongly support anti-environmentalist views. It is the latter position that remains in place to the present day, despite quiet challenges by some who cannot justify abandoning the long-standing theological call to protect the earth.

Beyond examining conservative evangelical views on environmental protection, this book explores how the community utilized two different concepts of nature, largely throughout the 1970s, to help create the religious right movement. The first involves the dichotomy between what they considered to be "natural" versus "unnatural." This perspective was not a basis for understanding environmental protection; rather it was used to justify political causes such as their fight against abortion and gay rights. Activists for these issues, they argued, were trying to destroy God's intended order as created in the Garden of Eden. Legalizing abortion or gay marriage, they reasoned, signified an "artificial" or "unnatural" change that would undoubtedly lead to an imbalance of the natural order that God designed as described in the creation story of Genesis. In this way, conservative evangelicals employed perceptions of creation as designed by God to support their most cherished political positions.

The second way conservative evangelicals went beyond ideas regarding nature protection also took place during the 1970s, when they constructed a sense of nationalism by reimagining the United States' historical origin stories using romanticized conceptions of humanity's relationship with natural landscapes. These stories contributed to the development of a unique identity that provided a common culture, or a connective historical tissue, that bound together conservative evangelicals nationwide to ultimately lay the philosophical foundations for what became known from the late 1970s to the present as the religious right. Through such an approach, the community came to think of themselves as "real Americans" who earned the land and therefore legitimized their movement as a stark rejection of societal changes often led by the 1960s counterculture. Again, these two ways of utilizing concepts of the natural world were not environmental policies of the conservative evangelical community. These perspectives go beyond the origin story of the group's current anti-environmentalist position to exhibit previously unexplored ways they used understandings of humanity's relationship with the nonhuman natural world to shape their political movement.

This book matters to our national understanding of American politics and culture because it explains why and how the religious right's conception of the natural world contributed to the movement becoming an important political barrier against nature protection initiatives, including solutions to global warming. In this way, *The Nature of the Religious Right* encourages a general audience of voters, environmental advocates, and especially evangelicals of the religious right to understand the present by exploring the past. With a clearer understanding of the past, people from diverse political and social backgrounds might be able to find mutually agreeable solutions to environmental problems, which would ultimately benefit our national and global communities. As sociologist Elaine Howard Ecklund says of her studies of evangelicals, "If we use research to humble the attitudes we might have towards another group . . . we will be more likely to approach that group and ask the question, 'how can I collaborate in a way that benefits others?'" In this way, she hopes her work will break down stereotypes and thus allow for future co-operation between seemingly diametrically opposed groups. She wisely reminds the public, "We're not just talking about abstract ideologies, we're talking about real groups of people."[1] Indeed, in this current climate of intense political polarization, it may be easy to "other" those with whom we disagree, but perhaps by understanding the history of the religious right, we can gain a more nuanced perspective of its logic. Mike Pence may espouse anti-environmentalist rhetoric common among conservative evangelicals today, but as this book demonstrates, such views were not preordained. They evolved over time and although not prevalent, elements of their eco-friendly philosophies survive in the present day.

In addition to informing the general public, *The Nature of the Religious Right* challenges two fundamental ways that scholars traditionally understand the relationship between the religious right and environmental protection. This relationship is presently understood in the following two ways: The first suggests that politically conservative evangelicals developed anti-environmentalist views on the basis of their biblical or theological beliefs, which includes the view that the world would end soon (premillennialism) and/or that humanity should have "mastery over nature"; the latter perception stems mainly from an interpretation of Genesis 1:26–28, in which God commanded Adam and Eve to "subdue" the Earth and have "dominion" over all living things. The second is that the community opposed environmentalism not due to biblical interpretations but out of loyalty to conservative politics often connected with choosing a strong economy over the health of nature.[2] Both explanations undoubtedly have merit, but they are usually presented as reasons that always existed within the religious/political community, or that the issue was simply ignored until they decided upon environmental opposition.

Unlike the politically and theologically conservative evangelicals of today, other Christians who proved eco-friendly have traditionally received most of the attention from historians. For example, Mark Stoll's *Inherit the Holy Mountain* largely focuses on those from Calvinist and Presbyterian backgrounds who supported environmental efforts in the nineteenth and twentieth centuries and thereby helped set the foundations for the modern environmental movement. Other scholars have also recounted the journey socially progressive evangelicals took to embrace eco-friendly actions in the 1990s and 2000s.[3] The politically conservative evangelicals who today make up the religious right, however, have yet to receive a historical account regarding how they came to hold anti-environmentalist views, including a refusal to support climate change. This book fills that void.

To capture unfolding events and understandings of the natural world, *The Nature of the Religious Right* draws on conservative evangelicals' church sermons, television ministries, and published works disseminated to a national audience, as well as the leadership's private correspondences. Likewise, sources from the group's grassroots, including correspondences, polls, interviews, and reports from newspapers highlighting individual church activities as well as pastor sermons, are also analyzed. One of the most fascinating sources is k–12 educational material written by politically and theologically conservative evangelicals and consequently purchased by the growing number of independent Christian schools nationwide. These parent- and pastor-approved materials show how the community intended its worldview to inform the next generation of religious right supporters. They also demonstrate how the politically conservative evangelical community's attitudes toward the environment have changed over the past fifty years.

All these sources show that the community accepted and / or espoused eco-friendly values until the early 1990s. Educational books published by the quintessential politically and theologically conservative evangelical press known as A Beka Book (or Abeka since 2017), which operates in connection with Pensacola Christian College, stands as an example. In 1986, one chapter book for older elementary school students featured a story praising preservationist and Sierra Club cofounder, John Muir. The story, titled "Land that I Love," depicts a young John Muir begging his father not to cut down a particular very large oak tree. The story concluded, "As John's eyes followed the mighty trunk up, up to where the branches laced against the sky, his soul stirred with its splendor. And in his heart, the promise took root, never to be forgotten. This was his land—not by birth, but by love. He would fight all his life to preserve its richness for children yet unborn."[4] The accompanying illustration depicted Muir saving a tree from his axe-wielding father who wanted to cut it down. This story and / or similar sentiments were not reprinted in the next decade. Instead the same publisher released a high school science textbook in 1993 denying the reality of global warming accompanied by the poem "Roses are red, violets are blue, / They both grow better with more CO_2."[5] The reasons for this change in environmental views are found within the very pages of these texts and are furthermore supported by the wider conversation occurring among conservative evangelicals at the organizational and grassroots levels.

Another group of sources central to this story derive from two case studies involving the executive director of the Southern Baptist Convention's Christian Life Commission, Richard Land, and the NAE's vice president of governmental affairs, Robert Dugan.[6] Although Land and Dugan may be considered leaders at the organizational level, their journey to anti-environmentalism reflects the struggle experienced by the wider grassroots community as demonstrated in their discussions with peers, the organization's membership, and the information they chose to read. Like most other conservative evangelicals, they began the decade promoting or being open to widespread eco-friendly activity, but they ultimately abandoned and opposed it.

Indeed, this history does not portray the stereotypically militant and closed-minded conservative evangelical voting demographic as preordained opponents of environmental protection efforts. Instead, this book reveals that those in the religious right attempted to find a compassionate balance between humanity and the nonhuman natural world, but due to a variety of factors, they found themselves opponents of views they once, at least philosophically supported. In short, the present day animosity toward environmentalists held among those associated with the religious right evolved over time and is truly complex.

The Nature of the Religious Right begins just before the birth of the modern environmental movement on Earth Day 1970. This popular event brought the environmental issue into the conservative evangelical community while confirming the importance of the issue among a few of their intellectual elite who previously discussed the topic.[7] Initially, the community, including those who held politically conservative views, constructed an eco-friendly theologically based philosophy known as Christian environmental stewardship. Simultaneously, however, the secular environmental movement accused Christianity of perpetrating the ecological crisis. In answering such allegations, both politically liberal and conservative evangelicals were forced into a defensive posture and therefore lost the momentum toward possibly developing a solid position that produced pro-environmental activity. This dilemma, however, did not prompt conservative evangelicals who later became the religious right, to label themselves "anti-environmentalist." Instead, they continued in their acceptance of Christian environmental stewardship and furthermore connected to ideas of nature in alternate ways stemming from Christian Reconstructionism and dominion theology.

The primary way Reconstructionism and dominion theology will be used in this study is through its connection to politically conservative evangelical understandings of the natural world. This relationship is explained in chapter 2 by unpacking Reconstructionist ideas with dominion theology concerning the Genesis creation story in which God set up a hierarchical relationship with humanity and the rest of the natural world. According to the primary founder of Reconstruction, Rousas John Rushdoony, getting back to this original hierarchy would bring balance and harmony to all areas of life. *The Nature of the Religious Right* utilizes such an aspect of Reconstruction as it proved attractive to the founders of the religious right movement. They factored it into their arguments to challenge the counterculture-inspired social movements of the late 1960s, such as women's and gay rights, whose advocates they perceived as lobbying for the social acceptance of "unnatural" or "artificial" lifestyles. The differentiation between "unnatural" and "natural" justified, in the eyes of politically conservative evangelicals, their quest to socially and politically support God-ordained separate gender roles, traditional marriage, and fighting against abortion, the latter being a product of what they saw as destroying the ordained hierarchy by replacing God as creator with humanity's medical science. Therefore, politically conservative evangelicals believed that when humanity restored its God-ordained design or natural design, then all social ills would be remedied. It was these views, framed as "God's creation" versus "manmade artificial," that in part drove conservative evangelicals to form the religious right movement. Reconstruction's recipe for a better future in part conflicted with the group's accepted premillennialist prediction that the world would end soon and was therefore never accepted in its entirety. The religious right nevertheless, cherry-picked useful aspects of it to help fuel their social and political efforts.[8]

Reconstruction theology is additionally furthered in chapter 3 and 4 by demonstrating that the idea of nature played other roles in the quest to save humanity's proper place in God's hierarchical creation, such as through the religious community's construction of Christian nationalism; another platform from which they launched the religious right movement. During the 1970s, they built a unique history of the United States by making their faith a primary reason for the success of the country. The idea of humanity as a creation of God and the idea of earth's wilderness as the realm where humans were meant to dominate, but not abuse, both had important roles. Politically conservative evangelicals, for instance, depicted the "unconquered" forests of North America as healthy obstacles, which encouraged "real Americans" of the past to conform to their God-ordained gender-specific family norms. Moreover, it was during this struggle with the wilderness that politically conservative evangelicals believed their religious ancestors gained ownership of the land that became the United States. Thus, in this understanding of humanity's relationship with the landscape, politically conservative evangelicals learned to think of themselves as those who set the foundations for the United States. This narrative was commonly taught in the ever-growing number of Christian and homeschools throughout America. Accompanying and in harmony with these views until 1989, Christian school publishers supported eco-friendly messages of Christian environmental stewardship that demanded respect for God's earth. During these decades, their eco-friendly views did not clash to any great degree with the group's long-held love for free enterprise.[9]

Anti-environmentalism, in short, did not become an accepted standard and mainstream theological or political position of the religious right during the 1970s or the 1980s. It was present, but remained the exception, rather than a leading position among politically conservative evangelicals.[10]

In contrast to previous decades, the 1990s, as demonstrated in chapter 5 and 6, saw the attempt by segments of the conservative evangelical religious right to turn past eco-friendly philosophies into social action. Secular conservatives, however, crushed the effort with the help of an increasing number of conservative evangelical allies. Among other examples, these chapters particularly focus on the experiences of Richard Land and Robert Dugan. Due to a variety of factors, both Dugan and Land evolved from holding or leaning toward eco-friendly sentiments to supporting a strong anti-environmentalist position.

Chapter 7 analyzes the struggle's aftermath by exploring the newly adopted anti-environmentalist views of Land, Dugan, and others in the wider community. This chapter also shines a light on the impact of the progressive Evangelical Environmental Network (EEN) that helped spur the publication of the religious right's first official anti-environmentalist documents published in 2000. Although these statements represent the accepted and currently held conservative evangelical anti-environmentalist position, the EEN and others continued in their quest for Christian environmental stewardship, which has never disappeared and remains quietly active to this day.

Overall, the adoption of anti-environmentalism was achieved only after a lengthy struggle between eco-friendly and anti-environmentalist advocates within the politically conservative evangelical community. In short, present-day religious right opposition to environmental protection policies is the product of a complicated history that took place over a period of years. Unlike those with an entrenched and unwavering position on abortion, the people associated with the religious right did not come to open antipathy toward environmental protection efforts until the early 1990s.[11]

Terminology: Defining the Religious Right

As Michael McVicar notes in his biography of Rousas John Rushdoony, putting labels on individuals and religious communities can be tricky and may lead to alienating readers who through academic training or personal experiences disagree with the author regarding what category an individual or group fits in. Properly defining theological beliefs and the political identity of those in the religious right is indeed important.

To understand the religious beliefs, this book will use same lens as Brian McCammack, who cites religious scholars Mark Noll and David Bebbington in his article "Hot Damned America: Evangelicalism and the Climate Change Policy Debate." McCammack writes that American evangelicals, generally speaking, share three key theological elements. The first is "conversionism (an emphasis on the 'new birth' as a life-changing religious experience). Second is Biblicism (a reliance on the Bible as the ultimate religious authority), and third is crucicentrism (a focus on Christ's redeeming work on the cross.)"[12] Perhaps the most important of these three key factors is that evangelicals interpret the Bible as the inerrant and literal word of God. For example, they believe that God literally created the earth as described in the book of Genesis. In this way, it is common for conservative evangelicals to reject scientific understanding of evolution and to take the Bible as truthful in every way: scientifically, morally, and as historical fact. Thus, they are different from "liberal" or "moderate" evangelicals, who may understand the Bible in a more figurative spirit and not take the Bible as factual in every way. Furthermore, understanding the Bible as the inerrant word of God, as stated by McCammack, may categorize evangelicals as theologically conservative, but this group can further be split into those who are socially liberal and conservative. It is the social or rather politically conservative evangelicals who will be at the center of this book.

Within the theologically conservative community are fundamentalists. Fundamentalists throughout the twentieth century are traditionally understood as separatists. Like others in the wider conservative evangelical community, they believe in the inerrant Bible but are not comfortable working alongside others who may not share their strict theological interpretations. This group, however, became involved in "secular" affairs, particularly through the religious right movement beginning in the late 1970s and will therefore in addition to other politically like-minded evangelicals be simply labeled "conservative evangelicals." This name should be similarly understood to what Michael McVicar terms "Neoevangelical" as understood by Harold John Ockenga, Westminster Theological Seminary graduate, first president of the National Association of Evangelicals, and cofounder of the Fuller Theological Seminary. It is Ockenga who noted that "neoevangelicalism" is a rejection of fundamentalist separatism "and [a] summons to social involvement."[13]

It is precisely this call to social involvement that led conservative evangelicals as a whole to create the religious right, which should be understood as a virtually all-white evangelical social and political movement. The foundations of the community date back to the post–World War II period, but it was the objectives of late 1960s counterculture that consolidated the religious right into existence. In reaction to the counterculture movements, during the 1970s conservative evangelicals discussed what they stood for, which over the decades have become known as pro-family (including but not limited to heterosexual married couples) and pro-life (life deserving protection begins at conception).

Up to the present, the religious right movement remains organized and partly energized through a web of communication networks driven by a number of hubs or epicenters located largely in the American South. These hubs include think tanks, private advocacy groups, megachurches, colleges or universities, and national church organizations.[14] Perhaps the best-known hub is the movement's virtual headquarters in Lynchburg, Virginia, which consists of megachurch Thomas Road Baptist Church, a k–12 private school, Liberty University, and the now defunct political organization known as the Moral Majority. Through these institutions, their leader and pastor, the late Jerry Falwell, reached conservative evangelicals both regionally and nationally. In addition to employing a variety of media such as television, fax machines, email and websites, Falwell utilized the effective strategy of direct mail campaigns to raise millions of dollars and inform sympathizers regarding social and political issues, which all contributed to the movement's vitality and growth. Recipients could buy into the movement's philosophies and were expected to arm themselves by registering to vote in the hopes of attaining certain goals via the ballot box. Other key epicenters throughout the country continue to function similarly to Falwell's organization; these include televangelist's Pat Robertson's Christian Broadcasting Network and Regent University in Virginia Beach; Coral Ridge Ministries in Ft. Lauderdale, Florida; the National Association of Evangelicals in Washington, DC; the Southern Baptist Convention in Nashville, Tennessee; Pensacola Christian College (connected with A Beka Book educational material) in Pensacola, Florida, and Bob Jones University and its press located in Greenville, North Carolina; and the Chicago-based magazines *Christianity Today* and *Moody Monthly* as well as the Philadelphia-based *Eternity* (the two latter magazines are no longer in publication). From the 1970s to the present day, these hubs participated in a continuing conversation with each other as well as with millions of conservative evangelicals nationwide regarding social, political and religious issues. Thus, the religious right does not have a specific "leader" who conducts the movement. Instead consensus among participants is found via discussion.

The sources utilized in this book reflect the nationwide discussion to understand the mood and interest of the community's evolving and nuanced relationship with nonhuman nature as something that may or may not hold value as a product of God, and furthermore, the way they think of themselves and the world and their relationship to it.

The Historical Background and Importance of the Religious Right Movement

The religious right and the environmental movement did not both originate during the 1970s by chance. Each should be understood contextually as products of the 1960s counterculture backdrop that included a continuation of the civil rights movement, anti-Vietnam protests, women's rights, and the gay rights movement. The impact of these wider movements cannot be overstated and will therefore be briefly summarized to frame the emergence of environmentalism and the religious right. Indeed, the religious right's cofounder, Jerry Falwell, once reflected on the period, saying that "America almost went to Hell during the 60's and 70's. We call those two decades the dark ages of the 20th century. Why? Not because of liberals and not because of pornographers and abortionists or jurists or legislators but because of the deafening silence of the pulpits in America."[15] This statement did not mean the counterculture progressive movements were blameless. Indeed, Falwell found their ideologies and goals abhorrently evil. But instead of simply focusing on the problems, Falwell offered a solution by accusing his own community for sleeping while the wolves attacked the fold. Thus, his countermovement, officially organized in 1979 under the name the "Moral Majority," would "save America."

The social changes that led to the religious right movement emerged in part from the civil rights movement, which began in the mid-1950s. It represented one of the first major philosophical challenges to white social and political hegemony. Until then, many whites presumed that African-Americans could only be servants or low-wage laborers who lived in substandard housing and received little support from social services including education and health care. Mississippi civil rights leader Amzie Moore once reflected on the preexisting philosophies that undergirded these social norms. He stated, "Listen, for a long time, I had the idea that the man with white skin was superior, because it appeared to me that he had everything, and I figured that if God would justify the white man having everything, that God put him in the position to be the best."[16] These ideas were challenged, however, in post-World War II America, due in part to African-Americans fighting and dying in the war effort to keep Americans free. The blinding hypocrisy of returning to a segregated nation that fought precisely for opposite ideologies helped ignite the Civil Rights Movement, which led to the Supreme Court decision of *Brown v. Board of Education* in 1954, along with countless non-violent demonstrations led by Dr. Martin Luther King Jr. These events were publicized to Americans through the mediums of radio, print, and television, powerfully portraying the unjust nature of white hegemony. Many whites, including conservative evangelicals, found this challenge to the status quo uncomfortable to say the least, and this feeling increased as the quest to overturn social inequalities intensified throughout the 1960s and into the 1970s.

In 1967, the CBS television network ran a documentary awkwardly titled *The Homosexuals*. One segment featured a bewildered man watching demonstrators with signs that read "QUARTER MILLION HOMOSEXUAL FEDERAL EMPLOYEES PROTEST CIVIL SERVICE COMMISSION POLICY" and "REVISE INSULTING MILITARY REGULATIONS ON HOMOSEXUALS." The onlooker stammered into the camera "I'm a country boy I guess, because I couldn't believe this. I mean I didn't know this was a problem over here or at least I didn't think anybody would have a sign out about it."[17] Indeed, vocally promoting gay rights challenged social norms. The topic was so controversial that companies did not want to associate with it in any way, and none stepped forward to sponsor the documentary. Several years later however, gay rights expanded into a national movement when a riot broke out in response to police raiding a gay bar in Greenwich Village in New York City. Those present recognized the arrests as a consequence of systemic social inequality and gained support to challenge such views from across the country. As Eric Marcus writes in *Making Gay History*, "By the early 1970s, the number of gay and lesbian organizations soared to nearly four hundred, ranging from politically oriented groups with names like Gay Liberation Front, to chapters of the predominantly gay and lesbian Metropolitan Community Church."[18] Marcus specifically pinpointed college campuses as places where these organizations often found homes. If educational institutions refused to recognize them, lawsuits were filed. The gay rights movement gradually gained steam, and in 1979 the Jimmy Carter administration invited representatives from the gay community to participate in the White House Conference on Families.

The gay rights movement, although visible, was not as prominent as the Vietnam War protests of the 1960s and 1970s, in which thousands of young Americans were mobilized into political action. Antiwar sentiment went beyond public demonstrations and into popular culture as reflected by the financial success of a number of antiwar and pacifist songs, including Barry McGuire's "The Eve of Destruction," which went to number one on the Hot Billboard Charts. The lyrics, sung in McGuire's raspy voice, highlighted the hypocrisy of politicians sending others off to war who could not vote:

> The Eastern world it is explodin'
> Violence flarin', bullets loadin'
> You're old enough to kill but not for votin'
> You don't believe in war but what's that gun you're totin'?[19]

Indeed, these were not sentiments listened to by a few people. Young Americans challenging apparent inequalities became the hallmark of the late 1960s and early 1970s period.

The first student teach-ins protesting the war in Vietnam began at the University of Michigan in March of 1965 and the cause was subsequently amplified by a more organized effort led by Students for a Democratic Society (SDS), who met in Washington, DC, and were supported by 20,000 protestors. By 1968 the need for social justice along with calls to end the conflict in Vietnam reached a climax, when students seized campus buildings at Columbia University, which inspired further demonstrations at colleges across the nation. The media covered former soldiers publicly throwing away their medals in protest against the war, while draft dodgers left the country, and young men burned Selective Service cards. Not only were young people demonstrating against the war, but also the inequalities of the draft itself. Young men with financial means, for instance, avoided the draft by attending college, but Selective Service officials tried rectifying the disparity in 1969 when numbers attached to one's birthdate were drawn via lottery on national television. This new draft lottery targeted all young men of military age, regardless of their status in life. High lottery numbers drawn received deferments whereas low numbers were to be drafted first. On December 1, 1969, Americans watched strangers decide their fate on live television as officials carried out the lottery. At the University of Massachusetts, Amherst, for example, anxious student-residents of Cance Hall crammed into a dorm room to watch the results. Upon seeing their birthdate drawn, some sat stunned and silent while several cried. For days afterward on campus, students asked each other, "What's your number?"[20]

As Vietnam protesting continued, women recognized and confronted gender inequality within their own social activist groups. In response, they fueled a movement already gaining momentum for women's rights. Developed in 1960, the birth control pill offered women greater control over their bodies and the 1963 book *The Feminine Mystique* by Betty Friedan attacked the traditional and expected position of women in society as caretakers of the family and home. Women needed to find out who they are, Friedan wrote, and should have the right to explore other opportunities beyond that of homemaker. The 1964 Civil Rights Act outlawed gender discrimination, and later feminists led by Ti-Grace Atkinson pushed for more radical changes. The women's movement claimed other victories such as the Supreme Court decision of *Roe v. Wade* in 1973 and later the near realization of the Equal Rights Amendment.

Coinciding with these social movements grew another cause that sought to protect the earth and all of its creatures. In 1962 biologist Rachel Carson published *Silent Spring,* and the conclusions sent shockwaves throughout the United States. She warned that the pesticide chemical DDT was not the miracle product it was thought to be. It killed birds that consumed DDT-ridden pests, as well as reducing their ability to procreate because the compound compromised the integrity of eggshells. In several Wisconsin communities, for example, biologists found DDT responsible for a 30 to 90 percent reduction in total breeding-bird populations.[21] After the book's release, chemical companies spent hundreds of thousands of dollars trying to discredit Carson. However, experts and the public increasingly became convinced of her arguments after noticing declining bird populations and, in connection to water pollution, witnessed massive fish kills. In 1969, the media furthered environmental awareness by displaying alarming images of Cleveland's Cuyahoga River, which was so polluted that it caught fire. The same year Americans read about and witnessed television reports of California's Santa Barbara oil spill. It seemed that the environment was dying, and nothing was being done. To end this ecological crisis, the following year, college students organized to form the first Earth Day observance on April 22, 1970. Teach-ins were held across the United States, Fifth Avenue in New York City was shut down, and Congress recessed. Twenty million people participated in Earth Day activities, propelling a nationwide movement to protect nature. Directly in response to popular demand for action, Republican President Richard Nixon established the Environmental Protection Agency and signed into law a number of environmental regulations including the Clean Air and Water Act.

Unlike other movements of the late 1960s, calls to protect the environment enjoyed massive support among different demographics throughout the U.S., including conservative evangelicals. Even before Earth Day 1970, the community was quietly developing theologically-based eco-friendly philosophies, but these efforts were somewhat eclipsed in contrast to their vehement reactions to other social changes proposed by the counterculture. Starting in the 1970s Falwell and others shifted from speaking about largely spiritual matters to directing a political movement later known as the religious right. Other organizers included charismatic televangelist Pat Robertson, think-tank organizer Paul Weyrich, popular theologian and writer Francis A. Schaeffer, the NAE's Robert Dugan, and Harold Lindsell, the head editor of *Christianity Today.* In his autobiography, Falwell specifically credited the Supreme Court's decision in *Roe v. Wade* as the defining moment when he realized that other Bible-believing Christians must get involved in politics. According to the book, he met with his family and told them what the Court's decision meant. His family agreed and Falwell's sermons increasingly incorporated themes regarding current events tied in with morality and politics.[22]

Beyond *Roe v. Wade*, Falwell and fellow conservative evangelicals expressed anger about a variety of other contemporary issues stemming from a rapidly changing culture. Almost anything new could draw their ire: men sporting long hair, the drug culture, rock music, gay culture, free love, or women trying to find acceptance in the work place. These issues, combined with preexisting vitriol toward the early 1960s Supreme Court decisions that banned prayer and scripture reading in public schools, helped motivate the conservative evangelical community to expand the number of k–12 Christian schools and to establish higher education institutions. In 1971, Falwell founded Lynchburg Baptist College, which later became Liberty College and then Liberty University. Three years later Pensacola Christian College opened its doors and Pat Robertson founded the Christian Broadcasting Network University (later Regent University) in 1977. The new institutions did more than just provide students with a "safe" learning environment devoid of what evangelicals considered to be cultural dangers promoted by the counterculture. The schools also functioned as platforms to develop the politically potent religious right movement. Liberty University, for example, became a destination for politicians to seek votes and for other Christian and secular conservative notables to share their faith. During the span of one month in 1983, Liberty College hosted Vice President George H. W. Bush, NASA astronaut Jack Lousma, and Secretary of the Interior James Watt.[23]

Additionally, those behind Pensacola Christian College and the much older fundamentalist Bob Jones University realized the k–12 Christian and home-schools needed tailored education materials and in response founded lucrative publishing companies. Their publications were designed specifically to give Christian students information that their parents endorsed. Students could now be taught that communism, evolution, drugs, premarital sex, and liberal values were not only anti-Christian but un-American. These educational materials explained in depth the fundamental elements that would later make up the religious right movement otherwise discussed by pastors such as Falwell in general terms during Sunday morning services or at his patriotic and politically inspired "I Love America" musical programs held nationwide. In a way, this educational material served as a detailed and evolving Christian American manifesto that prepared the next generation of conservative evangelicals to fight for their causes here on earth.

The Moral Majority, cofounded by Falwell in 1979, acted as the first official representative of the religious right, which burst on the national political landscape in 1980 by taking credit for Republican Ronald Reagan's upset of incumbent Democrat Jimmy Carter. In response, the media published numerous articles about the movement, while political scientists debated the organization's effectiveness. It was not until the congressional election of 1994, however, that experts finally agreed that the religious right actually affected election results in the political world. Researchers found that 75 percent of evangelicals voted Republican in 1994 and that they were likely to cite what was and continues to be the religious right's hallmark issues of family values (47 percent) or abortion (29 percent) as their most important concerns.[24]

Due in part to strong religious right political currents in today's conservative evangelical churches, as reported in Mathew J. Wilson's *From Pews to Polling Places*, many congregants say that it is impossible for any of them to be Democrats.[25] It is precisely the latter sentiment that helps clarify that conservative political leanings are ingrained in the social and religious fabric of the conservative evangelical community. This statement does not mean that all conservative evangelicals are "card-carrying" religious right members. No such thing exists. The religious right is a movement, not a club of registered members and therefore identifying who is part of the movement and who is not will be another aspect of this book that may be troublesome for some readers. Nevertheless, it is conservative evangelicals who make up the movement and vote en masse for common social issues. Thus, for the purposes of clarity, those who support classic pro-family and pro-life positions are associated with the religious right in this book.

Prior to acknowledging statistics from the 2016 presidential election, it may have been somewhat easy to dismiss the religious right as simply the radical fringe. The 81 percent of conservative evangelicals who voted for the GOP ticket, however, is a powerful reminder that this group was and is affecting elections on a national scale. Presidential candidates are aware of this fact and actively court their votes. The higher education institutions operated by self-proclaimed fundamentalists are common speaking destinations for Republican candidates today. George W. Bush, for example, delivered a speech at Bob Jones University in 2000, and Mitt Romney spoke at Liberty University in 2012. Moreover, the evangelical vote has been credited with destroying candidate John McCain's promising campaign to become the Republican nominee in 2000 after he made disparaging remarks about the need to pander to Christian voters.[26] George W. Bush, on the other hand, brandished his born-again identity and gained the endorsement from the religious right, which had grown in political importance and effectiveness throughout the 1990s.

After Bush secured the White House in 2000, his campaign manager, Karl Rove, observed that the Republican Party had captured 14 million evangelical votes and planned to garner more in the next election.[27] More recently, GOP candidate Ted Cruz launched his 2016 presidential campaign at Liberty University and the school also secured visits from candidates Jeb Bush and Donald

Trump. After winning the presidency, Trump returned to address Liberty University students and reportedly offered the school's chancellor, Jerry Falwell Jr., an invitation to lead an official education task force.[28] Perhaps most importantly, after the 2016 election, the Pew Research Center reported that 81 percent of white, born-again/evangelical Christians (the demographic known as the "evangelical vote" or religious right) voted for Trump. Polls for 2020 largely reflected similar results.[29] These numbers surpass or equal the percentage who claimed they voted for fellow Christian George W. Bush in 2004.[30] This finding strongly implies that the religious right movement continues to significantly affect the national political landscape.

The conservative evangelical community is politically effective because its members are a cohesive, passionate demographic dedicated to bringing their vision of a better world into reality. Robert Putnam alludes to their ceaseless efforts in his seminal book *Bowling Alone: The Collapse and Revival of American Community*. He writes that since the 1960s and 1970s, participation in American religious communities fell nationwide by between 25 to 50 percent.[31] Evangelical membership, on the other hand, grew during the same time period by one third.[32] This group, he states, is also three to five times more likely to be active in civic and political life, and as Putnam further observes, "Religious conservatives have created the largest, best-organized grassroots social movement of the last quarter century."[33] Studies by other scholars also found that conservative evangelicals, are the most devout among Christians in the United States.[34] Sociologist James Davison Hunter explains throughout *The Culture Wars: The Struggle to Define America* how this politically motivated religious community continuously fights a very real culture war in today's world.

The Nature of the Religious Right analyzes the frequently misunderstood and politically potent religious right community in the United States and particularly its views on nature and the environment. Although well-known religious scholars such as George Marsden have a point when they say that conservative evangelicals are in some sense "militant reactionaries," at least with regard to the environment, they do not fit easily into such a clear-cut package. Indeed, while the religious right responded with animosity toward most progressive counterculture movements, the call to protect nature avoided such a fate—at least for roughly twenty years.

Presently, scientists and politicians repeatedly tell the American people that the environmental problem of global warming is the most important issue of our time. Thus, understanding the roots of the religious Right's opposition should be considered vital to finding mutually beneficial avenues into the future.

CHAPTER 1

Conservative Evangelicals Respond to the Founding of Earth Day

In post–World War II America, economic stability along with technological and scientific progress made it easier for humanity to feel it now possessed unprecedented tools to conquer and control nature. Advertisements praised American capitalism by showcasing vast assortments of commodities available at newly built shopping malls and grocery stores. For the inundated housewife, no-fuss frozen TV dinners were ready to eat after a quick trip to the oven. Beyond the kitchen, travelers enjoyed using jet-propelled airplanes to reach far-away destinations. Americans also looked forward to a future of plenty with the aid of miracle insecticides that promised larger crop yields. It seemed the "howling wilderness" that once daunted the Pilgrims and early pioneers was a thing of the past.

Rachel Carson's 1962 book *Silent Spring* soon put the brakes on mankind's notion of unfettered rule. Apparently, there were side effects to all this wonderful "progress," and people began wondering just what gave Americans the hubris to believe they could reshape nature for human convenience without consequences. Then, in 1967, Lynn White Jr., a medieval historian, neatly explained the root cause of environmental degradation in his article "The Historical Roots of Our Ecologic Crisis." White plainly blamed environmental destruction on Christian philosophies pertaining to the God-ordained human relationship to the natural world. White argued that Christianity supported and promulgated a Christian hierarchical view of mankind that separated humans from nature and justified human dominion over it. He employed numerous examples to back up this conclusion, including the Bible's Genesis creation story in which God gave man the right to name the animals, which symbolically made humanity superior. White continued in this vein of thought, asserting that Christians think they were made in God's image, and thus are "gods" over the created order, which was intended to serve them. He claimed that monotheistic Christianity also conflicted strongly with nature-friendly traditional European pagan beliefs in which each tree and body of water should be respected and revered since each held spirits. As Christians took it upon themselves to cut down trees and make nature work for humanity, in the process they destroyed the earth and paganism.[1] White believed that although modern America might be in a post-Christian era, society continued to hold this Judeo-Christian mindset. The article, which first appeared in *Science* magazine, was reproduced in other publications, including those of various Christian denominations, which issued answers to White's accusations.

One of the most noteworthy individuals to respond to White's article was Francis A. Schaeffer, a trusted conservative evangelical intellectual.[2] During his early career, Schaeffer worked with fundamentalist and political radical Carl McIntire, but the two parted ways in the 1950s and Schaeffer moved with his family to the mountains of Switzerland. There, he founded an institution called L'Abri (the shelter) in which visitors could participate in a welcoming atmosphere dedicated to an intellectual exchange of all topics connected with faith, including how it is applied to everyday life, and, most importantly to Schaeffer, how the answers to life are found only through Christianity. Building on the intellectual conversations at L'Abri, Schaeffer began lecturing on various issues, publishing books and producing film documentaries that were well received among the American Christian community.

Schaeffer is perhaps best known for two film documentaries he produced in the late 1970s, in which he articulated philosophies used by the religious right movement. Although Schaeffer was not as heavily involved in politics ten years earlier, his development of Christian environmental stewardship between 1968 and 1970 became the accepted perspective used by fellow conservative evangelicals as the "right way" or "proper way" that humans should relate with the nonhuman world. Thus, Schaeffer's environmental views served as the standard environmental position among conservative evangelicals associated with and within the religious right for roughly two decades. In early 1990s, for example, political and theological conservative Richard Land, of the Southern Baptist Convention's (SBC) Christian Life Commission, specifically and repeatedly utilized Schaeffer's environmental views to encourage peers and SBC members to incorporate environmental protection activities into their everyday lives.

In response to White's accusation that the Christian worldview is responsible for the ecological crisis, Francis Schaeffer constructed a conservative evangelical environmental position using foundational ideas explored in two books he published in 1968: *The God Who Is There* and *Escape from Reason*. Both volumes included an in-depth account of humanity's proper relationship to God. He explained that everything, including mankind and nature, from the universe down to the soil, was connected and that only God as the creator was autonomous. At the same time, because humans were made in the image of God, they were not only part of the physical world but also of the supernatural. Therefore, humanity shared an important relationship with God as well as creation. He underscored the understanding that people must accept their place within this hierarchy and respect it. If people met this requirement, he argued, life would have meaning because humans were designed by God to live within this framework. Schaeffer repeatedly brought this concept up throughout the rest of his career, weaving the message into his lectures and books, sometimes reminding audiences that they needed to read his other publications to truly understand and grasp the deep knowledge he offered. His other late-1960s book, *Death in the City*, also reiterated the God-human relationship and by 1976 all three volumes combined had sold nearly a half million copies.[3]

To spread his understanding of Christian environmental stewardship, Schaeffer took to the lecture circuit. While addressing an audience in St. Louis in 1968, he explained that although humanity may be a higher creation of God, people are also a part of the natural world. Mankind, he said, was not "autonomous" or absolute ruler of the earth; only God held such a high position. "Isn't it true," Schaeffer asked, "that all too often we act as through we are sovereign towards the tree? We're not sovereign over the tree. . . . Only God is sovereign over the tree. All I am given is that I am made in God's image. But I'm not king of the world. This must be the thing to be understood."[4] Schaeffer continued in this vein, saying that nature has value simply because it was created by God. He wrote, "I hike through the mountains around my home and often I go to places nobody goes. I go up there and see some of the most beautiful flowers one could ever see. They are tremendous, I love it. . . . I know, from a human viewpoint that if I did not pass that way, no human being would ever see that flower. . . . But of course, a Christian knows that somebody else sees it; God sees it."[5] Thus, Schaeffer reasoned that nature was not intended simply for humanity's benefit. Instead, nature held value because it was created and enjoyed by God regardless of humanity's existence. Overall, Schaeffer argued that if God was the creator and God made both humanity and nonhuman nature, then humanity must value nature as a fellow creation of

God. It was this fundamental philosophy that Schaeffer offered to the conservative evangelical community in the late 1960s.

While lecturing in 1968, Schaeffer speculated that maybe in fifty years the need to protect the planet would become "one of the central battle grounds," and he hoped Christians would be those on the frontlines.[6] His prediction came true just two years later when the first Earth Day observance ushered in the modern environmental movement. The development likely pleased Schaeffer because his lectures on ecology had just been turned into a book titled *Pollution and the Death of Man: The Christian View of Ecology.*

As in his lectures, so in the pages of this short book, Schaeffer laid the foundations for "Christian environmental stewardship." Observing again that humanity is a part of the created order while being separate from it, he reasoned that humanity was made in God's image and therefore existed on a higher plane with supernatural beings, while at the same time people also existed on an equal plane with the rest of creation. Therefore, he argued, people should not treat nature as an impersonal resource, but should recognize that there exists a connection between humanity to nonhuman nature. He wrote, "Psychologically I ought to 'feel' a relationship to the tree as my fellow creature. . . . We should realize, and train people in our churches to realize, that on the side of creation and on the side of God's infinity and our finiteness-we really *are* one with the tree!"(emphasis in original)[7] Additionally, according to Schaeffer, people were not the only thing that mattered on earth. Humanity was undoubtedly important and he would say that people came first because they were God's crowning achievement, but in no way was Schaeffer paying lip service to environmental protection only to later focus on the larger need to sacrifice nature to enjoy a strong economy. The singular goal of this book was changing the way Christians understood humanity's relationship with the natural world, and Schaeffer did this by asking them to take a step back from an anthropocentric cosmic view and realize that God's creation mattered as well. Within this argument, he specifically addressed the debate that pitted free enterprise against caring for nature.

Schaeffer was a capitalist, but not one who sided with profit at all costs. In *Pollution and Death of Man*, he asked readers to factor in the health of the environment when making economic decisions. Indeed, later in the 1970s, when Schaeffer became a bigger name in the evangelical world, he relied on wealthy donors to help finance films such as *How Should We Then Live*. Still, in the case of his eco-friendly views in 1970, he did not believe in unfettered free enterprise. Rather, he bemoaned the dark side of humanity's love of money. He wrote, "Why does strip-mining turn the world into an absolute desert? Why is the 'Black Country' in England's Midlands black? What has brought about this ugly destruction of the environment? There is only one reason: Man's greed."[8] Schaeffer did not denounce capitalism; instead, he promoted a delicate balance between laissez-faire free enterprise and the value of the environment. Schaeffer described his approach through an analogy of a business owner and a consumer: "I am to treat the man I deal with in business *as myself*. I am to 'love' him as my neighbor, and as myself. It is perfectly right that I should have some profit, but I must not get it by treating him (or exploiting him) as a consumer object."[9] In short, he demanded that a Christian capitalist should not maximize profit by sacrificing the value of the created order. "He [a Christian] has a limiting principle, and in doing less, he has more, for his own humanness is at stake." By keeping our humanity as a variable within the formula of capitalism, Schaeffer argued, Christians would extend respect not only to other humans, but also the nonhuman world. In the process, he concluded that both would reap positive results because it is what God intended.[10]

In sum, *Pollution and the Death of Man* offered readers a Christian approach to environmental protection. It was not a secular environmentalist message of preservation, but it was also not an apologetics piece for free enterprise and humanity's superiority over natural resources that were placed on earth for humanity's desire for riches. It was this view that would become the foundation for Christian environmental stewardship, which other conservative evangelicals reiterated from the first Earth Day observance until the early 1990s when the community attempted to turn Schaeffer's accepted eco-friendly philosophies into action.

Pollution and the Death of Man served as the first major environmental policy position produced by a biblical literalist and future religious right sympathizer. However, when placed alongside his other publications of the time, Schaeffer's environmental argument did not necessarily make nature protection a top priority. Rather, it provided further support for the God-human hierarchical relationship, which he consistently promoted in his other books. Schaeffer's larger focus was saving human souls and teaching Christians the basis for effectively living their faith and fulfilling the meaning of life. *Pollution and the Death of Man* was a complex exploration into the place of the natural world in relationship with humanity and God, which was otherwise a footnote within his larger philosophical and theological arguments.[11] Furthermore, it was a nuanced argument that was and perhaps remains hard to follow for some who may want a hero and villains story line such as capitalism as being all good or bad or humanity as a blessing or curse on the earth. Schaeffer indeed left much up to the reader, especially when it came to actually finding solutions to balance capitalism and natural resources. Twenty years later, the conservative private advocacy group, the

John Birch Society, used Schaeffer's trusted name to tell people that Earth Day 1990 was an earth worshipping communist plot and cited a section from *Pollution and the Death of Man* in which Schaeffer wrote about the importance of people. Schaeffer did believe that humanity was God's crowning achievement, but such a position, he argued, nevertheless demanded that Christians embrace environmental action and curb greedy impulses.

Pollution and the Death of Man was a first step to motivate an otherwise silent church (as Schaeffer accused Christians of being) into protecting God's natural world. After the popular Earth Day observance on April 22, 1970, many others in the conservative evangelical world wanted to get their community actively participating at the very least in a movement parallel to secular environmentalists. The most popular conservative evangelical magazines, *Eternity, Decision, Christianity Today,* and *Moody Monthly,* as well as the National Association of Evangelicals' (NAE) *United Evangelical Action,* jumped on the bandwagon to make saving God's earth a top priority.[12] *Eternity* magazine, as just one example of many, devoted an entire issue to ecological awareness in its May 1970 edition, with a cover photo depicting a pristine mountain lake with discarded beer cans in the foreground and a caption asking: "WHAT ARE WE DOING TO GOD'S EARTH?" The feature story, titled "When You've Seen One Beer Can You've Seen Them All," described the author's disappointment upon seeing littered beer cans during a trip to the Yosemite Valley. It inquired of the reader, "Does the elimination of the brown pelican from our shores through the indiscriminate use of the 'miracle insecticide' DDT reflect God's love? Does the bite of a chain-saw into the flesh of a towering 2000-year-old redwood prove His majesty?"[13] The author, Ron Widman listed humanity's sins against nature such as producing carbon monoxide, the recent fire on the Cuyahoga River, the over-use of Minnesota's Superior National Forest, and the somewhat comical occurrence of the Royal Air Force having to parachute cats into Malaysia in hopes of controlling disease-carrying rodents, which had proliferated because the indigenous cats had died from eating DDT-ridden cockroaches.[14]

Echoing Schaeffer's criticisms, Widman also noted that Christian churches had not previously adopted policies of ecological responsibility. He supported Christian eco-friendly activity with biblical verses and listed actions that Christians could take on the individual level, such as teaching children how to be conscientious stewards by conserving resources and not polluting. He also raised the issue of how economics plays a key role in environmentalism. Widman admitted in his conclusion that being ecologically responsible might cost more money, but added "After all, we are the ones who stand to gain the most: clean air, clean water, open spaces. Why shouldn't we pay?"[15]

In another strong pro-environmental conservative evangelical example, three days after the official Earth Day observance, long-time pastor Leighton Ford delivered an Earth Day sermon during his brother-in-law Billy Graham's weekly radio show, *Hour of Decision*.[16] The program opened with the familiar tone of Cliff Barrows' voice announcing "The Billy Graham Evangelistic Association presents the 'Hour of Decision.'" A choir sang "How Great Thou Art" and after a few more formalities the nineteenth-century hymn "For the Beauty of the Earth," after which Ford spoke on "Good Earth or Polluted Planet?"

Ford delivered a solid pro-environmental Christian message. He grabbed the listener's attention by telling the story of a boy who was given a garden and told to take care of it. The boy instead spoiled what he was given by dirtying the water, cutting down trees, and polluting the air so much he could not see the sun. Ford reported that he told this story to his children, who replied that the boy had sinned by polluting. "Polluting," Ford told his radio audience, was a new term to his generation, but abusing the earth is what society was doing and that must change. Like Schaeffer, Ford explained the proper God-human-nature relationship, but in a simple, straightforward way. In his view, the environment was valuable not only because it was created by God, but because it was perpetually owned by God and not gifted to humanity. Ford was not the originator of such a view, but it was this understanding that expanded Schaeffer's eco-friendly understanding of creation, and it would become the mainstream conservative evangelical environmental position for the next two decades. Ford stated, "Yes God has put the earth under our dominion but that does not mean that man is the sovereign lord. This earth is not our earth. It is God's earth. We are not using our things, we are using the talents and gifts God has given to us. We are to have dominion, but under God's domain."[17] Like Schaeffer, Ford asked listeners to remember that although humanity was indeed superior, nonhuman nature was not simply a resource for human use. It is clear from the beginning of his sermon that Ford was not simply saying that humanity needed to live responsibly and curb the usage of DDT or stop polluting for the health of people and animals. In an attempt to motivate his listeners into environmental action, he instead articulated man's superior but humble place in creation, a view in harmony with what Schaeffer had been arguing for years.

By asserting that humans have an obligation to God to care for the earth, Ford attached his faith-based environmental argument to the traditional Christian understanding of "stewardship," which essentially means being a custodian. The idea of stewardship within conservative evangelical culture can be applied to a variety of situations, any of which involve a responsibility to care for something. Protestant ministers in general commonly speak about stewardship when it comes to church tithing or volunteering one's time for the upkeep of church grounds and buildings. Bible verses such as Leviticus 27:30–32, Mark 10:17–25, and Romans 12:1 are often cited to support this practice. Stewardship remains to this day as something that Christians should live by not simply to be a good person, but to fulfill a commandment by God. Through this approach, Ford made stewardship of the earth a religious edict.

Fundamentally, what Schaeffer and Ford articulated in their view of Christian environmental stewardship is a similar version of how secular nature conservationists think of the optimum human-nature relationship. In this latter view, humanity is a part of the natural world and can use it, but must use it wisely so that it will continue to support future generations. Preserving the beauty of nature may be an aspect of conservation, but the needs of humanity often remains paramount. The proposal and building of the Hetch Hetchy Dam in Yosemite Valley, California, during the early twentieth century serves as an historical example epitomizing conservationist philosophy. Both Forest Service Chief Gifford Pinchot and President Theodore Roosevelt appreciated the outdoors, but deferred to the needs of humanity when necessary. To increase San Francisco's water supply after the 1906 earthquake, they moved Congress to dam the Hetch Hetchy Valley despite passionate condemnation from preservationist and Sierra Club President, John Muir. Christian environmental stewardship, in a similar manner to conservationism, recognizes that humanity can use and shape the natural world, but must do it wisely for the benefit of future generations. What makes Christian environmental stewardship unique is the understanding that people are God's crowning achievement. People are therefore most important, but nature is also valued simply because it was created by, and remains perpetually owned by, God. This viewpoint continued as the accepted conservative evangelical position into the early 1990s.

In conclusion to his argument for stewardship, Ford connected his environmental argument to the most important duty of saving souls. Thus, he skillfully mixed stewardship of nature with the spiritual struggle of people trying to de-pollute their souls through the process of accepting Christ as their savior. "Like those ducks drenched in oil from the tanker on St. Petersburg, our sins defile us." He continued, "We need a spiritual detergent to cleanse our souls and that is why Jesus shed his blood. The blood of Jesus Christ, God's son, cleanses us from every sin. Faith in that blood and the living Christ can restore us to the fellowship of God, lead us to repentance and motivate us to clean up the mess that we find our world in."[18] The primary point of the *Hour of Decision* was to save listeners for Christ. Ford knew from the beginning that he was taking on a topic unfamiliar to his audience and one he had to validate to sell. Therefore, he chose to undergird his sermon with saving souls while making environmental stewardship a commandment from God.

Ford surely thought he had effectively molded a successful and inspiring Christian Earth Day message for his listeners. He concluded his sermon as a cavalry bugler sending troops out for battle. Notice that his rhetoric continued to highlight the themes of stewardship and saving souls: "Will it [Earth Day] stand for ego, estrangement, and exploitation?" he asked. "Or will E-Day stand for . . . 'entrust' that God has entrusted to us this world, 'economize' the careful management of our environment and 'evangelize' the good news of the greatest cleansing of all, that Jesus Christ can bring?"[19]

Ford's Earth Day message was moving, well thought out, energetic, and a step up from Schaeffer's more rarified philosophies. Nevertheless, the rhetoric never quite made it to the next step of cohesive action by his religious community. There were obstacles causing the discussion to stagnate. Interestingly, one of the problems was apparent right before Ford's sermon in a promotion for Billy Graham's *Decision* magazine article titled "On the Brink." Its topic was the "new radical revolution that is sweeping through many university campuses throughout our world today."[20] It was this problem, embodied by young people leading the late 1960s counterculture, and not the health of nature, that seemed more important in Graham's eyes. Nevertheless, others in Graham's circle furthered Ford's concerns for the planet, including Sherwood E. Wirt, who wrote an editorial in *Decision* titled "The Defilement of the Earth." Here, Wirt cited standard eco-friendly Bible verses from Genesis in which God created the planet and saw "that it was good," and from Numbers 35:34 that read, "Defile not the land which ye shall inhabit, wherein I dwell: for I the Lord dwell among the children of Israel." Wirt drew on this latter quotation to state that such a concept should be applied to the Earth as a whole and followed it with a list of ways humanity hurt the planet. Like Ford, Wirt wrote that winning souls for Christ is paramount, but warned, "Let's not foul the environment while we do it."[21]

Initially, Graham did not have a problem with the environmental sentiments communicated through his newspaper and radio broadcast; instead he was more worried about combating the counterculture led by the young adults of the baby boomer generation. Perhaps his concerns had merit, at least when it came to the messages stemming from secular environmentalists. While Schaeffer, Ford, and Wirt espoused Christian environmental stewardship, the environmental movement's college-age organizers directly accused Christianity of causing the entire ecological crisis.

The Environmental Handbook

Several months before Earth Day, the event's organizers distributed a manifesto in the form of a book titled *The Environmental Handbook: Prepared for the First National Environmental Teach-In*. The publication, which went on to sell 1.5 million copies, was to be, as the title states, a guidebook for those leading and participating in educating America on the ecological crisis. As environmental historian Adam Rome writes, "To many commentators, the handbook was the distilled essence of Earth Day."[22]

The Handbook promoted several ideas for fighting the problem of overpopulation, which were considered radical at the time. Garrett Hardin, author of the chapter titled "The Tragedy of the Commons," condemned the United Nations Declaration of Human Rights for supporting the freedom of couples to decide the number of children they wish to have. Instead, he urged concerned citizens to support Planned Parenthood to pressure the burgeoning world population into seeing the error of their ways.[23] Hardin suggested that reproductive freedoms should be curbed because overpopulation was a major cause of environmental degradation.[24] This theme was later repeated in a chapter by Keith Murray of the Berkeley Ecology Center, which stated that the government should help curb population growth by offering "massive" federal aid for contraceptive and sex education for all levels.[25] This latter proposal rubbed conservative evangelicals the wrong way, and once sex education was offered in public schools, it quickly became a hotly contested issue. Murray additionally went as far as to indirectly suggest environmental answers could not be found in traditional Christian beliefs and left them out of a list of nature-friendly faiths that readers might embrace.

> It seems evident that there are throughout the world certain social and religious forces which have worked through history toward an ecologically and culturally enlightened state of affairs. Let these be encouraged: Gnostics, hip Marxists, Teilhard de Chardin Catholics, Druids, Taoists, Biologists, Zens, Shamans, Bushmen, American Indians, Polynesians, Anarchists, Alchemists . . . the list is long. All primitive cultures, all communal and ashram movements."[26]

Perhaps most distressing to conservative evangelicals was that the editor reprinted Lynn White Jr.'s 1967 essay, thereby forcing the issue of Christian culpability back into popular debate and suggested to readers that they find an alternative more eco-friendly faith.

The Environmental Handbook as a whole presented many uncontroversial solutions and raised awareness of real ecological problems. For example, the authors urged Americans to take it upon themselves to clean up trash that other irresponsible people left behind. Still, despite mostly noncontentious suggestions, the book proved to be a wedge that forced conservative evangelicals away from the environmental movement. Perhaps the Earth Day organizers were looking for a scapegoat or straw man on which Americans could place blame for their ecological woes, or maybe they just lacked the interpersonal social skills to promote unity. In any case, *The Environmental Handbook* baldly accused Christianity of ruining the Earth while encouraging readers to find another faith. This insulting approach proved a defining moment when the secular environmental movement officially rejected the cautious but willing conservative evangelical community.

In response to the *Handbook*, conservative evangelical leaders such as Harold Lindsell felt obligated to fight the specter of White's accusations and argue how Christianity can be friendly to the Earth. Lindsell, an ordained Baptist minister who helped found the Fuller Theological Seminary, authored a variety of Christian books and served as the editor of *Christianity Today* (*CT*) from 1968 to 1978. Although *CT* should perhaps be understood as leaning socially liberal in later periods, what the magazine produced during Lindsell's tenure and what he wrote himself reflected his conservative evangelical theology, as well as the views of others who would later form the religious right movement. As religious historian George Marsden notes, Lindsell was specifically placed as the editor of *Christianity Today* because he was a devoted religious and political conservative who fused militancy into cultural and biblical questions.[27]

Like Schaeffer and Ford, Lindsell was aware of the growing ecological crisis throughout the 1960s. In response to citizens promoting an environmental movement, he directly told readers as a contributing author of *United Evangelical Action* magazine published in early 1970, that as the first of many problems, society was committing "ecological suicide." He began his argument by praising Rachel Carson's *Silent Spring*. "Let me illustrate this," he wrote, "We have polluted the atmosphere. . . . I suggest you read Rachel Carson's book, *Silent Spring*. . . . We have exploited and raped nature. . . . We have not only subdued and corrupted it and, if we continue at the rate we are going, the planet will shortly be uninhabitable."[28] In this article, Lindsell did not feel the need to dedicate any words to distance or downplay the environmental movement. Lindsell was not an environmentalist, but his rhetoric was certainly in line with broader calls to protect the ailing environment. Indeed "Suicide Ahead," represents a strong pro-environmental position, but this lasted for only a short period. Upon reading *The Environmental Handbook*, Lindsell never uttered such pro-environmental sentiments again.

In response to the *Handbook*, like Lindsell, his editorial staff at *CT* would have no part of the secular ecological movement and accused its supporters of worshipping the Earth. In the April 10, 1970 issue, the magazine ran an editorial lashing out at the handbook's authors in a piece titled "Ecologism: A New Paganism." The author wrote, "Unfortunately, at least a few persons appear to have gone beyond legitimate concern for our environment to pervert the science of ecology into what might be called *ecologism*" (emphasis in the original). The authors defined the latter term as the worship of nature; a heresy they accused the secular environmental movement of perpetrating. The author stated, "These people are uninhibited in their opposition to orthodox Christianity (as well as to such derivatives as humanism and Communism), and to replace it they urge what is essentially old-fashioned paganism."[29] To support this contention, the editorial directly cited Lynn White Jr.'s argument and quoted from the *Handbook*'s chapter in which author Keith Murray praised non-Christian and seemingly pantheistic faiths. "We too want to clean up pollution in nature," the editorial allowed, "but not by polluting men's souls with a revived paganism."[30]

In the May 8, 1970, issue of *CT*, Lindsell's staff again felt compelled to address the *Handbook*'s non-Christian eco-friendly faiths. The introduction of the article titled "De-Polluting Ecology" underscored the book's glaring problems. "Non-biblical theologizers have thrust before us a new view of man that makes him a part, rather than lord, of the created order. Those who urge less human assertiveness over nature fail to understand (or apply) Genesis."[31] Two years later Lynn White Jr.'s article continued to sting the evangelical community. Like others before him, James M. Houston, principle of Regent University in Vancouver, British Columbia, cautioned *CT* readers against following popular ecological solutions and experts, all the while specifically criticizing White's conclusions. Houston nevertheless concluded by demanding that Christians live not as individuals but as interdependent beings within ecosystems, which included redirecting our focus from income to a variety of important factors including the environment.[32] Other writers in the conservative evangelical community who wrote for *United Evangelical Action* and *Eternity* offered similar critiques of environmentalists.[33] Importantly, during each rebuke of the environmental movement along with aspects of *The Environmental Handbook*, the magazine authors typically supported an understanding of Christian environmental stewardship. Thus, they felt humanity should not follow environmentalists but could protect the earth nonetheless as God-mandated custodians or stewards. Until the later 1970s, Lindsell himself carefully made this distinction and publicly promoted such a view.

Garret DeBell and those who put together *The Environmental Handbook* were not the first to suggest that nature worship was the key to a healthier planet. Shortly after Lynn White Jr. suggested that people follow the nature-friendly philosophies of St. Francis of Assisi, sociology professor Richard L. Means mused about the benefit of following pantheistic beliefs. Both ideas were cited as problematic by Schaeffer in his book *Pollution and the Death of Man*.[34] However, such calls to find environmental solutions in non-Christian faiths did not cause even the most politically conservative evangelicals to entirely reject the need to protect the earth. Even the politically radical fundamentalist and one-time colleague of Schaeffer, Carl McIntire, responded to Earth Day somewhat positively in his own newsletter, the *Christian Beacon*.

Carl McIntire remains famous today as a fundamentalist preacher who was such a militant separatist that he even alienated himself from his own organizations. He had a constant need to be in charge, and any challenge from fellow members sent him into self-exile. McIntire was one of the first fundamentalists to whole-heartedly throw his religious faith together with present-day politics. His desire to separate himself from worldly enemies made him more than ineffective politically, but his views to a certain extent stand as political and intellectual precursors to the more public-friendly Christian groups such as the Moral Majority and the Christian Coalition. Thus, his views on environmentalism are important to take into consideration, rather than simply dismissing them as the ramblings of the extreme fringe.

McIntire titled the June 17, 1971, *Christian Beacon*'s cover story "ECOLOGY ANTI-CHRISTIAN." The article reflected the fact that conservative evangelicals were not against protecting nature, but rather felt under attack themselves. Instead of taking direct shots at *The Environmental Handbook*, McIntire raised similar concerns within the conservative evangelical community with respect to secular environmentalists who blamed Christianity for the ecological crisis. He cited Edward B. Fiske, a United Presbyterian minister, who reportedly lauded Buddhists and Taoists as having a better relationship to nature than Christians. McIntire also found problems with the secular environmental movement for leaving nature protection up to the central government and instead asserted that the issue should be for individuals to tackle. He stated that the ecological crisis was overblown, but wrote that something needed to be done. "Simply . . . there are areas that need to be cleaned up. There are some streams that have been polluted by the discharge of factories. There are cities, some of them, that need to give attention to this problem."[35] Like Lindsell, McIntire became upset at those who promoted alternative faiths as "good" eco-friendly religions over that of Christianity. He then paired this problem with his partiality toward limited government to discredit the environmental movement, but only up to a point. He still admitted that something had to be done to clean up pollution. Interestingly, he never raised the question that Schaeffer posited in *Pollution and the Death of Man*: What is humanity's proper relationship to God's earth? Should humanity work in harmony with nature or did God give natural resources to mankind to utilize at will? McIntire did not answer these questions, which strongly suggests he had no problem with the need to care for the environment in a compassionate way and did not see any reason to argue against the environmental movement's goal of preserving the Earth. Although the ecological crisis was real to McIntire, what upset him was those who blamed Christianity for destroying the Earth and suggesting that non-Christian faiths and the government had better answers.

In addition to Schaeffer, Ford, Lindsell and McIntire, another important reflection of eco-friendly views within the conservative evangelical community comes from a 1971 poll conducted by the 12 million-member SBC one year after Earth Day. Surveys sent to 312 pastors and 375 Sunday school teachers asking about their view regarding pollution produced an overwhelming response: 81.7 percent of pastors and 76.3 percent of Sunday School teachers reported "that a local Southern Baptist Church should 'lead church members to involve themselves and cooperate actively with authorities' in attempts to solve air and water pollution problems."[36] Slightly over half, however, of the 13.5 percent of respondents who felt air and water problems were none of the church's business classified themselves as politically conservative and one-fifth in this group said they were theologically conservative. These findings regarding the politically conservative Southern Baptists, could perhaps stand as a backlash against the endorsements of non-Christian faiths as reflected in the rhetoric by McIntire and Lindsell. Nevertheless, the vast majority of respondents demonstrate the existence of accepted eco-friendly philosophies at the mainstream grassroots level. These high percentages also imply that in these churches, Sunday school teachers and pastors at the very least likely spoke to parishioners about Christian environmental stewardship, as did Ford on Graham's *Hour of Decision*.

In harmony with the SBC's survey and the eco-friendly messages articulated by Ford and Schaeffer, a small, but noticeable number of conservative evangelicals at the grassroots level participated in environmental activities. John H. Townsend, for one, delivered an eco-friendly sermon to his congregation at First Baptist Church in Los Angeles, which the *L.A. Times* listed along with various religious communities that wanted to save the earth.[37] Beyond pastors delivering sermons, an article in the *Dallas Morning News* titled "Earth Day Sweeps Country" reported that, along with nationwide teach-ins at numerous schools and colleges as well as events in various states, the students at

Missouri Baptist College sought to set an example to others by organizing a cleanup event on their campus.[38] At Wayland Baptist College, the school's newspaper editor commented that environmental action must be taken immediately because time was a commodity that society did not have much of.[39] A year later, students of Houston Baptist College joined with city efforts to clean up litter and pollution.[40]

Elsewhere in Texas, individual Baptist church congregants proudly demonstrated eco-friendly efforts. David Bratcher, a Teenage Citizenship Award Program finalist and member of North Dallas Baptist Church, proudly organized an ecology seminar at his high school while participating in numerous other programs. Clearly, Bratcher did not see any conflict between his ecology seminar and his religious community. The *Dallas Morning News* listed his environmental event in front of a long list of religious-based activities, including Bratcher serving as the president of the Youth Council at North Dallas Baptist Church and being involved as a member of the Royal Ambassadors, a Baptist boys' mission organization. He additionally won the Dallas Baptist Association's Excellence Award while acting as a "youth pastor, Vacation Bible School worker, [and a]member of both youth and adult choirs."[41] Beyond his numerous activities, Bratcher's worldview paralleled that of his politically conservative religious community, including its growing impatience with the counterculture's influence on popular culture. Bratcher reported that young people were increasingly turning to Christianity and the organized church because trying to find the answers to life elsewhere proved unfruitful. Such views precisely mirrored messages from Francis Schaeffer and Billy Graham concerning the counterculture movement. In short, Bratcher, a devout member of his religious community who was in agreement with the viewpoints of the leadership, felt that no conflict existed between his faith and the need to maintain a healthy environment.

Beyond overachieving youths such as Bratcher, serious conservative politicians and members of Baptist churches did not feel that fighting for a cleaner environment threatened or compromised their careers. In April of 1972, James Wheeler of Mesquite, Texas, and a member of Oates Drive Baptist Church, sought the Democratic nomination for House District 33-I. His Democrat label aside, Wheeler promised to end cash welfare payments to mothers of dependent children, vote against raising taxes, and encourage quality public education on a neighborhood school basis while also promoting efforts to "clean up the environment."[42] Likewise, four years later Baptist and Texas politician Alan Steelman, ran for a U.S. Senate seat based on trying to limit big government, big business and big labor. Although he vocally promised to be an opponent to big business, others felt that "he almost always lands on the side of big business." He particularly wanted to cut down the power of the federal government to keep it from "harassing" individuals and businesses, big or small. In addition to his strong conservative political views, Steelman, as a Baptist and the son of parents in the Missionary Baptist Church, supported "strong stands for protection of the environment."[43]

The examples of Bratcher, Wheeler, and Steelman, as well as the eco-friendly efforts of the Baptist colleges, all support the idea that conservative evangelicals were not anti-environmentalists, and nor did they ignore the issue. Their activities reflect the fact that Christian environmental stewardship functioned as the accepted philosophy within the mainstream of the conservative evangelical community.

Despite these examples of environmental activity, there were nevertheless grumblings and to a certain extent, a backlash from a few in the religious community's leadership. Although the *Hour of Decision* featured Leighton Ford's eco-friendly sermon in 1970, Billy Graham told the public on the same show in 1972 what he thought of environmentalism. He dismissed the issue by saying the pollution he dealt with as a child was worse than it was in the present day. His argument paralleled McIntire's antipathy toward government regulation of pollution, but broke with him by totally rejecting the need for ecological action. When recalling his childhood in North Carolina, Graham said that his father's farm was "full of pollution" but that they took care of their own problems and did not call on the government to fix them.[44] Instead of telling his listeners to practice Christian stewardship, Graham accused the younger American generation of always complaining about something and criticized their inability to clean up their own messes. Thus, Graham rejected the belief that an ecological crisis existed, negating any need for Christian environmental stewardship and instead blamed the younger generation for social problems, which his show the *Hour of Decision* had also alluded to before Ford delivered his Earth Day sermon two years previous.

Graham's 1972 environmental position clearly indicates a break from earlier conservative evangelical environmental thought. Although his view remained the exception more than the norm, it was important in that it was a reaction not to environmental protection efforts but to extraneous events. Indeed, Graham's views were not expressed until two years after Earth Day, after the publication of *The Environmental Handbook* and after the counterculture progressed as a major movement in the public eye. Graham apparently did not have a problem initially supporting Christian environmental stewardship since he permitted his brother-in-law to deliver an entire sermon on his own radio show in honor of the Earth Day observance. When Graham refused to believe the reality of the ecological crisis, he did it within the framework of rejecting the counterculture movement. In other words, Graham primarily hoped to crush the counterculture movement and therefore rejected anything they stood for, including environmental protection efforts. Furthermore, Graham's rejection of the environmental crisis was an anomaly among the conservative evangelical community at the time. Individuals within this religious community, including Harold Lindsell, promoted environmental activism through Christian stewardship before, during, and after Earth Day 1970. Graham's refusal to accept the reality of the environmental crisis never proved salient among conservative evangelicals later in the 1970s, including the energy crisis of 1973.

By the time of the energy crisis of 1973, the push by eco-friendly leaders such as Schaeffer and Ford decreased in popularity, but did not disappear. New motivations arose to conserve resources, but these were more along the lines of being frugal model citizens rather than emotional appeals to protect the Earth as God's creation. Arguments for Christian environmental stewardship, however, remained in the background.

The Energy Crisis

It was mid-October 1973 when Arab members of the Organization of Petroleum Exporting Countries (OPEC) protested US support of Israel by cutting back on oil exports and soon thereafter halted all oil shipments to the United States. OPEC had found the Achilles heel of what was considered at the time to be the world's strongest country economically and militarily.

US citizens were shocked when the oil that had always seemed plentiful and cheap became in short supply. On November 7, 1973, President Richard Nixon addressed the public to explain his administration's plan to deal with the crisis. He stated that oil-run power plants would be converting to coal and that the federal government and military would ration fuel. Nixon assured his listeners that in the long run they would achieve energy independence from OPEC, but in the short term everyone must conserve. He called on states and officials at the local level to encourage carpooling and reduce speed limits.[45]

In response to President Nixon's recommendations, conservative evangelical churches across the country cut back on energy use. First Baptist Church of Van Nuys, California, formed an energy conservation committee and reduced the use of its busses by 20 percent. The church's other programs were downsized, including the teen ski outings, which were relocated to nearby resorts or ended altogether. Almost 1,500 miles away in Dallas, Texas, future religious right proponent W. A. Criswell's First Baptist Church encouraged members to carpool to Sunday morning services in addition to implement-

motive?,
necessity
nationalism

ing energy-saving policies in their various buildings. As the decade wore on, the church installed a central computer to maximize energy efficiency.[46] Elsewhere at the Christian and Missionary Alliance in Missoula, Montana, the members held Bible study in congregant homes, and to save gas, their pastor Norman Foss purchased a bicycle. First Baptist Church of Hammond, Indiana, restricted its fleet of 150 buses on Sundays and thereby saved one-third of fuel consumption. At Detroit's Temple Baptist Church, the pastor G. B. Vick reasoned that cutting back on bus transportation would only lead to congregants traveling by car and therefore would use more energy; thus, it would be counterproductive to downsize their bus ministry. The conservative evangelical Wheaton College in Illinois converted to natural gas and set thermostats at 70 degrees. The school also limited the lighting periods of its outdoor Christmas tree as a public demonstration reflecting agreement and participation in energy conservation efforts. Perhaps most noteworthy, even future religious right co-founder and one-day ardent anti-environmentalist Jerry Falwell's Thomas Road Baptist Church joined energy saving efforts by reducing their bus system and therefore reportedly saved 6,000 gallons of gasoline a month. The church additionally extended these efforts by reducing the number of social outings and youth activities.[47] On the national organizational level the Christian Stewardship Council, formed in 1975 and produced "A Code of Ethical Pursuit." The group's primary goal was to help sort out "worthy evangelical enterprises from those that were '"financially negligent and exploitative.'"[48] This organization was apparently short lived, but its very existence reveals action attempted at a higher level than individual church energy-saving activities.

Although conservative evangelical churches nationwide proactively reacted to the 1973 energy crisis, the decision to do so was not solely voluntary. President Nixon forced energy conservation by banning gasoline sales on Sunday, and energy prices across the board rose dramatically. Thus, decisions to conserve were a response to a mixture of government policies in an effort to save money. At the same time, however, the conservative evangelical community did not blame large government for the policies or call for more and cheaper energy. Instead, many Americans, including those of conservative evangelical backgrounds, vocally admitted that Americans were wasteful in their resource consumption and argued that the gluttony needed to cease. In his November 7, 1973, speech Nixon acknowledged that "the average American will consume as much energy in the next 7 days as most other people in the world will consume in an entire year. We have only 6 percent of the world's people in America, but we consume over 30 percent of all the energy in the world."[49] Even before this speech and oil shortage, articles circulated throughout Christian magazines calling for a reduction in American gluttony and waste. In May of

1973 *CT* writer Addison H. Leitch wrote an article titled "Without Natural Affection," in which he warned Christians of the consequences of waning interest in the environment. In his view, although teenagers might be in the local news for their recycling efforts, the addition of an annual 12 million cars to the roads, the endless production of plastics, and the unseen consequences of food additives overwhelmed eco-friendly efforts. Leitch called for Christians to remove themselves from this unethical consumer culture and firmly declared, "The GNP is not God; it sounds more like the service of mammon."[50] Similar messages filled the pages of evangelical publications during the energy crisis like transportation minister Terry Spahr of First Baptist Church of Van Nuys, California, who clarified, "We'll be preaching on obeying the spirit—not just the letter of the law."[51] Likewise, conserving resources for stewardship reasons remained evident in other articles, including "Christ and Your Living Standard," "The Three Faces of the Energy Crisis," and "Smile When the Fuel Runs Low." All of these sources not only reflected the need to curb gluttony and conserve out of necessity, but also and importantly reiterated the moral duty of Christian environmental stewardship.

The message to conserve energy in the spirit of Christian environmental stewardship was celebrated specifically by the editorial team of *CT* led by the militant political and theological conservative Harold Lindsell. Between 1974 and 1975, Lindsell's editorial staff published "Living Better with Less" (1974) and "Waste as a Wrong" (1975). In the latter example, the editors reiterated Schaeffer's theological understanding that God created or designed everything to have a proper place, which was "entrusted" to humanity to value because it was God's creation. "Waste as a Wrong" stated that waste "is a moral evil. It is sinful because it is a misappropriation of resources that God has entrusted to his creation. Failure to put things to their proper, God-given purpose is something for which everyone will eventually be judged and held accountable."[52] The Bible, it continued, clearly promoted stewardship in its injunction to store grain in view of future famines, as well as preserving the leftover food after Jesus fed the multitudes. It then connected these points with the aim of April's Earth Day. The editorial stated, "An ecological emphasis has become traditional in April, perhaps because we are more inclined to be nice to Mother Earth. . . . Could not churches seize upon this seasonal consciousness for a monumental impact against waste?" Lindsell and his editorial staff were not pushing for nature preservation in the same way as secular environmentalists; rather, they were admonishing Christians who failed to value God's creation, while encouraging believers to actively implement Christian environmental stewardship into their everyday lives.

Although it is unclear if Lindsell personally wrote these eco-friendly articles, at this period in time, he at least endorsed their content. Furthermore, in 1976 he personally wrote an article titled "The Lord's Day and Natural Resources," in which he virtually reiterated the very same points and stressed the need to conserve resources because they were created by God. In short, the politically and theologically conservative evangelical Harold Lindsell, despite his intense rejection of the secular environmental movement, nevertheless championed Christian environmental stewardship long after Earth Day 1970 and the 1973 energy crisis. This was also true of conservative evangelicals nationwide who likewise pointed to stewardship in efforts to conserve resources in response to the energy crisis.

Conclusion

Contrary to previous popular and scholarly perceptions in which conservative evangelicals traditionally ignored or opposed environmental protection, during the late 1960s and early 1970s, the community discussed the subject and developed an eco-friendly view that Christians could help save the Earth. Lynn White Jr. introduced Christians to the issue by accusing their faith for the ecological crisis. In response, Francis Schaeffer took to the lecture circuit to excite fellow believers into embracing his understanding of Christian environmental stewardship. Schaffer's call received a boost of energy through the birth of the modern environmental movement in 1970, when Ford and multiple evangelical publications intensified and expanded the idea of stewardship as a way Christians could protect the environment. Almost simultaneously however, secular Earth Day organizers complicated and partially derailed the religious community's response by freely disseminating apparent anti-Christian messages, particularly through *The Environmental Handbook.* Thus, after Earth Day 1970 and the publication of the *Handbook*, conservative evangelicals were left in a defensive position expressing mixed opinions including occasional suggestions, as exemplified by Billy Graham, that the ecological crisis did not exist.

Conservative evangelical and *CT* editor Harold Lindsell is a prime example of someone who praised Rachel Carson just before becoming quite upset after learning about the environmental movement's attitude toward Christianity and its approach to understanding the natural world. This problem notwithstanding, Lindsell continued espousing Christian environmental stewardship and, in accordance with conservative political and religious extremist Carl McIntire, did not dismiss caring for nature to support the idea that humanity was ordained as the earth's absolute ruler. McIntire additionally fought the idea that other religions were better for the earth and disagreed with government regulation, all the while admitting that pollution was a problem that needed addressing.

Billy Graham's refusal to believe that the environment was in danger seems the beginning of the end for the conservative evangelical push to initiate a parallel environmental movement through Christian environmental stewardship. By this time, the idea had come under too much fire, whether it was through Schaeffer's subdued and complicated philosophy describing nature's secondary but important "proper place," or Lindsell warning that the environmental movement promoted nature worship. Furthermore, Graham's 1972 views were not a simple denial of the ecological crisis; but rather he dismissed the problem by framing it in his disgust for the looming counterculture movement that was challenging Christianity's hegemony over US cultural norms. Results from a Gallup Poll reflected that the counterculture's apparent challenge was indeed significant and real by reporting a sharp shift in views of religion from 1957 to 1970. The poll explained in 1957 that 69 percent of Americans felt that religion was increasing in influence and only 14 percent felt that it was declining. However, as the decade ended and the 1960s began, the two perceptions sharply switched positions. By 1970, they were almost opposite of what they once had been, with 75 percent of Americans saying religion was losing influence and only 14 percent saying it was gaining.[53] Thus, it was not hard for Christians in general to feel pressured by changing currents during the 1970s, and this went beyond environmentalists blaming Christians for ruining the earth.

Billy Graham, at least initially, did not find Christian environmental stewardship problematic as evidenced by his brother-in-law's environmental sermon on his radio program the *Hour of Decision*. Additionally, the eco-friendly article "Defilement of the Earth," written by his long-time associate and editor of his newspaper, *Decision*, Sherwood E. Wirt, shortly followed Graham's anti-counterculture piece "On the Brink." At the most, Graham was uncomfortable with Christian environmental stewardship only because of its association with the secular environmental movement and the 1960s counterculture. His dismissal of the ecological crisis came two years after Earth Day in a brief piece on the *Hour of Decision*. Such a view was not a repeated message by Graham, nor did it become an accepted position among the conservative evangelical community as evidenced by the rhetoric and actions taken by the larger community in response to the energy crisis in 1973.

Apart from the numerous examples of activity at the grassroots level to conserve energy combined with the 1971 SBC poll that found a vast majority of pastors and Sunday school teachers supported Earth protection, individual church sermons centering on environmental stewardship are difficult to find.

Many sermons at the time were not recorded or else have become lost. For example, conservative evangelical Adrian Rogers, the pastor of Bellevue Baptist Church, a megachurch located in Memphis, Tennessee, and future two-time president of the SBC, reportedly delivered a sermon in 1973 titled the "Theology of Ecology." The contents of his sermon unfortunately were lost and the rhetoric on the environment was somewhat too mixed by this period to be fairly sure what his view of the issue was. However, as previously discussed, CT's editorial staff led by Harold Lindsell used the similar term "ecology theology," which suggests that Rogers might have read their work and advised congregation members not to partake in the nature-worshipping ideas of the secular environmental movement. These feelings against secular environmentalists were in fact only a reaction to the *Environmental Handbook*, while at the same time they supported Christian environmental stewardship. Thus, in his 1973 sermon, Rogers likely advocated something close to what Schaeffer, Lindsell, and possibly Carl McIntire articulated at different times, in which they admitted environmental problems existed and something needed to be done because God's earth deserved respect, but with the caveat that Christians should always be wary of nature worship and big government. As of 2010, however, the roughly 30,000 member Bellevue Baptist Church does not recycle, but this fact should be tempered with the realization that conservative evangelical environmental views changed considerably since the 1970s. Lindsell embodies such a point. He initially celebrated tenets in common with secular environmentalists including the reality of the ecological crisis by encouraging readers to read Rachel Carson's *Silent Spring*, but then separated himself from them after perusing the *Handbook* while repeatedly endorsing Christian environmental stewardship. He would later turn his back on all nature protection philosophies in the early 1980s. Nevertheless, as argued, during the 1970s, it should be underscored that ignoring the environmental crisis or beliefs that it was humanity's right to freely use resources because of biblical commandments to "dominate" and "subdue" the earth cannot be blamed for being the direct cause of conservative evangelical failures to embrace eco-friendly actions at the birth of the modern environmental movement. In addition to Lindsell, the 1971 SBC pastor and Sunday school teacher poll particularly supports this latter point.

As the 1970s wore on, environmental protection dwindled as a topic of concern within the conservative evangelical world. There was, of course, a handful of articles sporadically published throughout the decade asking readers to practice Christian environmental stewardship and wondering why the Christian community was not taking action.[54] The ever-declining number of articles dedicated to the issue of environmentalism/ecology in CT speaks to the disappearance of the topic (see table 1.1).

Table 1.1   Declining interest in the environment

OCT. 10, 1969–SEPT. 25, 1970	OCT. 9, 1970–JULY 16, 1971	OCT. 13, 1972–SEPT. 28, 1973	OCT. 12, 1973–SEPT. 27, 1974	OCT. 11, 1974–SEPT. 26, 1975	OCT. 8, 1976–SEPT. 23, 1977
Ecology: 5	Environmental Crisis: 1	Energy Crisis: 1	Ecology: 5	Ecology: 1	Environment/ ecology: 0
	Ecology: 6	Ecology: 1	Energy Crisis: 5		

This information was compiled from the number of articles under the index headings found in the bound annual periodical volumes of *Christianity Today*.

Indeed, although enthusiasm for Christian environmental stewardship slowly withered within the evangelical community, it never entirely died, but stayed alive in different forms. As will be explained in following chapters, the natural world as well as Schaeffer's understanding of humanity's "proper place" in God's creation made the transition to fighting the beginnings of the what became known as the "culture wars." This was the same area of concern that Billy Graham alluded to, as evidenced by speaking about the revolution on college campuses while rejecting the need to preserve the earth.

Schaeffer: Christian env. stewardship
Env. Handbook : Xianity is primary
  – Lynn White   cause of ecological
                        crisis
                      /   \
          dominion   hierarchy

CHAPTER 2

Humanity's Proper Place between God and Nature

Although the first two decades after World War II were not devoid of unnerving issues such as the atomic bomb or the communist threat, the late 1960s and early 1970s ushered in unsettling and rapid social changes within America's mainstream culture. Protesting the Vietnam War, the drug culture, new contentious laws regarding racial equality, gay rights, and the women's liberation movement brought increased feelings of instability. There were those who embraced the changes, while some did nothing at all. Others tried to figure out ways to regain control and return to "normalcy." Conservative evangelicals took the latter approach by theologically explaining the developments and devised a game plan to take control of the future. Ideas of nature and a definition of what is "natural" played a major role in the strategy to return life to "normal."

To explore these responses, this chapter takes a step away from conservative evangelical engagement with environmental protection efforts, to explain how this community understood humanity as a creation of God as well as their relationship with the nonhuman world. It demonstrates that conservative evangelicals utilized ideas of nature connected with their understanding of creation in an attempt to comprehend and regain control of the tumultuous world surrounding them. This chapter is developed thematically around conservative evangelical rhetoric connected to nature and creation that percolated largely throughout the 1970s and early 1980s to assist in constructing the religious right first officially embodied by Falwell's Moral Majority (founded in 1979).

The way conservative evangelicals used ideas of nature in an attempt to regain control is somewhat similar to the ideology of a "back-to-the-land" or "back-to-nature" movement. The basic premise behind a secular back-to-land movement is that humans need to reconnect with what is "natural" by cutting out the "artificial" human-made things in their lives. Returning to nature for improved health is a timeworn philosophical idea, which underwent a revival in the United States during the late 1960s. Among the variety of books and articles that explore this back-to-the-land movement is *Kitchen Literacy: How We Lost the Knowledge of Where Food Comes From and Why We Need to Get It Back* by environmental historian Ann Vileisis. During the later part of the twentieth century, she explains, the knowledge that pesticides and additives were incorporated into mass-produced foods spurred a popular longing for the "natural" especially among counterculture groups. Supported by books such as *Diet for a Small Planet* by Frances Moore Lappé and *Food Pollution: The Violation of Our Inner Ecology* by Gene Marine and Judith Van Allen, back-to-landers believed they could improve their health by cutting out foods containing toxins that would "'violate' the 'inner ecology' of the human body."[1] Doing so also offered a solution to mounting environmental problems. The basis for this philosophy stems in part from French Enlightenment thinkers who saw value in adopting a "return to nature" existence instead of assuming that good came from all human-created developments. Jean-Jacques Rousseau, for example, reasoned that rejecting luxury and remaining "closer to nature" would result in a healthier life.

The conservative evangelicals of the 1960s and 1970s were not part of the counterculture or the back-to-land movement. A number of their intellectual leaders did, however, develop their own back-to-the-land or back-to-nature philosophy, which they believed offered a panacea for all the world's troubles. They promoted a back-to-God message that went beyond the traditional recommendation that one must trust in God and accept Jesus as one's personal savior. More specifically, they depicted God in his specific role as a creator of human and nonhuman nature. The idea was that if people followed God's created hierarchical design for their lives, then all personal problems would be solved (Francis Schaeffer argued a similar approach as covered in chapter 1). Furthermore, if society as a whole adopted God-designed lifestyles then the nation would prosper and even the ecological crisis would be remedied. If God's design was ignored, however, he would punish humanity and the world through personal setbacks, national failures, and natural disasters. This viewpoint challenged counterculture progressive movements, which, they believed, introduced artificial ways of living that went against what God intended for humanity. For example, conservative evangelicals interpreted changing gender roles, as supported by women's rights advocates as directly conflicting with what was natural, or, rather, intended by the creator. Such reasoning developed throughout this religious community to become part of the foundation for the religious right movement.

"nature"   "natural"

Getting Back to the Right Nature "artificial"

Conservative evangelicals expected to experience the end of the world as we know it through the ever-imminent Second Coming of Christ as predicted in the Bible. As premillennialists, they believed that problems on earth would grow progressively worse until Jesus returned, marking the "rapture" in which all saved Christians would, in the "twinkling of an eye," physically ascend to Heaven.[2] During this process, the deceased in cemeteries and even those decomposed in oceans would rematerialize and join the living believers on their journey to Paradise. There is much more to this belief, but the main point is that people in the present are living with a looming doomsday clock and that as it runs down, all aspects of life, including the spiritual, moral, and physical, will devolve to a tipping point when Jesus will return. Thus, all the "bad" news in the tumultuous late 1960s and 1970s could be explained as further confirmation of biblical prophecy.

This apocalyptic prediction existed long before the late 1960s and 1970s. For example, during World War I and World War II, fundamentalists tried to fit the current events with their end-of-the-world narrative.[3] One theory held that fascist Italian leader Mussolini was the Antichrist.[4] Later, the development of the nuclear bomb was seen as the possible method by which the world would one day be destroyed by fire. Likewise, the rapid social changes of the late 1960s set the stage once more for further apocalyptic speculation by Hal Lindsey, who tried to make sense of the world through his book, *The Late Great Planet Earth* published in 1970. By 1980, it had sold 10 million copies, making it one of the top sellers of the decade.[5]

In his book, Lindsey used current events to predict a grim future in which the United States would fall like Rome due to moral decay, and the ineffectiveness of the United Nations would guarantee the impossibility of peace.[6] Christians, he promised, would be spared because Christ would take them to Heaven when things reached a tipping point. The people left on earth would have to face the Antichrist for seven years until Christ returned a third time and restored mankind and the world back to a perfect balance in which the "glorified persons" would enjoy "only righteousness, peace, security, harmony, and joy."[7] He suggested that until Jesus came back Christians should live life to the fullest because time is short.[8]

This depiction of the future dovetailed with traditional premillenialism throughout the conservative evangelical community, but during the 1970s, many believers were not comfortable watching the world go to ruin. Instead they developed a formula to solve all earthly problems by using Schaeffer's idea of placing things into their "proper place" as originally designed by God in the Garden of Eden. This understanding was also closely connected with views called "Christian Reconstruction" and "dominionism," or dominion theology as developed by theological intellectual Rousas John Rushdoony.

As Michael McVicar observes, both Schaeffer and Rushdoony were influenced by the writings of a Westminster Theological Seminary professor named Cornelius Van Til, who in part argued that humanity should abandon man-made or, in other words, artificial solutions, for social problems such as relying on the government to mitigate poverty. They should instead ground their faith and life in following God's laws. More specifically, Rushdoony argued that people must follow the design for humanity as first outlined in the Genesis creation story of Adam and Eve—humanity's first parents who lived in obedience to God until they declared independence by listening to Satan and eating of the fruit of knowledge. Before making this choice, both had lived in accordance to God's rules, and consequently, life on earth was balanced and a paradise. According to Rushdoony, if humanity returned to living under God's rules as humanity was meant to, then life would return to a balanced and correct state. In this way, he argued, humanity in the present day could take back control of their lives and the world. This method of control became known as "dominionism" after God told Adam and Eve that they had dominion over the Earth. Rushdoony justified the basis of God's design for humanity through the creation story of Genesis. He framed the command to dominate the earth as something men were born or created for. It other words, it was a *natural* desire.

Man was created in the image of God and commanded to subdue the earth and to have dominion over it (Gen.1:26–27). Not only is it man's *calling* to exercise dominion, but it is also his *nature* to do so. Since God is the absolute and sovereign Lord and Creator, whose dominion is total and whose power is without limits, man, created in His image, shares in this communicable attribute of God. Man was created to exercise dominion under God and as God's appointed vice-regent over the earth. *Dominion* is thus a basic urge of man's nature." (emphasis in original)[9]

By this last statement Rushdoony meant that dominion is an innate and absolute behavior of humankind. It is, in other words, a part of humanity's DNA,
put there by God as the creator. Thus, denying what is natural for humanity, in
this case dominion, makes its rejection and other ways of living artificial and
therefore problematic.

In Rushdoony's eyes, the first step to exercising dominion was to take control
of the human world primarily by fulfilling God's expectations for a proper functioning family as laid out in the Genesis creation story. As Rushdoony read it,
God designed separate gender roles such as that women were the "helpmeet" of
men who were the head of the household and that children must listen and
obey their parents. The importance of this family structure, in Rushdoony's understanding, cannot be overstated. If the family functioned as set up by God,
there would be little need for a strong central government. Families would take
care of themselves, including educating their children at home, which would
instill in the next generation and subsequent generations the importance of exercising dominion over all aspects of life and would eventually lead to changing
society and implementing a reality that is centered under God and biblical law.

By following God's original design, or as Schaeffer similarly argued, living
within mankind's "proper place," all problems would disappear. Unlike Schaeffer, however, Rushdoony painstakingly combined New and Old Testament law
to specifically outline the rules that humans must follow to implement Reconstruction. These laws included capital punishment for homosexuality or disobedient children. Needless to say, most Americans found these rules appalling.
Moreover, Rushdoony's argument that the U.S. government should be altered
to the point of the country becoming almost a libertarian state was met with
skepticism and outright disapproval. These latter aspects of Rushdoony's Reconstruction kept the ideology from becoming widely accepted among conservative evangelicals. Nevertheless, as McVicar makes clear, elements of
Reconstruction remained attractive and were adopted piecemeal throughout
the community. Schaeffer, for example, particularly liked the idea of taking
control of the present and future by understanding God's design for humanity. As discussed later in this chapter, this plan of action offered a formula to
correct the momentum of the modern progressive social movements led by
the late 1960s counterculture.

The importance of the family under the authority of God proved very attractive to conservative evangelicals, especially in the 1970s, when women's
and gay advocacy groups became more active and influential. Consequently,
conservative evangelical leaders fought the progressive movement's proposed
changes by repeating Rushdoony's views surrounding the family. Religious
right cocreator, pastor Jerry Falwell was one of the most ardent supporters of

this belief, telling audiences that as the family goes so does the fate of life on earth. His sermons were saturated with the importance of the family and the proper place each individual plays in the unit's structure. For example in a 1976 sermon titled the "Characteristics of a Christian Home" Falwell stated, "The most heavenly thing on earth is the Christian home."[10] It is a place he said, where the members respect each other and follow God's rules. Problems such drugs and crime, were in his view, the consequences from a lack of strong family homes in afflicted communities.[11] Falwell, like Rushdoony, also saw the family as a creation first established in the Garden of Eden. "To even stop to define the family indicates that we've forgotten what the family is," he said in 1982. "We've forgotten basic, conceptual principles. That family in the Garden of Eden became a reality when God brought together a man and a woman—one man for one woman for one lifetime."[12]

In his efforts to invalidate the counterculture movements, Falwell used the idea of God's intended design for the family. Thus, in a 1976 sermon Falwell accused women's advocacy groups of trying to "negate and completely circumvent God's plan for the home." He went so far as to say that those who refuse to support a good Christian home where the husband is the head of the family have failed in life.[13] Women, he later repeated, were intended to be in the home loving their husbands and attending to their children. However, he understood family financial problems and knew not all could meet the ideal. "I'm not against women working, but I think that the family is the first priority."[14] In short, he believed that men working while women stayed in the home gave the best chance for a healthy and well balanced family, which created a healthy community, nation, and world. It was the way things were "meant" to be. A few years later in 1980, Falwell invited Phyllis Schlafly of the conservative private advocacy group the Eagle Forum to address his congregation. After listing goals of the women's liberation movement, she used God's role as flawless creator to attack gender equality. "One of their [women's liberation] dogmas basically is that God goofed in making two different kinds of people and that we should use the Constitution and legislation to ignore the eternal differences in the roles that God has ordained between men and women."[15] In other words and in accordance with Falwell's beliefs, Schlafly stated the goal of women's liberation was to upset God's design and make such liberation a reality through legislative law. Schlafly in contrast, pointed out that doing so went against the immutable or "eternal" differences that God had designed between men and women. These views directly echoed aspects of Rushdoony's Reconstructionism.

Similar arguments to Falwell's and Schlafly's reverberated elsewhere in the conservative evangelical community, furthering the idea that gender roles in the family were not only inflexible, but that no one could opt out of them and lead a fulfilling life. It was, they believed, human nature to fit into specific gender norms within a God-ordained family structure. The newspaper the *Christian Activist*, produced by the Schaeffer family's media production company, highlighted the innate gender roles in their summer 1984 edition by targeting the "shortcomings" of the women's liberation movement. In the article "The Feminist Mistake," the author Mona Charen felt the feminist movement had led young women astray leaving them as well as men "miserable." To support her case, she summarized the lonely lives of three of her smart, well-educated, single, but unsatisfied and unhappy friends. Her point was that marriage would solve her friends' many problems. She wrote, "In return, it [women's lib] has effectively robbed us of one thing upon which the happiness of most women rests—men."[16] In another issue, the newspaper reprised this message in an article by Mary Pride, who after earning a bachelor's degree in electrical engineering and master's degree in computer systems engineering, chose to become a homemaker and a Christian. After settling into her new lifestyle, she wrote a book titled *The Way Home (Beyond Feminism—Back to Sanity)*, in which she argued that the modern woman is at odds with biblical inerrancy. Like Falwell, she used Genesis 1 to argue that God's design for humanity to procreate through a man and woman requires their becoming husband and wife under the holy bond of matrimony. She explained that in the Garden of Eden, Adam was made complete only with the creation of Eve. "Adam" she wrote, "was alone: incomplete . . . He needed a helper, He needed a woman." In a later subsection titled "Back To the Garden" she continued this vein of thought by noting that marriage and gender fulfill roles within God's created hierarchy. If people followed God, then rewards would follow. Pride concluded, "As with all of God's designs, our needs do get met, but by the route of faith. *First* we do what God commands, then to our surprise we find ourselves blessed (emphasis in original)."[17]

To support God's design for the family, conservative evangelical churches and colleges strongly encouraged marriage. Falwell, for example, was quite vocal about supporting the opportunity for new Christian couples to meet and have a successful marriage—but it must, he warned, function in a particular order. Similarly to Rushdoony's understanding of Reconstruction, following this precise formula of the family was the solution, Falwell stated, to solve the "problem in America." On Easter Sunday, March 23, 1977 Falwell complained, "Do you know what the problem in America today is? We are totally neglecting the home." He then told listeners of his ministry's efforts to confront this shortcoming. "We are trying to raise up a generation of young people who know what a Christian home is about." He then defined proper gender roles. "Young men who know what it means to be the head of the home; to be under the Lordship of Jesus Christ and how to be the spiritual leader." Next he explained the correct role of women: "We're trying to raise up young ladies here who know what it means to be in the subjection to Jesus and in subjection of her husband." This formula is what a strong marriage consisted of in Falwell's eyes, and he believed young Christians had an opportunity to build such relationships through his church and Christian college. "And these young people come here [to Liberty College] admittedly looking for a Christian husband, a Christian wife." He concluded this point by citing what gave his view credibility, which mirrored Rushdoony's philosophy about the family: "We believe the Christian home is the basic unit of society."[18]

Beyond using what was designed by God to define the family, Falwell explained what was "unnatural" when making his case against homosexuality. In 1977, an upset Falwell complained: "Without natural affection, [Romans 1] verse 3 and of course this is very obvious. This means men not interested in women, women not interested in men, but men with men working that which is unseemly, women with women, lesbians, homosexuals, without natural affection. Now if God says something is unnatural and in Romans 1 calls it reprobate and perverted then we needn't call it anything else." He then accused secular Americans of violating God-created separate gender spheres through contemporary fashion and the women's liberation movement: "And yet, today, there's a real effort to create a unisexual society, where the men all look like women and the women all look like men and you can't really tell them apart. And where, very often the women work and the men keep the children." By the end of the rant, he was furious with those who were turning God's creation upside down. Homosexuality and lack of gender distinctions "were just a total reversal in every strata of life, a disintegration of the home, without natural affection."[19] Here, Falwell simply was not rejecting homosexuality and inseparable gender distinction, but justified his argument by stating that such lifestyles overturned the proper role humanity was intended to play as designed by God. It was "without natural affection." Similar statements centering on what God intended or natural for humanity were not uncommon during Sunday morning services at Thomas Road Baptist Church.

Although Falwell cited New Testament scriptures to support his views on homosexuality in his 1977 sermon, the terms he used were connected with humanity's proper place within God's designed hierarchy as structured at the time of creation in the Garden of Eden. He would make such a statement nearly verbatim several years later while at a seminar in 1982 when defining the family: "Family in the Garden of Eden became a reality when God brought together a man and a woman—one man for one woman for one lifetime."[20] It was at this moment at creation that God structured the family and any deviation was a perversion in Falwell's eyes. This understanding is what upset him so much during his sermon in 1977 and caused him to conclude that alternative marriage roles were a "total reversal in every strata of life." A total reversal was an unnatural change in what God had intended or designed for humanity at creation.

Schaeffer's Magnum Opus

While Rushdoony's idea of Reconstruction suffered from certain problems, such as capital punishment and disbanding the government, and was in part rejected by the conservative evangelical community, fellow theological intellectual Francis Schaeffer presented a more generalized and friendlier version of the ideology in a book that he turned into a film documentary titled, *How Should We Then Live?* The conservative evangelical community considered the book and film astoundingly insightful and enlightening. It made sense of the 1970s by validating the Christian's faith and cultural understanding of where humanity, God, and the earth fit within their long-held beliefs in the Judeo-Christian hierarchy. Moreover, it revealed what happens if humanity strays from its proper place and does not live in subjugation to God's design. Schaeffer presented the film documentary version of *How Should We Then Live?* as a ten-part series. Each episode chronologically analyzed important periods in Western civilization from Rome to the present.

How Should We Then Live? explained the present by examining history through the lens of humanity's proper relationship with God. Schaeffer began by comparing the United States to the Roman Empire. He said Rome was not based on absolute truths as handed down by God and thus people functioned on self-interest instead of acting on what was best for society. Rome's primary mistake was that their gods were created by men and thus were finite and too weak for a society to function on. Christianity, however, had an infinite God that always was and always will be. Morality and rules descended from God to humans were a product of God's creation. Deviating from what God intended led to ruin as exemplified by the fall of Rome.

The rest of the documentary primarily followed the pattern of Schaeffer's analysis of Rome. Any period in history that went "well," Schaeffer concluded, was a consequence of humanity living in accordance with the intended God/human/natural world relationship. He determined that the era of the early Church was pure. People lived modestly, he said, and gave frequently to the church, which led them to set up charitable institutions, support the elderly, and create hospitals. However, as time went by, early Christians moved away from the design by dividing the church and the Bible and mixing human fabricated philosophies with scripture, which replaced God with mankind. This human-centered philosophy remained predominant and, according to Schaeffer, is reflected in Renaissance art such as Michelangelo's David, a humanist portrayal of the power of man. Similarly, Leonardo da Vinci understood humanity merely as a machine. This worldview changed again during the Protestant Reformation, when people moved away from society's humanistic elements to embrace the absolute truth of the Bible and restore God's place over humanity.

During the Revolutionary age, Schaeffer explained, new philosophies from the likes of Thomas Jefferson were the product of a circle of Christian consensus.[21] What the founding fathers of the United States built was a direct result of the Protestant Reformation, a time when people successfully implemented humanity's proper place in creation. Thus the United States was successful because it was produced from a "balanced" and correct idealism. In contrast, Schaeffer found the French Revolution was not based on biblical principles: its Rights of Man, for example, lacked any acknowledgment of God. Furthermore, he stated that because the French Revolution alienated religion, the consequence was sad events such as the taking of thousands of lives during the Reign of Terror. Schaeffer connected the French Revolution with the Red October 1917 revolution in Russia and remarked that communism was based on the same principles of ignoring God.

Schaeffer then spoke about the problems that the scientific age brought mankind, including Darwin's theory of evolution. He argued that evolution takes God out of His place as creator and puts humanity on the same level as animals. The idea of survival of the fittest allowed people to lose the belief that man is totally unique and a creation of God. With this new philosophy nothing is sacred; it led to eugenics, allowed for the Holocaust, and could lead to harvesting organs from humans in the future.

During the rest of *How Should We Then Live?* Schaeffer explained that modern society has increasingly accepted humanism and evolution by replacing God with man-centered philosophies. As a future consequence, society would theoretically break down and the government will grow in an attempt to control people. However, chaos will be the only result. Schaeffer's documentary used dramatizations depicting a society bereft of a relationship with God, whose only option is to turn to an all-powerful manmade government. To keep the people under control, Schaeffer speculated, government agents would one day put LSD in the water supply and select who should reproduce with genetic engineering. In conclusion, Schaeffer warned that humanity was at a crossroads where society could either turn back to restore everything to its proper relationship with God, or people could incessantly try to maintain a society that had no bearings or absolutes, where only chaos and perversion reigned.

Within the first five and a half months of publication, Francis Schaeffer's son Franky reported that the book sold 114,000 copies.[22] To this day Franky, now Frank, receives royalty checks for writing, producing, and directing the film version in addition to his other feature, *Whatever Happened to the Human Race?* amounting to several thousand dollars a year.[23] The reason for such a response from the conservative evangelical community was that *How Should We Then Live?* concisely explained societal problems by using the Christian faith. Additionally, it offered a prediction of what the future would look like if secular society continued its present course of ignoring God's design and embracing a society directed by manmade constructions. Conservative evangelical churches wrestled with these issues during the 1970s, and Schaeffer gave them faith-based solutions in his book and film documentary, which were sold throughout the world.[24]

In 1979, Schaeffer once again reiterated his concept of humanity's proper place by centering on the "unnatural" practice of abortion in his book and film documentary, *Whatever Happened to the Human Race?*, which he co-wrote with President Ronald Reagan's surgeon general, C. Everett Koop. In one scene within the first episode, Koop stood next to a salt lake surrounded by plastic baby dolls. Koop explained that he was in the Middle East, standing on the same ground where Sodom and Gomorrah once existed. The symbolism is clear. Abortion is a corruption and perversion of modern man, not unlike the social norms set by people in the biblical depiction of Sodom and Gomorrah thousands of years ago, which God found reprehensible and destroyed with fire. While at the ancient site, Koop commented on the upset of creation's hierarchy by reporting that a million abortions are performed each year while advocate groups fight to protect baby seals from being slaughtered. Furthermore, he noted that other species of animals are protected by the endangered species list and that quotas are followed for whale hunting. This argument Koop proposed underscored the hypocrisy of modern society's acceptance of abortion while protecting animals, which represented, in the eyes of conservative evangelicals, a clear attack on humanity's intended "proper place" in the God-ordained hierarchy of life. Other scenes in the film conveyed the message that abortion also destroyed the hierarchy of creation by showing animals and infants adjacent to each other in laboratory testing cages.

Beyond Schaeffer, the place of humanity in God's hierarchy was also important to Falwell. In 1982, he gave a sermon centering on abortion and repeated the analogy between unborn babies and animals that Koop had made. However, before making his point, Falwell made sure his congregation knew he was an "animal lover" and believed in "animal rights." He said that he once had seventeen dogs until his neighbors complained, but he still continued to have them in and out of the house. Falwell then cited an ad he saw in an unspecified magazine. "I love animals," Falwell began, "But let me read this to you in a nation that's aborting, murdering by suctions, by saline solution, and by any other means beating and destroying little babies to death at the rate of one and half million a year. Here's what the ad says. Each year some one hundred and eighty thousand baby harp seals are clubbed to death by Canadian and Norwegian seal hunters. Using our tax dollars—um, sounds like Planned Parenthood." He then backtracked, validating animal rights but not if they upset the hierarchy. "Now I want to say that I respect what they're doing, but isn't it a tragedy that in a nation where one a half million little babies are being torn to pieces [seals are receiving more attention] . . . I believe the baby harp seals ought to be saved. I believe the baby children ought to be saved too."[25] Here, Falwell was not dismissing the value of animal life. Instead he was reassessing the situation by factoring the value of humans into the creation hierarchy. However, Falwell completely abandoned this more nuanced approach to nonhuman nature in the 1990s.

Speaking to the same point as Koop who argued that abortion upset humanity's place in the created order, pastors sermonized against elevating people to the level of the creator. In the sermon "The Law of Sowing and Reaping," Falwell spoke about divorce and warned that it was a reason for social problems. Next he stated, "Down here in Norfolk [Virginia] and other places where we have genetic engineering going on, in vitro fertilization and so on, scientists are playing God. That is no less a criminal activity than ministers who play God like Jim Jones [the cult leader who led followers in committing suicide]. . . . Better leave that to God Almighty."[26] He then went on to speak out against homosexuality in the same breath.

In 1980, Bellevue Baptist Church pastor Adrian Rogers also spoke against science creating life in his sermon, "The God of Creation." He mused, "I read in the newspapers a while back where the newspaper said, 'Scientists Create Life in Laboratory.' Whoopee do. . . . No scientist ever created anything." Rogers warned that mankind was playing in the realm where only God should tread: "And I'm fearfully afraid in, in ah, of what mankind is able to do and what mankind will do with his so-called vaunted knowledge and wisdom. But only God has the power to create."[27] Schaeffer had also warned against creating life in the laboratory as well as abortion in episode 10 of *How Should We Then Live?* He argued that since humanity had removed the laws of God from society, the authoritarian elite would use science to replace God. Schaeffer expected genetic engineering to be very popular in the future and thought that the elite would decide reproduction rates.[28] Falwell believed that science's role in procreation was so important that he brought it to President-elect Ronald Reagan's attention in a meeting soon after the election of 1980. Among the "ethical issues" discussed with Reagan on December 29 were "Artificial Insemination, selective breeding, genetic engineering and euthanasia."[29]

God Speaking through Nature to Define Humanity's Proper Place

Conservative evangelical Harold Lindsell's 1970 article "Suicide Ahead?" (discussed in chapter 1) not only highlighted the ecological crisis, but also argued that it was a consequence of humanity's move away from the created hierarchy under God. Lindsell understood the ecological crisis as a punishment from God, much as Koop's symbolism of using Sodom and Gomorrah as evidence of God's punishment on humanity when God's rules are broken. He furthermore wrote, "We who are indebted to Scripture know that man is rooted and grounded in God. When God dies [due to abandoning faith], then man of necessity must also die." The laws of the hierarchical relationship between God and humans, he continued, are universal and affect unbelievers as they do Christians. "If they [unbelievers] disregard or disobey those laws, which are intrinsic to God's creation, they still destroy themselves."[30] In parallel with Rushdoony's and Schaeffer's views, Lindsell argued that this disconnection between God and mankind explained the turmoil in the world, including being the direct cause for the ecological crisis.

Lindsell furthermore described the breaking of the relationship between God and humanity as a "perversion" and as being "unnatural," and he supported such views through historical comparisons. He compared the United States to Rome and Greece, writing, "When those nations [Rome and Greece] at last perverted and disobeyed those laws [of God as absolute creator], those cultures perished." Like Schaeffer in *Death in the City* and *Pollution and the Death of Man*, Lindsell blamed this upset hierarchy for causing problems among humanity and the various troubles that plagued the nonhuman natural world. He concluded: "Man is cutting himself off from his Creator and he is also cutting himself off from God's creation by the abuse and disobedience of those laws which relate to God's creation under common grace."[31] To Lindsell, the secular environmentalists were on the wrong track in blaming only human indifference and greed for the degradation of the natural world. In agreement with Rushdoony and Schaeffer, Lindsell argued the deeper cause was upsetting the intended hierarchical relationship that humanity should have with

God. The ecological crisis was a consequence of God letting humanity know they needed to return to His rules; if not they would receive additional punishments from God.

Religious right cofounders Pat Robertson and Jerry Falwell held similar views as Lindsell and Schaeffer when it came to explaining pestilence on the earth. Robertson in particular described the repercussions of God's displeasure with humanity's refusing to live God-centered lives and used nature as an exemplar. In 1981, he wrote, "One historic measure of divine judgment is poor weather leading to poor crops. Famine serves as a warning. We can expect further drought in 1981 and a reduction in grain output. By 1982, unless there is a further turning to God in our land, we may well experience alarming drought and crop shortages."[32] These problems, he believed, were the result of the movement away from God to embrace law made by mankind: "A new rule of law is emerging. No longer do judges seek to make decisions based on the Bible, the Constitution, natural law, or historic precedent. . . . We have ceased to be a government of law and have become a government of men."[33] For Robertson, who echoed Schaeffer's view of American history, the United States was founded on the immutable laws of God. "The United States was founded as a Constitutional Republic with the concept that its laws, rights, and privileges came from a higher power—'the Creator.'"[34] Such views were common for Robertson. He often predicted pestilence and decline, but such an understanding was not absolutely inevitable. Like Rushdoony, he reasoned that if people turned to God, health would return to society and the earth. These feelings were common in his writings and could be witnessed years later in 1991, for example, when he speculated about the build-up that led to the 1991 Gulf War, earthquakes, and the eruption at Mt. St. Helen. These bleak events, Robertson argued, were divine retribution for humans ignoring God. "America has held a unique place in the world's history because we have been a Christian nation. Now as a nation we have forsaken God and His commandments. Will our Friend and Protector become our enemy and our avenging judge? Will tragedy and suffering be needed to return us to Him?"[35]

Similar views depicting a supernatural conversation between humanity and God were seen elsewhere during Sunday morning services. Pastor and former Liberty College seminary student Jerry Johnson opened a sermon speaking out on the sins of the United States, including homosexuality and pornography, and then suggested that God would judge the nation as He did in the biblical story of Sodom and Gomorrah. To prove God had dispensed punishment to mankind since biblical times, Johnson told the story of Jacksonboro, Georgia. He reported that the town was full of sin and that after the townsfolk rebuked a traveling preacher, God sent a flood to destroy the whole community.[36]

Jerry Falwell likewise explained national hardship, including the energy and ecological crisis, as God punishing humanity for not heeding His laws. In a 1976 sermon titled "America Back to God," He reasoned, "What about the energy crisis? Three years ago, from out of the blue we're out of oil. Strange, all of our lives we've never heard of such a thing. Now we're hearing about food shortages in the future. Our air and water are polluted. This is all, I believe, the wrath of God upon a nation who has inside her borders a sleeping church."[37] By 1979, however, he started thinking the energy crisis was a fabrication but still thought environmental issues needed to be addressed.[38] What was more important to Falwell was getting the United States as a society back to Bible-believing Christians and protecting the God-ordained construction of the family. When these first crucial steps were accomplished, all other things would fall into line.

Rushdoony, along with Falwell and the others proposed that the nonhuman natural world was a thermometer of God's relationship with mankind. In his second volume of the *Institutes of Biblical Law* published in 1982, Rushdoony examined the proper relationship between humanity and wilderness. Once again, Rushdoony set the "right" relationship at the point of creation. "Because God created man in His image to exercise dominion over the earth and to subdue it (Gen 1:26–28), God gave to man a relationship to the earth similar to His own relationship to His total creation. . . . Man's relationship to the earth is subject to the absolute Kingship of God, but, in a secondary sense, it is one of dependence: the earth depends upon man." Rushdoony meant that the health of the Earth depended on mankind living accordance to God. "The ground is cursed because of man's sin (Gen 3:17). The earth flourishes and is blessed as man is holy and obedient to the Lord; it is cursed and profane when man is disobedient (Deut. 28)."[39] He further illustrated this understanding by describing how a captain commands a ship:

> This influence [between sin and the earth] might perhaps be compared to that of a ship's captain upon his ship; the captain's dereliction affects the ship. This comparison however, proves too much. *First*, the relationship between a captain and his ship is mechanical in operation, and, *second*, it involves a very different kind of command than man exercises over nature. . . . The relationship of man to the earth is not mechanical; it is *religious*." (emphasis in original)[40]

Therefore, the health of the planet, in Rushdoony's eyes, depended on following one's faith. He was not advocating followers to reconstruct the earth by physically changing it, for it would change toward the negative or positive as humanity either remained sinful or turned back to God. He repeated and expanded this same view in his book's next two sections, "Sin and the Earth" and "Land, Holiness, and Dominion."

Conclusion

Biblical literalists fought publicly against the theory of evolution in the famous Scopes Monkey Trial of 1925. Although the fundamentalist side won the case, the group was visibly humiliated and did not make waves on the same national level until the emergence of the religious right in the late 1970s. The origin story of the religious right is found in the later 1960s when a series of social movements further challenged the conservative evangelical worldview of humanity's proper place within creation. This came in the particular form of women's and gay advocacy groups. Additionally, the tumultuous period of the later 1960s, which included Vietnam War protests, race riots, the impending ecological crisis, and the threat of a nuclear attack by the Soviet Union, was very unsettling to all Americans, including conservative evangelicals. In response, throughout the 1970s conservative evangelicals repeatedly told themselves that the end of world was coming, inspired in part by Hal Lindsay's *The Late Great Planet Earth*. While this religious community could agree that doomsday was indeed coming, Rushdoony, Schaeffer, Falwell, Robertson, and others encouraged a proactive movement to return humanity to its divine place in the universe. Their plan was structured as something very close to what might be called a Christian "back-to-the-land movement."

This Christian "back-to-the land" movement that Falwell and others offered conservative evangelicals in the 1970s, consistently repeated that health of life in general could be attained if people just get back as close as possible to God's structure as resembled in the Garden of Eden: live as Adam and Eve did in the garden, one man for one woman bonded in marriage; understand that the family is the unchangeable basic unit of society; acknowledge that humans are of God's creation and science cannot take the place of God as creator; and realize that when humans deviate from the ways of the Garden of Eden, only disaster awaits in the form of problems and pestilence. For conservative evangelicals, resolving problems such as the ecological crisis required that people return to God's laws and cease their human-created or artificial lifestyles. As in the biblical chapter of Isaiah, the only way to save the crumbling nation of Israel was not to be found in human developments in the areas of economics, science, or technology but through worshiping God and living "correctly."

Bible messages similar to that of Isaiah, such as Noah and the flood as well as the story of Sodom and Gomorrah, helped provide the foundations for the

conservative evangelical belief that God, humanity, and nature are intercon-
nected. According to the Bible, with the exception of Noah and his family, mankind had forgotten God and His commandments. As a consequence, God
decided to start the world anew by sending a natural disaster via a worldwide
flood. This account is very similar to the other Genesis story about the destruction of Sodom and Gomorrah. The fate of these two cities remained regularly cited in conservative evangelical culture to show what happens when
humanity misbehaves. The key importance to the idea of "misbehaving" is that
it signifies a perversion or a departure from mankind's proper place in creation
and therefore merits retribution from God. Conversely, if humanity respects
and follows God's biblical laws, then society as a whole will function in harmony and people will reap blessings from their creator.

Indeed, conservative evangelicals formulated a holistic view of creation and
its health, including family, community, nation, and the environment, in which
all depended on maintaining mankind's proper place in God's hierarchical creation. The formula for a better earthly existence was quite plain to Rushdoony, Schaeffer, Falwell, and Robertson throughout the 1970s. All they needed
was organization and support to effectively turn it into a movement. During
this process, their understanding of the nonhuman natural world continued
to evolve.

"natural order"

consequences → ecological disaster

CHAPTER 3

Nature in a Religious Right Perspective

As editorials encouraging Christian environmental activism virtually disappeared from the pages of the religious community's most popular magazines, commentaries on homosexuality and abortion—sometimes linked to pollution and natural disasters—filled the void. Between October 10, 1969, and September 25, 1970, *Christianity Today* published three articles on homosexuality and eleven on abortion. These numbers steadily rose over the years. As shown in table 3.1, between October 8, 1976, and September 23, 1977, homosexuality garnered fifteen articles, and abortion rose to sixteen. Indeed, it was these issues and their evolving place in wider society that greatly concerned conservative evangelicals. In response, leaders including Falwell and Robertson blamed related social changes for the world's problems and argued a solution could be found through humanity returning to its natural and proper relationship with God. The formula for "normalcy" however, needed a vehicle for implementation. Thus, conservative evangelicals required a movement of their own.

Falwell took the initiative by trying out various approaches on his congregation, the attached k–12 Christian school, the college, and his television broadcast, *The Old Time Gospel Hour*. While the philosophy of humanity's proper place in God's creation percolated throughout the conservative evangelical world, the community constructed other ideas to help build an identity for the religious right movement, which included sustained messages of eco-friendly Christian environmental stewardship throughout the 1970s.[1] This identity should be understood as a developing sense of nationalism that allowed conservative evangelicals to believe they were direct religious descendants of early American settlers who earned or legitimized their place in the New World by struggling with and overcoming the wilderness. It was through this historical perception that those who became the religious right legitimized and justified their special status as "real Americans," charged in the present to save "their" country from secular and liberal political forces. This imagined history was normal fare during Sunday church services and was clarified in detail within the educational material used by thousands of Christian schools throughout the United States. In parallel with this Christian nationalist message, eco-friendly nature sentiments remained the religious group's standard environmental view. Thus, evidence demonstrates that instead of neglecting the environmental issue or marginalizing nature's value by believing humanity should dominate and therefore use the earth as a simple economic resource, conservative evangelicals continued holding an environmentally sympathetic philosophy of Christian environmental stewardship. At the same time they were using ideas of nature to construct their own political identity.

On the evening of April 4, 1975, thousands of the faithful streamed into Thomas Road Baptist Church in Lynchburg, Virginia. In addition to a full sanctuary, two other church buildings were filled to maximum capacity, including the gymnasium. The youth program alone counted over 2,500 in attendance. It was "patriotic day" for pastor Jerry Falwell's megachurch, and the service was later televised in the United States and Canada.[2] The choir was decked out in red, white, and blue, ready to perform a fifteen-minute program titled "I Love America." The service began with one of the singers, Doug Oldham, requesting donations to fund the church's Christian school. While stirring piano music played, Oldham explained that he had recently received a letter from an elderly lady who was on a fixed income and donated only one dollar. The meager gift however, was worth far more, as it was found in her husband's

Table 3.1   Issues throughout the 1970s

OCT. 10, 1969–SEPT. 25, 1970	OCT. 9, 1970–JULY 16, 1971	OCT. 13, 1972–SEPT. 28, 1973	OCT. 12, 1973–SEPT. 27, 1974	OCT. 11, 1974–SEPT. 26, 1975	OCT. 8, 1976–SEPT. 23, 1977
Gay Rights: 3	Gay Rights: 5	Gay Rights: 5	Gay Rights: 8	Gay Rights: 6	Gay Rights: 15
Abortion: 11	Abortion: 13	Abortion: 17	Abortion: 10	Abortion: 14	Abortion: 16

This information was compiled from the number of articles under the index headings found in the bound annual periodical volumes of *Christianity Today.*

wallet the day he died. Oldham suggested that only the work of God is worth such gifts, and then he sang an old time favorite, "It Will Be Worth It All." Falwell followed with a few lighthearted jokes about the piano player and promised that congregants could sit on the floor if the church ran out of chairs. He asked his audience and those at home to purchase Bibles. Part of the proceeds would go into the Christian school.

His relaxed demeanor then turned more serious. Falwell directly contrasted his Christian schools with the late 1960s counterculture. "Lynchburg Baptist College and these other schools," Falwell began, "are unique in that unlike most American colleges and universities today to our shame, there is patriotism on this campus."[3] He continued in this vein: "Our young people love America, it's not just talk and music. It's not just bicentennial celebration. Yes, we're praying for revival. But, these young people love America." Falwell promised his schools were pro-American. "We don't have any draft card burners and American flag desecraters on this campus. It's not allowed. Our young people love America. Thank God for the freedom here. With all our problems, where else in the world can you see and hear, what you're about to see and hear right now. I love America."[4]

Straightaway the orchestra played the introduction for the chorus, who sang an upbeat, inspirational song about the love they held for the United States. During a pause in the music, a young woman cited Alexis de Tocqueville, who concluded during his time in nineteenth-century America that the source of the new nation's greatness was the Christian church. The speaker warned, however: "Today our nation has left her faith in God and the principles which laid the foundations of her greatness." The only hope was spiritual revival. A man spoke over the crescendo of the chorus repeating that people must not be dismayed because "The church . . . it's alive and doing well!"[5]

The introduction and "I Love America" program were not just a call for money and indeed, as Falwell pointed out, it was not only a bicentennial celebration. The entire introduction was expertly woven together into layered messages that advertised a specific brand. Besides selling the traditional evangelical spiritual message for the individual to form a personal connection with God (promising everlasting life), Falwell incorporated the idea that godly, salt of the earth Americans, could save their country from certain destruction. This goal would not be accomplished by sending missionaries to far-away lands. Instead, donations were invested into the building of a Christian educational establishment that consisted of a k–12 school and a college, which he promised would produce patriotic Christians. The audience had the opportunity not only to contribute by giving their money and attending services, but could also actively participate by sending their children to his schools.

Falwell was promoting a unique national identity known as "Christian nationalism." Combined with the conservative evangelical understanding of mankind's proper place in God's creation, this form of nationalism was meant to fuel the group into social and political action. Additionally, to help strengthen the nationalistic philosophy, conservative evangelicals incorporated new perceptions of the natural world, which were taught in the growing Christian school movement, including Falwell's patriotic k–12 academy. These views of nature championed a simpler time embodied in romantic notions of early colonists, eighteenth-century frontier families, and a nineteenth-century agrarian country, when people struggled against and worked closely with the land. This carefully constructed narrative of the past openly embraced the idea of austere early settlers as hardy subsistence farmers. Thus, although twentieth-century conservative evangelicals outwardly championed American capitalism, at least in their imagined construction of the past, affluence and ideas of the city were downplayed to create a more heroic narrative of who they believed were their religious ancestors. All of these ideas worked together into a formula for saving the God-ordained institutions of family, church, and nation. Falwell was not the only socially and politically active fundamentalist turned conservative evangelical or neo-evangelical promoting these philosophies, but he was undeniably the most prominent and the most successful of his generation, whom he guided to form the religious right movement.

Christian Nationalism

Christian nationalism is an imagined common national heritage that features conservative evangelicals as descendants of a glorious past who are charged in the present with saving the future of the country. Its leaders could not build a movement solely based on reactions that produced feelings of fear and hatred for the 1960s counterculture. They had to create something they hoped Americans would embrace and ultimately become. Conservative evangelicals had a basic idea of what they wanted, and it was not just what came before the late 1960s. In 1962 and 1963, the Supreme Court prohibited prayer and Bible reading in public schools and, before that, their community was embarrassed on the national level by media coverage of the Scopes Monkey Trial in 1925. Perhaps the key to building a Christian national identity was to go beyond living memory. They settled on pre-industrial America, and the best place to build this ideology was in the already developing Christian school movement. The material taught in these schools had to make sense of the world from a Christian perspective. Its authors also did not have the luxury of pastors who could skip over or generalize issues as was possible in Sunday sermons. Their published educational products required specific messages supported by "factual" detail and far more importantly, they must be parent and pastor approved.

The Christian School movement began during the 1960s and rapidly increased between the late 1970 and the early 1980s, with the addition of up to 1,000 Christian schools founded annually. By 1987 there was an estimated 15,000 Christian schools in the United States.[6] In 1988, Robert Smith, executive director of the Council for American Private Education, estimated the Christian school enrollment to be about 700,000 students, while the executive director of the Association of Christian Schools International, Paul Kienel, speculated that they numbered around 1 million. These figures should be tempered by the fact that Christian schools represent only 2–3 percent of the entire k–12 educational system.[7] Even so, as of the turn of the twenty-first century, Christian school attendance consistently amounts to over 1 million students.[8]

As Christian and home schools expanded during the 1960s and into the 1970s, Bob Jones University and the founders of Pensacola Christian College stepped in to meet the educational material needs of the classroom through their publishing arms: BJU Press and A Beka Book. The two became among the most popular publishers and were commonly utilized not only by conservative evangelicals, but also other Protestant schools. As educational historian Adam Laats explains, the Christian school movement was instigated by the 1962 Supreme Court decision regarding school prayer, which led to a backlash among evangelical and fundamentalist churches and extended to other Protestant denominations including Lutherans and Mennonites. Each group needed basic religious-oriented educational material attractive for a "wide-evangelical basis," which A Beka Book and BJU Press provided.[9] Thus, these publishers cast a large net to connect with readers, and their material was commonly mixed together in classrooms throughout the Christian school community. This situation meant that the Christian educational material from A Beka Book and BJU Press were employed not only in fundamentalist classrooms, but also throughout the entire Christian school community. Therefore, and most importantly, the educational messages produced by these publishers constituted the educational foundation of the classroom experience for "thousands of Christian day schools opening throughout the 1970s and 1980s."[10]

As a historical source, the Christian school material should be understood as representing the conservative evangelical, and soon-to-be religious right, mainstream community. As previously mentioned, the material was tailored specifically for evangelical and fundamentalist students, but it also had to be parent approved, and even Christian schools found pleasing parents to be difficult. One fundamentalist Christian school, for example, allowed students to use older secular history textbooks to take up the slack of the Christian publishers that had not yet produced material for all levels.[11] One older "secular" textbook used at this particular school apparently did not meet the standard of at least one parent who censored a section by hand probably in the late 1970s or early 1980s.[12] In this instance, glue and black construction paper covered President Franklin Roosevelt's biography likely in reaction to his support of big government through the New Deal. These parents, after all, cared enough about their child's education that they had deemed public schools untrustworthy because of their "liberal ideologies" and in response wished to ensure their children received a Christian-centered education. In other words, these parents were serious about the material their children read in school and wanted to ensure that each message relayed from author to audience was carefully calculated. Thus, this educational material should be understood as one of the most accurate and important sources reflecting the worldviews and ideologies of the conservative evangelical community in the 1970s, which later became the religious right movement. In sum, the publishers designed the information in textbooks for k–12 students as common accepted truths and not as unsettled and controversial debates among conservative evangelicals on the national level.

During its first years as a publishing company, A Beka Book scrambled to get "readers" out to elementary school audiences and soon realized that they did not necessarily need new material. They began by reprinting literature from the eighteenth, nineteenth and early twentieth centuries that promoted acceptable values. This included old standards such as *Pilgrim's Progress* and especially the well-known McGuffey Readers of the nineteenth century. The latter was a series of primer booklets produced for elementary school students beginning in the 1830s by a Protestant traveling preacher named William Holmes McGuffey. The stories all had religious-friendly morals and took place in rural areas or small towns. The venue for the stories is not surprising given that McGuffey intended his product for a predominately agrarian nineteenth-century audience. But what remains peculiar is that later twentieth-century conservative evangelicals who sent their children to Christian schools could fancy themselves being of the same ilk.

Many members of southern churches were first- and second-generation urban dwellers, who had relocated from the farm to industrial centers in places such as Los Angeles. That is, whereas two-thirds of the South's population lived in rural areas during the 1940s, by 1960 less than one-half remained and only 10 percent worked on farms.[13] Now separated from agrarian life in the 1970s, these people could romanticize the bucolic landscapes depicted in the Mc-Guffey stories read by their children and imagine a simpler time of moral and hard-working Christian Americans who settled the frontier by constructing and maintaining family farms. In other words, parents approved of the reading material that championed the hard work and long-held respected morals learned on the family farm, frontier settlements, or small town life. These places were devoid of technology that made life easy along with the vices and problems of the present-day cities.

What is unique about the educational material is that it was not intended just to educate, but to build barriers against the changes in late-1960s American society while at the same time promoting a nationalistic identity throughout the Christian school community, one in which the relationship between humanity and the nonhuman natural world played an important role.

A Beka Book made its nationalist message paramount in a series of readers intended for elementary students titled "The OF AMERICA Reading Series." The introduction to one of the books stated, "The purpose of the OF AMERICA Reading Series is to return to the nation's classrooms the great patriotic and character-building classics which have become a part of our national heritage, but which have been almost universally excluded in textbooks in the recent years."[14] In short, while learning to read, students received precise messages supporting a particular "national heritage." The vast majority of the stories used to accomplish these ends took place in a pre-twentieth-century America, when pioneers earned their homes by struggling with and overcoming the obstacles in a wilderness environment.

Earning the Land

Producing educational material gave A Beka Book the opportunity to rewrite history. Their OF AMERICA Reading Series did exactly that by offering stories, poems, and illustrations that not only relayed moral and patriotic messages, but also portrayed the origins of the United States as God-ordained and earned through hard work. The books often used a common formula emphasizing that the first colonists and later westward migrants did not just relocate to start a new life, but were on a mission to find a new land where they could worship freely. This goal was given value by emphasizing the settlers' courage, faith, independence, and hard work, which enabled them to overcome environmental obstacles, including crossing oceans and taming the wilderness. Perhaps most importantly, authors portrayed settlers earning their home within a reciprocal process in which they carved out farms from the wilderness while the necessary hard work and unstable environment made them strong God-fearing people in return. Thus, the landscape played a central role in the way twentieth-century conservative evangelicals wanted to remember the founding of the United States. It was these origin stories that helped lead to a sense of nationalism and in consequence the development of the religious right movement.

For their history, the authors of the OF AMERICA Reading Series chose the story of the Pilgrims to demonstrate the nation's Christian roots and identify their religious and national ancestors. In the booklet *OF AMERICA, Volume II*, published in 1975, such a message came through in the poem "The Landing of the Pilgrim Fathers" by Felicia Hemans, first written in the early nineteenth century. The poem's sentiments dovetailed with the new nation's interest in building a sense of unity and identity. Such a goal fit perfectly with what A Beka Book editors needed to tell their readers about how their religious ancestors were responsible for the creation of the United Stated and earned the land by their faith and hard work.

The terms "landing" and "fathers" in the title already suggested an origin story and the first lines described the dangerous environment facing the Pilgrims:

> The breaking waves dashed high,
> On a stern and rock-bound coast,
> And the woods against a stormy sky,
> Their giant branches tossed.

The untamed elements presaged a daunting and insecure future for the Pilgrims, who met their new land with bravery and faith while singing hymns of "lofty cheer." The author asked: Why had these people come from their homeland and risked their lives? Not for riches, she answered, but to freely worship God. As a result, the poem concluded, the Pilgrims created a home or rather a "holy ground" in the New England wilderness.[15]

This poem embodied the essential theme of the OF AMERICA Reading Series, minus a description of the hard work it would take to make a home in the wilderness. It offered an origin story for the United States, depicting a God-ordained holy land and conveying messages of hope, religious faith, and bravery in the face of dangerous obstacles—lessons the A Beka Book editors desired their young readers to carry into adulthood. The last question written by the editors in the subsequent student activity section pertaining to the poem asked, "What can you do to leave this land unstained for those who come after you?" This question did not implore readers to keep from "staining" the land through environmental pollution, but rather to continue the laudable goal of the

Pilgrims who survived natural threats to find a "holy ground" on which to practice their faith. The editor asked of the student readers in home and Christian schools to draw parallels and emulate Pilgrim virtues for the benefit of future generations because the brave and successful Pilgrims were their religious ancestors and founders of America.

The wilderness of North America played the role of a dangerous obstacle in many stories beyond "The Landing of the Pilgrim Fathers." The first historical story within another of A Beka Book's OF AMERICA Reading series *Flags Unfurled*, for example, was titled "The First Fight." Here, the authors retold the common narrative regarding the Pilgrims' struggle to feed themselves during their first winter in the harsh New England environment. The desperate situation led to some of their number dying, while others barely survived. During this dire period, the authors explained, the Pilgrims nevertheless persevered, demonstrating strength, bravery, and hard work in a daunting landscape where danger lurked. Like the accompanying illustration showing a skulking Native American coming upon a log cabin in a snowy forest, the prose explained the perilous conditions and the Pilgrim's response: "A swift dart shot from an Indian bow in the forest, or the echo of a savage yell terrified" the Pilgrims, but "they went on hunting and staking off plots for gardens and houses, and cutting logs and stalking game in a fearless way that interested the Indian tribes." Although Indians might be dangerous, the reader learned that the Pilgrim heroes ultimately controlled the environment and their future by following Squanto's instructions. The conclusion explained that through the hard work of creating successful farms and thereby earning their place in the wilderness, the Pilgrims enjoyed their first Thanksgiving with their Indian neighbors. The text interpreted the Pilgrims' success in enduring a harsh environment as the historic beginnings of what became the United States. As the last sentence stated, "It was a very good foundation which the Pilgrims had laid for building their stronghold of hope, a land of liberty."[16] Thus, the very struggle to reshape wilderness into a pastoral land played an integral role in the nation's origin story carried out by the Pilgrims, who twentieth-century conservative evangelicals understood to be their direct religious ancestors, and consequently, this story made them heirs to the nation or rather, "real Americans."

Within the pages of the book *Flags Unfurled*, the editors went so far as to explicitly tell their audience what makes a "real American" by including another reprinted piece titled "Pioneers." It began, "Some of our poets and thinkers have tried to tell us what it means to be a real American." Like the other stories, the authors centered on the struggle to control or shape the wilderness as the formula that produced these "real Americans." "No doubt the work of making a living in the depths of the vast American forest developed strength of body and mind in the pioneers. . . . Every blow aimed at trees that surrounded his cabin in the forest made the backwoodsman safer in his hold upon the wilderness." As in "The First Fight," the settlers in this story overcame the obstacles that faced them to become rightful owners of the land they had earned. They controlled their surroundings by bending nature to work for them, and in the process became strong individuals and therefore an ideal people to lay the foundations of a new country. "Such was the life of the settlers in the clearings of the great forests of the New World. Of stern, hardy stuff, they worked hard and fought bravely to keep their hold on the land they had won. This was the way the adventurers and colonists from the Old World countries became Americans."[17]

Of the different stories depicted in A Beka Book's Of AMERICA Reading Series, the story "Pioneers" is a prime example of the formula of combining hard work and individualism. The series gave young readers the understanding that it was their religious ancestors who created the United States by taming the wilderness and believing in God. This process gave conservative evangelicals in the 1970s the heritage to imagine themselves heirs of the United States.

A Beka Book material also created a sense of Christian nationalism through accompanying illustrations. "The Landing of The Pilgrim Fathers" featured an full-page reproduction of a watercolor showing brave, sturdy Pilgrims walking through a snowy forest. The men carry firearms and surround a woman and her daughter who clutch Bibles as they make their way forward. Three other illustrations in the book feature full-page color portrayals of the human struggle to control the environment. Although George Washington meets guests at a formal dinner in one illustration, others depict Columbus's ship tossed about in a heavy storm at sea and American frontier legend Davy Crocket plowing a field, his gun and powder horn leaning against a freshly cut tree stump in the foreground, all of which signified power to defend oneself (the gun) and control over nature (the cut tree stump and plowing the land). Most if not all the other stories followed suit, presenting settlers in poses of courage taking on or shaping the world around them. The illustration in "Pioneers" portrays a man chopping trees while his wife tends to the children near the cabin. Similarly, in a story about Daniel Boone in the same volume, a boy is shown about to take aim at a bobcat that is ready to pounce. The book's cover illustrations along with others in the reading series suggest the nationalist-inspired contents by patriotically featuring monuments or icons of the United States. Some examples include illustrations of Mount Rushmore,[18] an unfurled American flag,[19] and the Liberty Bell with the following words written into the yoke: "gratitude," "honesty," "industry," "initiative," "adventure," "beauty," "contentment," "courage," "patriotism," "respect," "self-discipline," "faith," "justice," "kindness," "laughter," "service," "forgiveness," and "aspiration."[20]

Another important feature that A Beka Book authors implemented in their reading material included separate gender roles as understood within dominion theology and the frontier myth. For example, dominion theology stipulated that men are the God-ordained head of the household and of nature. As Michael McVicar observes of Rushdoony, who helped lead the Christian homeschool movement, "when Rushdoony wrote of the Christian *man*, he specifically meant *men* and not men and women. God's commandment that man exercise dominion over the earth required multiple forms of work—including 'manual labor, agriculture, and science'—that culminated in Adam's classification of creation in Genesis 2:19" (emphasis in original).[21] At the same time, however, nature in A Beka Book material also gave men the opportunity to prove themselves as rugged individuals who could prosper on the North American frontier. In other words, the rough landscape of colonial America served as the perfect backdrop for a narrative spotlighting men's physical strength in taming the wilderness and therefore assuming dominating roles while being assisted by their obedient wives and children. Within this understanding, men and women were kept within their separate gender spheres as they turned the howling wilderness into a pastoral country. The authors of "Pioneers," for instance, focused largely on the important role of men who were carving forests into farms and building fortifications for community protection. In contrast, because of the environmental dangers, women merely processed what men brought to them, such as deer hide to be turned into clothes.[22]

The only way women or children could take a lead role in the stories was if men were not present. In these stories, women prove strong and brave thanks in part to their frontier upbringing. In "The Dangers of Pioneer Life," the husband and father, Johnathan Prebble, leaves his wife, Patience, and daughter, Drusilla, in their log home for a few days. During the night two Indians come upon the cabin. Drusilla is not afraid, however, because as the story explains, "She had been born in the wilderness. No village children had told her curdling stories of Indians. Now she was natural again, no more afraid than she had been with the wounded fox her father had brought in and nursed to strength last winter."[23] In this example, the landscape offered unique strength for Drusilla: She had been born in the wilderness, which afforded her the asset of not being afraid and not being corrupted into fear through the stories from village children. Thus, she was "natural again" insinuating that perhaps momentarily, she had become fearful of the Indian visitors but tossed the feeling away by remembering her identity as a frontier settler and therefore was not to be afflicted by weaknesses people often succumb to in more populated areas such as the village. Subsequently, Drusilla and her mother are able to take care of themselves, but even though Patience demonstrates a high level of self-reliance, she so relieved upon her husband's return that she bursts into tears. Such a formula supported the idea that strong Americans of both genders were created in the wilderness while at the same time maintaining a patriarchal narrative.

During the 1970s, A Beka Book's competitor, BJU Press, focused its efforts on accumulating original educational material largely in biblical studies, math, and some of the sciences. By 1978, it published *Bible Truths for Christian Schools* (elementary level) and *Bible Truth for Christian Schools/Secondary Level*, as well as textbooks for junior high and high school dealing with earth and physical science and chemistry.[24] These latter textbooks could also be purchased with supplemental educational aids. The only material dealing with history before their first full-length textbooks published in the 1980s, came in the form of two edited volumes titled *America in Person*, which featured firsthand accounts from American heroes such as George Washington or the story of how Indians captured frontiersman Daniel Boone, who later escaped. The other text, *American History in Verse*, was a truncated reprint of an earlier book titled *Poems of American History*, collected and edited by Burton Egbert Stevenson.

In *American History in Verse* the editors explained their logic for publishing this book in nationalistic terms not unlike A Beka Book's OF AMERICA Reading Series. They wrote in the introduction:

> The great events of American history cannot be retold too often, for man's memory is short, and even the recent past soon grows blurred and dim. So with the principles upon which the Republic was founded and the ideals which have grown up about it. They should have frequent restatement, not only because they are admirable in themselves, but because they form the foundation of what has come to be known as Americanism—that devotion to justice and liberty and human rights which has ennobled the country's past and by which its future will be shaped. . . . No nation exists today of which its people have a better right to be proud than these United States.[25]

The authors furthermore knew exactly what they were doing regarding their efforts to push an inspiring patriotic tale of America's past to their readers and acknowledged that it would be "absurd" to think that these poems offered a "balanced history": "but they do at least, illuminate those gallant and dramatic incidents which appeal most strongly to American patriotism which

Americans have most reason to remember."[26] Moreover, the authors addressed the contemporary "unpatriotic" social currents at the time (the 1970s) in a similar fashion as did the OF AMERICA Reading Series, by reminding their readers that the country "has no reasons to be ashamed of any of her wars," a likely reference to Vietnam War protestors, who upset Falwell, for one, who told possible donors that draft-card burners and flag desecraters do not attend his schools.

Like the OF AMERICA Reading Series, *American History in Verse* and *America in Person* were unabashedly patriotic, but the role of the wilderness was not as pronounced in these volumes, which focus on warfare and the blood shed of its American patriots. The stories, particularly those set in early American history, nevertheless, made the struggle with the untamed wilderness a secondary, but important, reason for earning the land. Numerous poems imparting such a message include Joaquin Miller's "Columbus," "Columbus and the MayFlower" by Richard Monckton Milnes, "John Smith's Approach to Jamestown" by James Barron Hope, "To the Virginian Voyage" by Michael Drayton, "Song of the Pilgrims" by Thomas Gogswell Upham, and not surprisingly another reprint of Felicia Hemans's "Landing of the Pilgrim Fathers." The messaging within these poems communicates that overcoming the wilderness was akin to patriotism produced by winning battles against other nations. In the preface for the poem titled "Our Country" by Julia Howe for example, the editors reiterated the remarks of the editor of the 1922 publication that "in the four years that followed (after the 1631 thanksgiving), the worst hardships of the new plantation were outlived and nearly four thousand colonists were distributed among the twenty hamlets along and near the seashore." The BJU Press editors added: "The fight for a foothold in the wilderness had been won."[27] Indeed, the struggle against the wilderness remains easily visible as a theme that allowed the conservative evangelical educational publishers to depict how the New World was won and claimed by their historical and religious ancestors and can be witnessed in the multiple stories and poems they reprinted. BJU Press continued this theme in the 1980s once it began publishing its own history textbooks.

Outside of A Beka Book and BJU Press, two independent authors, Peter Marshall and David Manuel, wrote a popular history book intended for Christian schools, which delivered the same nationalist message as the OF AMERICA Reading Series and BJU Press's *American History in Verse*. Their book, *The Light and the Glory: Did God Have a Plan for America?* (1977), offered a chronological history suitable for high school readers and adults. The introduction indicated the authors' inspiration with its list of a host of recent problems, including the assassination of John F. Kennedy, student riots, a faltering economy, a disintegration of morality, and the loss of the American Dream.[28] The authors believed life in the United States had been wonderful at one time, but this was before the twentieth century, before modern science and before living memory. Thus, they told the story of the founding of the United States, which, they argued, began not with Jamestown, but with the Pilgrims and Puritans who came to the New World's pristine environment to freely practice their religious faith.

As also reflected in the stories distributed by A Beka Book and BJU Press, in *The Light and the Glory* the wilderness functioned as the obstacle settlers overcame and in doing so developed strength and morality. The authors explained that unlike the Spanish who succumbed to greed, Pilgrims and Puritans inhabited a North American landscape that offered a healthier life. "America" they wrote, "was obviously the right place—virginal, wild, as yet untainted by the godless corruption that had befouled the known world."[29] The harsh winter and howling wilderness offered challenges the Pilgrims overcame by faith, hard work, and sometimes violence. After surviving the first winter and learning how to control their environment by planting crops, the Pilgrims earned their place in the New World. Their place in North America, however, was more than just earned; the authors understood the Pilgrims' suffering in the wilderness as the catalyst that brought them closer to God. "Something special had been born among them in the midst of all the dying—they had shared the love of Jesus Christ in a way that only happens when people are willing to suffer together in His causes. This was what they had come to the wilderness to find, and now none of them wished to leave it."[30]

Fellow conservative evangelicals in the late 1970s and those who became religious right leaders praised *The Light and the Glory* in terms that mixed religious faith with a sense of nationalism, and their comments were printed on the back cover of the book. Tim LaHaye, writer of the lucrative *Left Behind* books wrote, "*The Light and the Glory* reveals our true national heritage and inspires us to stay on God's course as a nation." Bill Bright of Campus Crusade for Christ said, "*The Light and the Glory* gives us new appreciation and inspiration to fulfill God's plan for us as a nation." Falwell also recommended it from the pulpit in 1979 saying it was the "most thorough" study "of the heritage of America." He agreed with the book that the United States was a chosen nation "raised up by God to be a base for world evangelization." It was imperative, he continued, that the students from his church and school carry on American Christian traditions by becoming the leaders of tomorrow who will "bring this nation back to you [God]."[31]

Indeed, the goal was to save America by making it great again. Their educational material depicted their "religious ancestors" as struggling against the frontier, working hard, adhering to faith, and practicing proper gender roles and in the process earning the land and God's favor. Additionally, the pastoral or wilderness settings of the stories projected a sense of purity and escape from the present-day problems of the 1970s. With increasing crime in larger cities, the country at least sounded like a wholesome place where morals could be learned. Thus rural life figured prominently in A Beka Book stories, as reflected in titles such as, "The Proud Oak Tree," "The Fly and the Moth," "The Flax," or "Catching the Colt."[32]

Nostalgia for country living connected with Christian nationalism was an attractive story to buy into and it would be echoed throughout the conservative evangelical community by celebrated leaders such as Billy Graham. In 1976 on his radio show the *Hour of Decision,* Graham reminded his audience that early Americans (he defined largely as Pilgrims and Puritans) did not have the luxuries of modern technology, including "telephones, radio, television, electricity, automobiles, airplanes, inside plumbing, or refrigerators." "Yet," he continued, "they succeeded—where we seem to be failing. They scratched, dug, worked, sweated, and prayed to build a nation from New York to San Francisco." With these images, Graham combined Christian religious faith with a preindustrial rural lifestyle requiring direct physical labor with the landscape. Like the messages from A Beka Book and BJU Press, it was this formula that built the nation that present-day Christians were about to lose. At the end of his message, and one the religious right would later loudly repeat, Graham encouraged followers to become politically active because "America is too young to die."[33]

Christian Environmental Stewardship and Education

Accompanying the Christian nationalist themes throughout the 1970s were eco-friendly messages of Christian environmental stewardship. Unlike secular environmentalists of the period, Christian environmental views depicted the "correct" relationship between people and nonhuman nature as a hierarchical one, with people above nature, yet also a part of God's creation.

Beyond the views of conservative evangelicals and among the wider American populace, the question regarding what is the "correct" or "proper" relationship between humanity and nature continues to be discussed within national discourse. One of the most influential essays that explained and challenged traditional environmentalist thought remains environmental historian William Cronon's 1994 conference paper and subsequent book chapter,

"The Trouble with Wilderness; or Getting Back to the Wrong Nature."[34] In this piece, Cronon convincingly argued that "untouched nature" or "wilderness" as understood by many environmentalists is only an idea, a creation of the imagination that ideologically separates humanity from nonhuman nature. He wrote that environmentalists often define wilderness as a spiritual place that may be visited but not lived in.[35] Moreover, within this traditional environmental perception, humanity is often depicted as a disease that should be stopped from impacting the nonhuman pristine wilderness.[36] Such a view, Cronon noted, stemmed from environmentalists who understand humanity as inherently bad and nonhuman nature as good. Here, the relationship is situated as a simple dichotomy—basically a heroes and villains scenario in which environmentalists lament the passing of the majestic wilderness landscape, as did Henry David Thoreau in his writings.[37] Cronon, in contrast, argued that valuing nature as a place "devoid of humans" while regarding human development as destructive of the environment is not reality and is dangerous because individuals stop valuing nature in their own communities. Humans, he stated, have impacted all environments and therefore pristine or untouched "wilderness" is a myth constructed by the human imagination. Therefore, all environments should be valued, not just ones that seem devoid of humanity.

Although environmentalists are not all wilderness preservationists, in "The Trouble With Wilderness" Cronon correctly criticized their understandings and aspirations for the natural world, which has been, at least in part, a reason for its success but also a limitation of the movement since its beginnings in 1970. Due to Cronon's critique and a younger generation of environmentalists pushing for new directions of advocacy, as exemplified in Michael Shellenberger and Ted Nordhaus's "The Death of Environmentalism," the idea that humanity is separate from nature is presently changing, but nevertheless, striving to make wilderness a reality remains a primary goal within the mainstream of environmentalist thought.

In contrast to environmental wilderness preservationist views, conservative evangelicals in the 1970s were not comfortable with the idea that humanity was separate from nature or that human-caused pollution should be stopped at all costs. The community did believe that abuses to nature should be curbed, but at the same time they thought that the needs of humanity must be met. In 1974, BJU Press published its first physical science book for high school students and dedicated a chapter to "Pollution and Chemistry." The chapter promoted environmental protection with the caveat that the needs of humans should not be ignored when making eco-friendly decisions. Such an idea conflicted with environmental preservationist thought and seemed more in tune with the understanding that humanity had a right to impact nature, but should do so wisely because as also argued in Cronon's "The Trouble with Wilderness," people and nonhuman nature do not exist in separate spheres.

BJU Press's views on nature in which humans factored into environmental decisions were evident throughout the textbook's chapter. For example, one caption above photos depicting a landfill, a fish kill, and smoke stacks read, "Where there are people, there will be pollution. The only way to completely rid the earth of pollution would be to rid the earth of people. This is hardly a suitable solution."[38] Here, the authors directly challenged the environmental movement's perspective that humanity is a disease to the natural world. They did not, however, propose that unchecked pollution was justified for the greater good of humanity and the economy. Pollution, they wrote, "can become a serious problem. Air pollution can cause the death of physically weak people. . . . And polluted water can cause the death of many water-dwelling creatures, as well as humans."[39] They listed several historical examples of humans impacting the landscape, including how Native American tribes burned land to hunt and sometimes "irresponsibly" left campfires burning, which led to forest fires.[40] They also offered the example of Donora, Pennsylvania, where in 1948, 4,910 people became ill and 20 people along with 800 domestic animals died due to air pollution. They nonetheless held that "the clamor for an immediate end to all air and water pollution can be carried too far too fast." They continued with this nuanced approach by asserting that the insecticide DDT for instance, had positive and negative consequences. They confirmed the pesticide caused problems with reproduction rates in fish and birds, but warned that legal bans resulted in an increase in insect-borne diseases and may lead to the use of another pesticide, which would have unknown consequences. The authors concluded later, "Man's involvement with his natural environment can no longer be regarded as all good or all bad. 'Pollution-free' solutions are impossible. Pollution should be held to a minimum but at a reasonable cost."[41] Here, the authors were not marginalizing the health of the environment as an excuse for financial profits or asking the reader to simply ignore the problem, but instead promoted a balance. Such views are not dissimilar to Cronon's concluding arguments in "The Trouble with Wilderness." In sum, BJU authors Williams and Mulfinger's argument cannot be interpreted as a rejection of eco-friendly protection efforts nor as a supporting view of secular environmentalism. Rather, it promoted a future where humanity lived *with* and cared for the nonhuman natural world.

The rest of the textbook's chapter covered different types of air and water pollution while explaining different ways these problems were being rectified. Williams and Mulfinger concluded with a section titled "What God Has Given

Us." Here, they promoted a proactive ecological position by asking the reader, "Should we not try to show our respect for what God has given us and do our utmost to preserve and maintain it?" They additionally pushed students to raise the alarm if they knew of environmental abuses in their area. The authors, however, reminded the reader in their last concluding remark that the pollution problem is only temporal whereas spiritual matters are eternal.[42]

The physical science textbook published by BJU Press was not an anomaly. In the OF AMERICA Series book titled *Liberty Tree* (1974) by A Beka Book, one featured piece was written by the nineteenth-century nature lover, John Burroughs. The story titled "The Bluebird" promoted the idea that nature was God's creation and therefore beautiful and valuable. Most notably, the terms "she" and "nature" were used interchangeably when referring to the "creator" or as understood by conservative evangelicals, "God." The story began, "When Nature made the bluebird, she wished to make the sky and earth friends. So she gave him the color of one on his back, and the hue of the other on his breast. . . . He [the bluebird] is the peace bringer."[43] Burroughs reference to nature as a female and as the creator of the bluebird was perhaps commonplace for general audiences, but it is striking that conservative evangelicals included the story in a publication intended for Christian school audiences. As stated, the messages from A Beka Book editors were carefully constructed and perhaps more so for the OF AMERICA Reading Series. For conservative evangelicals, the creator is undoubtedly God and is traditionally referred to in the masculine form. Conversely, and in this case, the A Beka Book editors approved of the story's message that nature is to be appreciated and they did not recoil at the idea that nature created the bluebird. Liberty Tree's "The Bluebird," however, would not be seen again, as will be explained in chapter 5.

Although environmental messages from A Beka Book were few, other stories from the press promoted an emotional attachment to nature. *Exploring God's World*, for example, published in 1976 for third-graders, cautioned readers about humanity's ability to ruin what God created. "To man, the tree is a friend that provides him with lumber to build. But man can also be the tree's worst enemy. In places where man has cut down too many trees, the soil begins to wash away. The wildlife that used these trees as homes must find other homes. . . . Trees are one of God's wonderful gifts to us, and we should take care of them."[44] For second-graders, environmental protection was not focused on so heavily, but materials still stressed nature appreciation and the importance of a healthy ecosystem.[45]

Throughout the 1970s the conservative evangelical community continued to occasionally support environmental protection beyond Christian school educational material. Engineering professor Henry M. Morris left his position at Virginia Tech University and in 1970 founded the Institute for Creation Research (ICR) dedicated to undermining Darwinian evolution. The organization produced a monthly publication titled the *Impact Series* in which the authors, many of whom held graduate degrees from accredited secular schools, argued primarily against evolution but sometimes moved into other issues, including traditional family values as well as the environment.

In April of 1974 Morris promoted a strong Christian environmental stewardship view praising nature as "God's unique handiwork," while stating that remedies for pollution can be found in "a sound creationist philosophy."[46] Furthermore, he blamed secular science and industry for the environmental crisis, writing, "Ecological problems developed entirely within a period when the scientific and industrial establishments were totally committed to an evolutionary philosophy!"[47] While making a reference to the energy crisis, Morris went so far as to criticize the burning of fossil fuels, directly stating that "these organisms were not designed to serve as fuels for man's machines, and it is not surprising that the efficiency of heat engines using them is low and the waste products are high. Furthermore, they are exhaustible and even now, the imminent end of economic oil and gas production is a matter of great concern."[48]

Later during that same year, Morris somewhat curbed his eco-friendly views by drawing the line at population control. He dismissed warnings of overpopulation by quoting Genesis 1:28 and speculated that the earth could hold 50 billion people before it reached maximum capacity. Morris, however, seemed unsure of how to confront the problem. He suggested that before overpopulation occurred, humanity might find technological solutions or Christ might return before humans were forced to disobey the command to be fruitful and multiply. After these speculations, however, he admitted that protecting the environment was a real issue that must be addressed. He again blamed the ecological crisis on evolutionary thought and vilified industry: "It is very significant that all of earth's serious environmental problems, even its population crisis, have developed during that one century (say, from about 1860 to the present) when the evolutionary philosophy had replaced creationism in the thinking of practically all of the world's leaders in education, science and industry."[49]

Conclusion

"And Jesus sat over against the treasury, and beheld how the people cast money into the treasury: and many that were rich cast in much. And there came a certain poor widow, and she threw in two mites, which make one farthing. And he called unto him his disciples, and saith unto them, Verily I say unto you, That this poor widow hath cast more in, than all they which have cast into the treasury."[50] Every conservative evangelical who grew up attending Sunday school knows this story. During Falwell's "Patriotic Day" service, Doug Oldham told an updated version of it by making the widow endorse Thomas Road Baptist Church with the donation of her husband's last dollar. Her gift, however, was specifically for the church's schools that promised to produce a new generation of Christians who identified with the "right kind" of United States, a concept later explained by the "I Love America" program. Who would not want to be associated with a present-day biblical heroine who gave her beloved husband's "last" dollar in an attempt to stand up against the detrimental social movements tearing the country apart? The idea of joining arms with other frugal and self-sustaining godly Americans proved very attractive and worked well with the larger narrative, which Christian educational material presented to their audiences. The story was a nationalistic romantic history of a pre-industrial Christian country, where people struggled against the wilderness to earn their place in the New World and set the foundations for what became the United States.

This construction of a Christian sense of nationalism, however, posed a problem. By placing these stories in rural areas and setting them in pre-twentieth-century America, the authors did not offer a way for Christians in the present to recapture or practice the elements they believed made America great. Marshall and Manuel's book *The Light and the Glory* even targeted modern science as causing more problems than it solved. Indeed, these books including those from A Beka Book and BJU Press intended for Christian and home schools told students that things were better in the past in part because people were molded into good citizens as they shaped the frontier landscape. The Christian book publishers would need to find a way to connect their romanticized sense of nationalism to the present if they wanted to show how "real Americans" could be made in the modern era.

In the 1980s, these publishers found ways to update their material. Since the closing of the frontier in the later nineteenth century, they chose a new avenue to explain how Americans could embody the qualities of the Pilgrims and other setters who struggled against the wilderness. The goal was achieved by focusing on the hard work and innovations accomplished during the industrial revolution while praising free enterprise and condemning government regulation. The stories telling of the struggle between settlers and the wilderness, however, did not disappear. They remain to this day a primary theme to teach early American history, and more specifically the nation's exceptional and God-ordained origin story told to students in thousands of Christian schools throughout the United States.

Beyond this sense of nationalism's role in establishing the religious right, the Christian school education material in the 1970s, although not in tune with secular environmentalist messages, did not depict the environment simply as a resource for the use of mankind. Rather, it argued nature should be valued and cared for because the earth was created by God. John Burroughs's story "The Bluebird," featured in the *Liberty Tree* and BJU's *Physical Science for Christian Schools*, for instance, were not oversights or mistakes on the part of the publishing companies. This Christian environmental stewardship message remained visible in tandem throughout the 1970s with the nationalistic idea that godly settlers struggled against the wilderness in both BJU Press and A Beka Book publications and continued as conservative evangelicals built the religious right movement throughout the 1980s.

nature as operative category

CHAPTER 4

The Moral Majority Finds Favor in the Republican Party

During the late 1970s, the general public's support for the environmental movement declined. Western landowners, known as the Sagebrush Rebellion, along with fellow conservative allies, vehemently countered attempts to sway politicians to preserve large swaths of land and nature protection goals in general by using a variety of tactics including attacking the public image of environmentalists. Environmentalists, they argued, despised capitalism, freedom, humanity, and the very concept of private property. As the economy struggled in the late 1970s and high-energy prices remained, this depiction seemed increasingly realistic. Americans also tired of President Jimmy Carter's message, which like those from environmentalists told the public they must conserve resources and find renewable forms of energy. Carter led by example—wearing sweaters, installing solar panels on the White House and telling the public that consuming material possessions would not make them happy. As the ailing economy and pressure to use less wore on Americans, alternative attitudes vilifying environmentalists while offering a future of plenty proved alluring to voters. In response, during the 1980 presidential campaign, GOP nominee and future president, Ronald Reagan, garnered public support in part by favoring a strong economy even at the expense of the environment. "Conservation" he said, "is desirable . . . but not the sole solution to our economic needs."[1] Thus, by the late 1970s, it seemed environmentalists were standing in the way of a better future offered by the Republican Party.

While this discussion unfolded on the national landscape, Jerry Falwell formed the Moral Majority in 1979, which functioned as the first active political organization of the religious right. Officially the movement claimed it was nonpartisan, but in reality it quickly forged an alliance with the Republican Party and supported many of the same issues, including a strong economy. This partnership, however, did not mean that they also chose to abandon the philosophy of Christian environmental stewardship. Except for a handful of individuals, from the late 1970s to the end of the 1980s, conservative evangelicals as a whole did not embrace the idea that they must sacrifice the environment for the economy, but instead made room for both to coexist. Voices from the leadership, including religious right co-founder, Pat Robertson, along with Christian school educational material, consistently espoused Christian environmental stewardship. Members at the grassroots level were not as enthusiastic but went about conserving energy and thought of themselves as good "stewards." For them, Christian environmental stewardship was perhaps a distant afterthought, but nevertheless they did not simply follow GOP talking points championing further energy exploration as proposed by Reagan and his controversial secretary of the interior, James G. Watt. Overall, high energy prices, the increasing popular depiction of environmentalists as anti-American extremists, the religious right's alliance with the Republican Party, and the environmental movement's apparent attack on Christianity through the publication of *The Environmental Handbook* in 1970 all weakened calls for Christian environmental stewardship. As will be demonstrated, however, this philosophy clearly survived at both the leadership and the grassroots levels, particularly among Southern Baptists.

The Southern Baptist Convention (SBC) is today the largest Protestant denomination in the United States. It originated in 1845 when a group of independent Baptist churches broke off from those in the North following an argument over the issue of slave-owners becoming missionaries. The organization remains a loose confederation of autonomous Baptist congregations in which each church follows its own doctrine and decides how much money to donate to the SBC and whether or not they wish to remain a member. The chief advantage in unification is to fund seminaries that produce missionaries. The SBC is also able to produce and disseminate Baptist literature through different organizations such as the Christian Life Commission (now the Ethics and Religious Liberty Commission) or the Sunday School Board (now Lifeway).[2] In the early twentieth century controversy arose among members concerning the interpretation of the scriptures. The two conflicting sides were labeled conservatives and moderates. Conservatives argued that the Bible should be taught as the infallible word of God and inerrant throughout. Moderates also believed that the Bible is the word of God, but felt areas of scripture may be left open to interpretation and that some Bible stories did not necessarily happen as fact. This latter group, at least until the late 1970s, was largely comprised by those in leadership positions, particularly at seminaries. Conversely, the majority of those at the individual church level (pastors and congregants) supported a biblical inerrancy perspective. Nevertheless, even with disagreement causing noticeable rifts among the participants, the Convention continues today as a community rich in opinions on a diverse range of subjects.

As demonstrated in chapter 1, conservative evangelicals, supported in part by the SBC, initially wanted to protect the natural world. Beyond the messages of Schaeffer, Ford, or Lindsell, an SBC 1971 survey found that among member churches, over 81 percent of pastors and 76 percent of Sunday school teachers felt that individual congregations should cooperate with authorities to "solve air and water pollution problems." This enthusiasm waned as a schism grew between themselves and the secular environmental movement, but the idea of Christian environmental stewardship continued to survive. In a 1975 poll of 233 SBC member churches, stewardship was a common justification for conserving energy. Some pastors specifically responded, "It is poor stewardship to build very costly facilities to be used only a day or two per week," and "It is better stewardship of the building if it is needed."[3] These responses do not necessarily reflect a congregation's intense devotion to Christian environmental stewardship. Nevertheless, in agreement with the survey comments from pastors, the poll's report author Jerry A. Privette attributed stewardship awareness for congregations choosing to conserve "the world's resources as well as building and energy resources of their local churches, houses and other facilities. Such a consciousness naturally emerges from a basic understanding of the Scriptures and a Christian commitment to good stewardship."[4] In this vein, he felt that such conservation practices would become common in the lives of church members and congregations as a whole.

Beyond philosophically supporting stewardship, Privette's report also revealed that energy conservation measures were implemented in the majority of churches contacted. Of the 233 SBC churches, 70.4 percent reduced energy by turning down thermostats, 80.3 percent turned off unnecessary lighting, and 63.5 percent diverted meetings and or services to specific areas to "avoid heating/cooling the whole building." A smaller number invested money into other energy-saving improvements, including 19.3 percent who installed weather stripping on doors and windows, while 18 percent switched to lower wattage light bulbs. A majority of the pastors (62.7 percent) also said that church pro-grams should be scheduled to permit "greater use" of buildings. These actions may be easily explained as a response to high-energy prices, but over 50 percent of pastors disagreed that new multiuse church buildings should be planned or based purely on economic reasons.[5] Furthermore, the fact that pastors pointed toward stewardship as their cause demonstrates that they perceived the prob-lem of high energy costs not only in economic terms but also as a spiritual issue in which they vocally accepted responsibility as custodians and not owners of the Earth's resources.

Additional reports in the late 1970s, such as by the Texas SBC, alluded to stewardship by treating energy conservation not as an economical imperative but as a "moral and spiritual matter."[6] North Carolina's SBC leaders held sim-ilar sentiments writing that wasting energy was not only financially negligent but a sin. The state convention's building consultant hoped to "call North Car-olina Baptists to a mature and biblical understanding of the stewardship of energy." The leadership also tried leading by example and adopted energy-saving policies in their buildings while advising member churches how they might face high-energy demands during the harsh winter of 1976–1977. The state convention lowered its building's thermostats to 68 degrees and cut elec-tricity use by 25 percent. To further save energy, it reduced the workweek from five to four days. Organizers also cooperated with the governor to re-quest that individual churches do the same. In this spirit, they reported that "many" congregations canceled Sunday evening services. Although most churches adopted energy conservation measures, enthusiasm for doing so was lacking. Indeed, calls to conserve were wearing thin on congregations, but stewardship as a moral and spiritual matter, not only financial pragmatism, remained the reason behind conservation efforts.[7]

Although challenged, the theme of stewardship continued at an energy con-servation conference held by the SBC in August of 1977. A few months earlier, future religious right supporter and pastor of First Baptist Church Dal-las, W. A. Criswell, proudly stated in a mass mailing focused on saving energy, "We shall be happy to have a part in making our dear church an example to the whole world as good stewards of the manifold gifts of God."[8] During the event his church reported that in 1973, at the beginning of the energy crisis, $100,000 was spent on utility bills, which increased to $200,000 by 1976; if noth-ing was done, expenses could reach $400,000 by 1981. To have greater control over the energy used, they installed a central computer programmed to shut off lights and to control heat and air conditioning. A representative from Criswell's congregation prefaced these energy saving decisions as a commit-ment to stewardship that should be present in all aspects of life.[9] Most at the conference relayed similar views of stewardship, while some, such as Cecil A. Ray, directly invoked Christian environmental stewardship, when he wrote in a section of his presentation titled "Responsible Use of God's Creation," that "God created both man and the material universe, He saw both as good. . . . Man's instructions to 'subdue, dominate' were never a license to exploit or destroy. By divine assignment, man is a conservationist."[10] In contrast, another participant named Gilbert Turner directly challenged the ideology of stewardship in a paper titled "Responses of a Baptist Businessman." Here, Gilbert complained about those who blamed business for the energy crisis and argued that free enterprise could find the solution "in a manner that will enable our great grandchildren to look upon the present-day crisis in much the same manner as we now view the whale-oil crisis of the nineteenth century."[11] Apparently, he was not concerned that multiple whale species were brought to the brink of extinction as a consequence of commercial whaling. Instead his thoughts centered on what kind of oil would replace the diminishing supply. Free enterprise, he thought, would get the job done. The example of Gilbert notwithstanding, the majority of voices at the seminar called for stewardship, not for energy exploration or other solutions offered by companies. Individual SBC churches proudly implemented energy conservation methods, and like Criswell's First Baptist Church Dallas, they justified such action through the moral and spiritual reason of stewardship.

Overall, despite high-energy prices in the mid- to late 1970s, conservative evangelicals at the grassroots level did not vocally promote economic growth, energy exploration, or a future of plenty at the expense of the environment. Their position was largely the conservation of resources for reasons that related to views of Christian environmental stewardship. Meanwhile, their children read about eco-friendly practices in Christian schools, and religious right co-founder Pat Robertson publicly supported the issue.

Between classic religious right arguments demanding that Americans "get back to God," Robertson from the late 1970s to 1989 promoted Christian environmental stewardship philosophies. During the 1970s, Robertson published a monthly newsletter titled *Pat Robertson's Perspective*. It consisted of a few pages filled with numerous short paragraphs, each containing musings and reflections regarding a wide spectrum of topics along with advice. These pages read like privileged information from an insider who explained where the economy was headed and what it meant for investments, while commenting on standard religious right concerns such as traditional family morals, school prayer, and the rejection of homosexuality. Robertson periodically wove Christian environmental stewardship into these published contemplations. In a response to those who doubted the existence or seriousness of the energy crisis, he clarified in

May 1977, "The energy crisis is real," and as a solution he promoted the use of nuclear power because he reasoned it did not have the same widespread polluting capabilities as coal. He admitted that the United States had a surplus of the commodity, but would rather avoid its use due to fears that American cities would resemble the English industrial centers of Manchester or Liverpool.[12] In further reflection on the matter, Robertson suggested the development of a massive program akin to the Manhattan Project with the objective of figuring out ways to harness new power sources such as the renewables of wind and tides.[13]

Robertson's comments in his May 1977 newsletter mirror classic environmental conservationist rhetoric aimed to meet the needs of both humanity and the environment.[14] Here Robertson reasoned that Americans could no longer continuously use limited resources, and he specifically noted that coal "pollutes the air." He also validated environmental advocates, writing that they would not permit the "scarring of the landscape that inexpensive mining techniques dictate." Such views held by Robertson were not an anomaly but resurfaced in subsequent publications addressed to followers of his television ministry as well as to the politically oriented religious right movement.

While Robertson publicly shared his environmental sentiments, the politically and theologically conservative editor of *Christianity Today*, Harold Lindsell, represented one of the few within the conservative evangelical community who, like SBC businessman Gilbert Turner, followed calls for a strong economy at the expense of the environment. Although Lindsell had once told his audience to read Rachel Carson's *Silent Spring* and promoted Christian environmental stewardship throughout most of the 1970s, by the end of the decade, he perused right-wing newsletters such as *America's Future*, which strongly stood in favor of the economy while dismissing nature protection. A 1979 issue complained that 20,000 employees at the Department of Energy were responsible for devising regulations to impede domestic energy development.[15] A month later, it cited automotive experts who claimed unreasonable environmentalists lobbied for federal policies that would force the auto industry to cut hydrocarbon emissions by 90 percent from what they were twelve years before, thus costing companies billions of dollars.[16] In December of 1979 *America's Future* lumped environmentalists with "welfare lobbyists" and "liberal politicians" who, with the help of the federal government, were putting a stranglehold on oil companies.[17]

In 1980, Lindsell read a book review in the October 17 issue of *America's Future* featuring James A. Weber's *Power Grab: The Conserver Cult and Coming Energy Catastrophe*. Weber, the review stated, refused to believe there was any energy shortage. The current crisis was only a self-imposed consequence of limiting energy exploration due to the Environmental Protection Agency (EPA) making drilling illegal in Alaska. The review quoted the author: "Why have our policymakers adopted an energy policy which means less rather than more energy? . . . instead [of economic growth, the conservationists/environmentalists are] attempting 'to create an 'environmental paradise on earth.'"[18] With pen in hand, Lindsell marked the following passage:

> The goal of these groups [groups that promoted conservation]is to achieve a society in America similar to that described by E. F. Schumacher in his 1975 book, *Small Is Beautiful: Economics As If People Mattered*. Mr. Weber describes the worldview inherent in this approach as calling "for enshrining nature . . . as sacred, while effectively repealing the Industrial Revolution, . . . The Schumacher vision is a beautiful, new world populated by human beings with low-technology, low-energy lifestyles of 'element frugality' sustained by the sun and the wind and the earth was just what the doctor ordered for environmentalists."[19]

Weber's *Power Grab* warned that trying to attain this idealistic paradise as suggested in Schumacher's book would in fact doom those on the bottom of the economic scale. He additionally suggested that those behind the environmentalist messages of using less were conspirators within a "small group of elitists" Weber labeled the "Conserver Cult."

Lindsell might not have embraced the conspiracy theory, but accepted the critique of *Small is Beautiful* and supported the basic argument that a stronger economy and in turn expanding energy exploration were more important than the health of nature. Such an understanding became a central argument in his upcoming book, *Free Enterprise: A Judeo-Christian Defense*, published later in 1982.

Lindsell was a theological fundamentalist who struggled with the concept and the need to safeguard the environment. He first thought Earth Day 1970 was a great idea, but quickly soured on it in response to what he read in *The Environmental Handbook*. However, he felt secure with the concept of Christian environmental stewardship, which allowed him to support nature protection while separating Christianity from the secular environmental movement and promoted it in *Christianity Today*, which he edited. In his own 1976 article titled "The Lord's Day and Natural Resources," Lindsell asked fellow Christians to stop driving on Sundays to save fuel—advice based not only on economics, but also in response to energy conservation and compassion toward nature.[20]

By 1980, however, Lindsell's opinion on the matter had changed perhaps as a consequence of reading pro–free enterprise rhetoric encouraged by but probably not only limited to *America's Future*.[21] While researching for his book, Lindsell found a list of sayings, presumably from Abraham Lincoln, which he felt could be useful to his pro-economic argument. He wrote the Library of Congress to validate its authenticity. The list consisted of classic socially and economically conservative maxims. Two examples included "You cannot help men permanently by doing for them what they could do and should do for themselves" and "You cannot bring about prosperity by discouraging thrift."[22] The Library of Congress responded, stating the list dated back to the nineteenth century but that Lincoln had been "assigned" as author later by the Committee for Constitutional Government, a 1940s organization that strongly opposed Franklin Roosevelt's New Deal measures.[23] Indeed by this time, Lindsell searched out such rhetoric and consequently abandoned his long-held argument for energy and resource conservation or "thrift" in connection with compassion for God's creation by replacing it with the importance of financial profits. Thus, he found comfort in information disseminated by private advocacy groups such as the Committee for Constitutional Government, and in turn followed the anti-environmentalist and pro-free enterprise rhetoric of *America's Future*.

Lindsell's disregard for the environment ultimately came through in his 1982 book, *Free Enterprise*, in which he declared his goal to counter the "arguments constantly heard about the depletion of natural resources, the ruination of the environment, and the need to defuse the propaganda favoring a return to the bucolic life of the farm."[24] He wrote that God mandated people create wealth and they should not be forced to live in the way advocated by E. F. Schumacher's *Small is Beautiful*.[25] This latter statement by Lindsell directly mimicked information offered in the 1980 issue of *America's Future* sent to his address. Although Lindsell evolved into an anti-environmentalist championing the economy at the expense of the environment, others including Pat Robertson, continued speaking publicly about Christian environmental stewardship even at religious right political events.

The Moral Majority

Officially, conservative evangelicals mobilized politically in June of 1979. Howard Phillips, a former Nixon federal appointee, founded the Conservative Caucus in 1974. He worked with other conservative right-wing notables such as fundraiser Richard Viguerie and strategist Paul Weyrich. Another acquaintance, a Colgate-Palmolive Company marketing man named Edward McAteer, who founded the conservative Religious Roundtable in 1979, introduced Phillips to Jerry Falwell the same year.[26] Until this time, the fledgling religious right functioned largely piecemeal; support for political mobilization existed but without a formal organization to lead members. Back in 1976 Viguerie noted the groundswell of conservative evangelical interest in politics through examples such as thousands protesting the Equal Rights Amendment in Houston, Texas. Preachers such as James Robison, Jerry Falwell, and Pat Robertson were undeniably disgusted with the progressive "liberal" and "humanistic" direction of the United States since the early to mid-1970s and consequently fanned the flames of opposition among their followers. In February of 1979 Phillips wrote to Falwell encouraging him to start a for-profit newspaper intended to reach millions of America's "moral majority." This letter reflected Philip's view, along with Weyrich's, that Falwell should turn their idea into a national movement that would serve, as the letter concluded, as a "'call to arms' for the entire 'moral majority.'"[27] They hoped the group would gain a large following by welcoming members from any denomination or faith that demanded politicians embrace and fight for moral issues. Falwell indeed liked the idea, and by June he announced the formation of the Moral Majority.

The Moral Majority did not try to convert people to Christ. Rather it was designed to use the brand of Christian nationalism that Falwell and others developed in previous years to combat upsetting social changes. They also took on some newer and more secular issues, such as opposing the Strategic Arms Limitation Talks (SALT II) and defense cuts while promoting free enterprise and a balanced budget. Although Pat Robertson claimed the religious right should remain bipartisan, as did Falwell, their rhetoric invariably proved pro-GOP.[28]

In August of 1980 the Religious Roundtable featured the most prominent conservative evangelical leaders to speak at the National Affairs Briefing, a rally held in Dallas, Texas, intended to help followers pick an appropriate presidential candidate in the upcoming election. The list of speakers included Jerry Falwell, Pat Robertson, W. A. Criswell, Adrian Rogers, Phyllis Schlafly, and James Robison. The highlight of the evening was for the audience, which numbered about 15,000, to hear directly from GOP nominee Ronald Reagan.[29] President Carter declined the invitation. Falwell's speech covered traditional religious right topics such as the importance of school prayer and the rejection of indecent programs on television. Robertson, who was also at the time a member of the Religious Roundtable, contributed something interesting to the discussion. Although he toed the line with normal religious right talking points, he threw in a message in support of Christian environmental stewardship:

> In the midst of the troubles of the world God says, be fruitful, multiply, take dominion. He says, my people have been called by my name to

establish dominion over the earth. He says, subdue it in My name. Not to rape the environment, not to spoil the air and pollute the rivers, but to bring My world to the peace and the harmony and the love and the order that I intended for it. And He said, I have given this to those who know my name.[30]

Robertson's environmental message directly touched on two aspects of Rousas John Rushdoony's idea of Reconstruction and its connection with how humanity should treat the Earth. As stated in chapter 2, Rushdoony, along with other conservative evangelicals who made up the religious right, believed that by living correctly under God's laws, all wrongs could be rectified. In his speech at the National Affairs Briefing, Robertson agreed with Rushdoony stating that humanity must follow God's law by exercising dominion over the Earth and by being fruitful and multiplying. Robertson, however, also highlighted that people must not spoil the air and pollute the rivers. Rushdoony made this latter point in his 1982 *Law and Society: Volume II of the Institutes of Biblical Law.*

Like Robertson, Rushdoony was very clear that humanity did not own the Earth and, moreover, dominion did not mean the Earth was at the will of humanity. Rushdoony wrote that even the wilderness outside of the Garden of Eden at creation was "good" and remained under the ownership of God. "*All the earth is the Lord's*"[31] Rushdoony wrote, and "Man is God's creature, God's property, and God's servant or slave. The earth is the Lords, and all of creation. The only law which can properly govern man and the earth is God's law. The premise of the law is set forth in Exodus 19:5: 'all the earth is mine.'"[32] In short, according to Rushdoony, there is no dominion of man where humanity was gifted the earth to use it at will. The real earth polluting culprits, Rushdoony believed, were those from the secular world, including environmentalists who lived by ignoring God. He wrote, "A very significant aspect of the lives of current ecology advocates is their deliberate pollution of forest and river areas. Paper, beer cans, feces and more mark their visitations to wilderness areas. If asked to be clean and orderly, they mock at such a request as evidence of a Puritan hangover." In contrast to environmentalists Rushdoony stated, "Thus, the purpose of the redeemed man must not be either the ruthless exploitation of the wilderness or its protection . . . but rather the careful development of all things under God. As the regenerate man obeys God and furthers His Kingdom, God blesses both man and the earth."[33] Although Rushdoony clearly felt that God's Earth must not be ruined, if humanity lived under God's rules, wilderness would be cultivated to create almost a pastoral landscape or a Garden of Eden. In return, mankind would receive blessings from God. Like Rushdoony, Robertson also believed the Earth was the Lord's and although at the National Affairs Briefing he echoed Rushdoony's view of Reconstruction saying that humanity must dominate and multiply, he also directly stated that polluting the land and rivers were not what God had intended. Here on a national stage in an official role as a leader for the growing religious right, Robertson cautiously advocated for a theologically-based eco-friendly relationship between humanity and the natural world.

The relationship between nature and humanity as expressed by Robertson utilized elements of Rushdoony's Reconstructionist views to encourage Christian environmental stewardship in similar terms articulated earlier by Schaeffer and Ford. Consequently, Robertson cannot be categorized as either an environmentalist or an unfettered free enterprise proponent. Nowhere was he saying that humanity must preserve the wilderness, but nor was he advocating the use of nature as a simple resource for economic profit. Instead, Robertson's nature views were nuanced and akin to Christian environmental stewardship as demonstrated by Francis Schaeffer in his book *Pollution and the Death of Man* and others, including Leighton Ford's 1970 Earth Day sermon as well as Harold Lindsell's statements until the late 1970s. Robertson's moderate environmental thinking in this example follow his previous eco-friendly sentiments as expressed in *Pat's Robertson's Perspective*. Robertson's environmental remarks went beyond the viewership of the Christian Broadcasting Network when he spoke at the very public and politically charged National Affairs Briefing held in Dallas, Texas, in August of 1980. That Robertson was not criticized for making this statement suggests that such a message was perfectly acceptable to and not uncommon among the conservative evangelical grassroots and the leadership. Furthermore, Robertson's remarks reveal that he chose either to ignore or to reject Reagan's message of a stronger economy at the expense of natural resources.

In addition to Robertson's address, the speech that proved the most memorable at the National Affairs Briefing was Ronald Reagan's, who famously declared to the evangelical audience, "I know that you can't endorse me, but I only brought that up because I want you to know that I endorse you and what you are doing."[34] This remark symbolically made him the candidate for the religious right, and they expected him to fight for their concerns as president of the United States. Although Reagan did not mention the environment that evening, he did criticize Jimmy Carter's "Crisis of Confidence" speech and refused to admit that the United States must "accept a condition of national 'malaise.'" Instead he encouraged an optimistic vision of the future via "unleashing America's economic power for growth and expansion." Later that year, during the GOP presidential nomination address Reagan warned, "Never before in our history have Americans been called upon to face three grave threats to our very existence, any of which could destroy us. We face a disintegrating economy, a weakened defense, and an energy policy based on the sharing of scarcity." He made it clear that conservation was a luxury that came second to economic prosperity: "Conservation is desirable. . . . But conservation is not the sole answer to our energy needs. . . . Economic prosperity of our people is a fundamental part of our environment."[35]

During the 1980s, Robertson did not alter his environmental views to follow or show support for Reagan. While Reagan won the nomination, Robertson promoted Christian environmental stewardship, writing, "If we refuse to make drastic cuts in our energy use, here is what lies ahead: . . . The substitution of more hazardous energy sources for oil and gas will present us with unacceptable environmental problems—air pollution, acid rain, aesthetic degradation or radiation hazards—which could menace entire populations."[36] Elsewhere in his magazine *Flame*, Robertson echoed his National Affairs Briefing speech: "Have we created a Frankenstein with our advanced technologies? Man has raped the earth of its natural resources, polluted the air, poisoned the waters and exhausted our energy supplies through greed and indifference." He advised his readers to pray to God that they might become "a better steward of earth's resources, as well as our personal resources."[37]

While Robertson preached for Christian environmental stewardship, other messages in agreement with Reagan's future of plenty and portraying environmentalists as the enemy of humanity circulated among the conservative evangelical grassroots. The same year as the National Affairs Briefing, a Baptist preacher named Lindsey Williams published a book and promotional pamphlet titled *The Energy Non-Crisis*. Williams described himself as a simple chaplain who traveled to Alaska to offer spiritual guidance to the workers on the Trans-Alaska pipeline in the 1970s. The companies declined his assistance when he arrived, but he persevered, and after a short time he was allowed to preach. Williams later befriended those at the management level who educated him on their situation. In the promotional pamphlets for the upcoming book, he wrote, "At one time I too thought there was an energy crisis. After all, that was what I had been told by the news media and by the Federal Government. . . . Then as I heard, saw and experienced what you are about to read, I realized that there is no energy crisis. There is no need for America to go cold, or for gas to be rationed."[38] The pamphlet and the book told of a visit from former Senator Hugh M. Chance who Williams claimed was an "outstanding Christian gentleman." Lindsey and Chance spoke to an oil expert, "Mr. X," who told them that there was plenty of oil in the ground, but that their efforts to extract it were prohibited. Free enterprise, Mr. X explained, has always come to the rescue of America in times of need.[39] Williams wrote that he once witnessed a monster oil strike but the next day found out the well was capped and the company had to withdraw from the area. "The excuse they [the Federal Government] gave was that some of the micro-organisms of that area of the Arctic Ocean might be destroyed if an oil spill ever happened."[40] He continued, "For one thing, the bureaucrats were working through the ecologists. Here is one instance: Construction of the Pipeline was halted one spring day when the ecologists stopped everything because a falcon's nest was in the way, and the birds hadn't hatched yet. They would have to wait a month, idling hundreds of men . . . which cost them an extra two million dollars!"[41] Overall, the promotional pamphlet praised American business, accused the media and environmentalists of obstructing and vilifying oil companies, and lastly offered the reader information on how to be saved. Williams concluded, "*Stand up* for God and Country! Pray, work, fight! . . . Let Freedom and hope continue in at least one nation on earth!" (emphasis in original).[42]

This book and promotional pamphlet circulated throughout the conservative evangelical community. Multiple copies of the pamphlet, for instance, found their way into the home of a devout conservative evangelical in Western Massachusetts known by the pseudonym of "Ferne."[43] Her collection of Christian reading material consisted of alarmist publications such as *Big Sister Is Watching You* (1993) by Texe Marrs as well as more theologically based and moderate devotionals like *A Life of Integrity: Right Choices* (1991) by James M. Grier, John E. Silvius, Irene B Alyn, and Lis K. Baker. Her reading material and page notes do not suggest she was an overt anti-environmentalist, but she also did not have a problem reading or possibly disseminating pamphlets promoting a new book that promised an inside look at how ecologists were harming the United States. The fact that Lindsey Williams was a Baptist chaplain was undoubtedly enough for Ferne to trust what he wrote, or at least the reason why multiple promotional copies found their way into her home.

While having access to Williams' views, she was exposed to conflicting messages regarding the health of nature's resources from other conservative evangelical writers. Besides the *Energy Non-Crisis* pamphlet, Ferne owned the 1982 book *Occupy till I Come: How to Spiritually Survive the Last Days* by Greg Laurie. The point of the book was to warn the reader that Jesus would soon return, and his proof was that the world's situation was progressively getting worse: "The military leaders are telling us that things are coming to an end. The ecologists are telling us that we are destroying our natural resources. The lawmakers are telling us that crime is at epidemic proportions, with no end in sight."[44] Later Laurie validated President Carter's *Global 2000 Report* (2000), a study conducted by the federal government to predict long-term environmental and population trends, by using it to legitimize his dismal view of the future. He wrote that, "the year 2000 the world will be more crowded, polluted, less stable ecologically and more vulnerable to disruption."[45] Unlike Williams, Laurie authenticated the ecological crisis to depict a deteriorating world and fewer resources. To insinuate that great wealth was not godly, Laurie also warned that the United States was like Sodom and Gomorra because, like them, it had an overabundance of food.[46]

The reality of the ecological and/or energy crisis was one issue among many that those in the conservative evangelical community such as Ferne talked and read about. It was not a major concern, but with the rising global awareness of environmental issues, it was becoming an area that warranted recognition. Stands were taken on the subject but they changed so much that even Falwell, who held strong opinions on just about every other issue, confronted the ecological crisis gingerly. In 1976 he used pollution and the reality of energy shortage to support an argument similar to Laurie's that the Earth was deteriorating because Christians were not fighting for a moral society.[47] However by 1980, in a sermon in which he promoted his upcoming television special "America You're Too Young To Die," he seemed uncertain at first about the energy crisis but then denied he ever believed it existed and echoed Williams: "What about energy resources? Yes we need to improve that situation. I'm not sure we have an energy crisis. I never have been. There's a shortage of what gets to the people. I don't think there's any shortage of what's in the ground."[48]

Until about 1980 few conservative evangelicals, including Falwell, questioned the reality of the energy crisis. Lindsey Williams was probably telling the truth that at first he believed what experts were saying about the scarcity of energy. Christians could see the energy bill rising, which prompted churches to action. However, after "secular" conservatives such as Howard Phillips and Paul Weyrich, with the help of Ed McAtteer, contacted and worked alongside religious right pastors such as Falwell, as witnessed in the origins of the Moral Majority, the topic of environmental protection and the related energy crisis began to be weighed with greater frequency against the benefits of capitalism. Nevertheless, although questioned, the feelings within the conservative evangelical community regarding caring for God's creation did not change to any great degree throughout the decade. Perhaps the greatest case in point was the religious right's response to born-again Christian James G. Watt who became secretary of the interior in 1981.

Watt and the Religious Right

People have a hard time analyzing the career of Secretary of the Interior James G. Watt (1981–1983). During his tenure in the Reagan administration, numerous articles were written about him and his environmental policies. Reporters followed Watt, and some were allowed special access. Such opportunities for the press were most likely granted with the hope that the populace would understand the secretary of the interior to be a reasonable person with a balanced approach to U.S. resources. However, these attempts failed and he remained a polarizing figure. As Watt reflected in a 2014 interview, the secretary of the interior is a position that attracts controversy and thus is an appointment frequently short-lived.[49] Nevertheless, Watt seemed to garner more controversy than others who held his position.

One of the first episodes that pushed Watt into the national spotlight was a remark made during his confirmation process in Congress. Representative James Weaver of Oregon asked Watt about his views toward conservation. Watt replied that he did not know how many generations would pass before the Lord returned, referring to the premillennialist belief in Christ's Second Coming, but until that time, he continued, humanity must maintain resources for the future.[50] Just about every scholar that examines Watt tells this story but even today some environmental writers such as Glenn Scherer only quote the first half, framing Watt as a religious radical.[51] After the hearing, environmental groups like the Sierra Club publicized the truncated remarks and sent out mass mailings portraying Watt as lacking rationality—a view that fit right into the other alarming portrayals of the religious right at the time. The People for the American Way, for example, produced a video in 1982 starring actor Burt Lancaster asking for donations to fight the religious right, a movement said to be working toward a theocracy.[52] What initially upset the Sierra Club was Watt's past employment as the head of a conservative organization called the Mountain States Legal Foundation, created by beer magnate Joseph Coors. In this role, Watt fought environmentalists who frequently sued to stall development and keep humans from "ruining" nature. This was the work that led to his name being brought to Reagan's attention when deciding on cabinet members. It seemed that Reagan found a kindred spirit—someone who understood that nature was a resource to use for humanity's benefit and more precisely to improve the U.S. economic situation.

As environmental studies professor Susan P. Bratton states in her article "The Ecotheology of James Watt," Watt's view toward nature was not a product of his religious beliefs. He grew up in Wyoming, where it was a continual struggle to manipulate the environment to survive. It was here that Watt adopted a strong utilitarian relationship toward the natural world. In his youth, religion did not play an important role in his life. Growing up and during college he attended mainstream churches, but then in the 1960s, while working in Washington DC, he became a born-again Charismatic Christian.[53] The conversion, however, did not change his relationship with the natural world, but rather he molded his interpretation of the Bible to fit his long-held views. While working for the Department of the Interior, he heard and came to embrace the term "stewardship" from Secretary Stewart Udall and used it throughout the rest of his career to describe how humans should interact with the natural world.[54]

In short, devout Christian Charismatic or not, Watt understood "stewardship" to mean mankind should use nature wisely but always for the benefit of people and a strong economy. One of the few times that Watt expressed views that one might deem close to environmental rhetoric was during Nixon's administration, when his job was to promote the policies of the president.[55] On March 24, 1970, Watt delivered a speech at an environmental-themed dinner at John Carroll University. Watt declared, "We can no longer afford to be exploiters of nature. We must become the trustee of our environment. Environmental considerations must become the central components of every decision we make because we are now aware that decisions we make will shape the future of mankind."[56] These views, however, later drastically changed and came to mirror Reagan's understanding that nature should be used to support a strong economy. As Reagan's secretary of the interior, Watt tried to win the public's favor but the environmental movement relentlessly attacked him and compared Regan's appointment of him to a farmer choosing a fox to watch the hen house.

While the controversy continued, his religious right allies such as Falwell and the Moral Majority never came to his aid, nor did they publicly endorse the administration's environmental policies. This divergence continued in spite of Falwell strongly supporting Reagan until Falwell's death in 2007.[57]

Beyond the seemingly unexplainable silence of the Moral Majority, Watt's relationships with other Christians were odd to say the least. The evangelical and very pro-environmental Oregon senator Mark Hatfield remained friendly with Watt and the two had lunch with Pat Robertson on at least one occasion in the 1970s.[58] Watt also appeared a few times on Robertson's television show the 700 Club in the early 1980s, but, as Watt later recalled, they talked about faith while the environment was not broached—or if it was, they did not delve into the nuts and bolts of the issue or controversy. Moreover, when Watt invited Francis Schaeffer to speak in Washington, DC, in 1982, he asked him to talk about humanism and national defense. Schaeffer, the man who wrote

Pollution and the Death of Man and delivered a string of lectures pushing Christian environmental stewardship in the late 1960s did not once talk about nature or stewardship in this speech to help the beleaguered Secretary of the Interior. The only clue available connecting the two and Christian environmental stewardship comes from a letter Watt wrote several months previous to the talk thanking a supporter who had sent him one of Schaeffer's books. In the letter, Watt noted that his wife recently attended several meetings with Schaeffer and that "unbeknownst to us, for the last several months, Dr. Schaeffer has followed our work in the Department and was very supportive of the change we are bringing in our commitment to stewardship."[59] Maybe Schaeffer had changed his views toward nature in the past ten years, but that is difficult to fathom. *Pollution and the Death of Man* promoted a much more compassionate relationship between humanity and the environment than that held by Watt. Since 1970 however, Schaeffer had largely dropped the issue, but underscored the heightened value of nature as the creation of God in his book and film documentary *How Should We Then Live?*

Beyond this peculiar meeting of Watt and Schaeffer, fellow Charismatic Pat Robertson neither denounced nor supported Watt. While the Moral Majority was elated in the early 1980s, claiming they had put Reagan into the White House, they were soon disheartened to find that few conservative evangelicals were appointed to cabinet posts. Watt, however, was one who indeed made it, but the Moral Majority did not show any organized attempt at letting the public know they approved Watt's interpretation of stewardship. Falwell, on his own, could have simply supported Watt in any public forum, and he actually did when it came to other topics beyond the environment.[60]

Falwell's lack of assistance for Watt cannot be attributed to the fact that the two followed different religious philosophies. Falwell liked the secretary of the interior, but was not sure what public environmental position to take. The closest Falwell came to supporting the secretary of the interior came during a sermon in 1982 when he delved, as he often did, into current politics. He first praised Watt as a godly man and then excused the controversial energy policies. After all, Falwell concluded, Watt was only doing what the president asked of him and was trying to make the United States energy-independent so that it would not have to "bow down" to Saudi Arabia or the Ayatollah in order to run automobiles or heat homes. He joked, "And he's [Watt] the fella that all the environmentalists are after his jugular vein. . . . God bless the environmentalists, everybody's gotta do something."[61] The comment garnered a little laughter, and he went on to say the country needs people who can take abuse but keep on going. These comments only suggest his personal feelings and lack substantial agreement with Watt's environmental position, an uncommon approach for Falwell, who was normally dogmatic and enthusiastically unapologetic in his political views.

Later in April of 1983, Falwell's newspaper, *Moral Majority Report*, featured an interview with Watt. In the article, Watt described nature as providing the necessary resources needed to survive as a nation in the face of the Cold War. He stated, "We must rearm America if we are going to live in peace. To rearm America, you've got to have energy. On the lands owned by the federal government, which are a third of America, we have enough energy to meet our needs for thousands of years."[62] He went on to say that Native American reservations were the picture of socialism in that they depended on social programs for support and that they should instead rely on political freedom and liberty. Thus he indirectly suggested that they should utilize natural resources on 50 million acres of tribal land. After the article was published, opinion pieces in support of Watt failed to appear in future issues. In essence, the *Moral Majority Report* allowed fellow religious right proponent James Watt to express his vision for America's natural resources but that seemed as far as the community cared to go.

Shortly after the article ran, Watt visited Liberty College to give a commencement speech on May 9, 1983. In promoting the event, Falwell placed Watt at the end of an impressive list of those coming to Lynchburg. At the Wednesday service, astronaut Jack Lousma talked about how God is everywhere in space; the following Wednesday the podium featured Vice President George H. W. Bush followed later by Watt. Falwell said he liked the secretary of the interior because he was "controversial." Furthermore, Falwell redirected any blame to the president, saying that Watt was just doing what Reagan wanted him to do, and "he's doing it quite well if you ask my opinion."[63] During the speech at Liberty, Watt totally circumvented the issue of environmental resources and the economy. He instead warned against large government that could stamp out religious freedom and accused public schools of pushing secular philosophies on students. Watt also urged Liberty College graduates to take action and stop the courts and legislatures that seek to destroy life for the unborn, born, old or crippled.[64] Here, amid his struggle to counter the environmental movement on the political stage, Watt once again chose to discuss other issues important to the religious right movement.

In 1982 Watt reflected on the dearth of support from members of his religious community but did not blame them. He wrote that they backed him by first supporting Reagan and thus he did not feel the need to directly ask for their assistance. After further thought, he reasoned that asking for help would look like he was using his faith as a political tool. He concluded, "The evangelical or fundamental Christian community with which I identify has traditionally not taken positions on political positions for which I am responsible in the Government." He thought it was inappropriate for the organized church to have a stance on every issue.[65] Watt's conclusions, however, seem at odds with the fact that the religious right, or at least its top leaders, did not have any problem taking sides on other largely secular political topics such as the handover of the Panama Canal or the proliferation of nuclear arms. Unfortunately for Watt's career, they were not willing to support his calls for a stronger economy at the expense of the environment.

Perhaps the strongest evidence of the religious right choosing to sacrifice the environment for a strong economy can be seen long after Watt resigned as secretary of the interior, when a group of religious leaders formed the Coalition for Revival (COR) in 1984. Over the years they produced resolutions such as "A Manifesto for the Christian Church Declaration and Covenant, July 4, 1986; An Act of Contrition and Humble Repentance; A Solemn Covenant; and A Statement of Essential Truth and A Call to Action."[66] Members of this group included Tim LaHaye, Franky Schaeffer, Adrian Rogers, Connaught Marshner, Ed McAteer, Rousas John Rushdoony, and Harold Lindsell. In 1986, COR produced another resolution titled "The Christian World View of Economics," written by the members of the organization's Economics Committee and edited by E. Calvin Beisner and Daryl S. Borgquist. The writers acknowledged that all of nature belongs to God, but then absolved believers if they failed in wisely using resources. The writers also neglected to support classic Christian environmental stewardship practices such as using resources sparingly or prudently. They did, however, feel that owners of private property should use the "principles of Scripture," but nevertheless left decisions regarding the use of resources up to the individual's or corporation's "conscience." The hallmarks of Christian environmental stewardship were further dismantled by the resolution's denial that "the amount of material wealth on Earth will ever prove insufficient . . . as long as people live consistently with God's laws."[67] The Rushdoony Reconstructionist-like caveat concerning "God's laws" was not discussed anywhere else in the twenty-three-page document. Instead, focus largely centered on protecting capitalism from socialism by supporting freedom of the marketplace; voluntary charity was also favored, while the right of government to support those in need was denied.

In general the resolution on economics only indirectly rejected eco-friendly views. The point was not to attack environmental positions but to reaffirm a financially conservative outlook. Furthermore, other COR members did not incorporate the resolution's economic statements into their messages to the conservative evangelical community. Like Lindsell's evolved view toward environmental protection in his book about free enterprise, the resolution merged into the background of conservative evangelical conversation. Conversely, the religious right's mainstream throughout the 1970s and 1980s continued supporting traditional Christian environmental stewardship philosophies as espoused by Schaeffer.

Christian Schools, Free Enterprise, and God's Earth

Although Falwell did not take a stance on environmental stewardship, the Christian schools he passionately favored continued to embrace it throughout the 1980s. Two of the top Christian textbook publishers, A Beka Book and Bob Jones University Press, expressed such viewpoints while simultaneously following the larger religious right's growing love affair with free enterprise and small government. During the 1980s, A Beka Book science books pointed out that humanity should "master" nature but added the caveat that it must be used wisely. Their other books however, as well as the material produced by BJU Press, maintained a stronger compassionate view for nature protection.

The BJU 1980 edition of *Biology for Christian Schools*, by William S. Pinkston, featured an entire section dedicated to ecology. Pinkston was a biology teacher who had taught at Bob Jones Academy since 1969. He understood that humanity is a part of nature and therefore has a right to use it, but must do so without waste. Humans, he wrote, can take the "consumer-manager role too far" and destroy the environment. Examples of humans abusing the Earth included frivolously using DDT, strip mining, dumping trash in the ocean, and pushing animal species to extinction. He also legitimized the worries of secular environmentalists without embracing calls for preservation: "It is inconceivable that God would place man on an earth that did not have natural resources to supply his needs. However, some sources give us the idea that no matter what man does, he messes up this world so badly that soon everyone will be starving, wearing gas masks, and drinking water out of cans." In this latter statement Pinkston was not minimizing or dismissing warnings from environmentalists. Instead, desperate times might come to fruition due to poor management. He wrote, "These sorts of things may happen; if they do, it will be because man has misused his environment, not because he has used it."[68]

In 1981, A Beka Book released *The Modern Age: The History of the World in Christian Perspective*. Along with the idea of Christian nationalism, such as the religiously motivated Pilgrims who set the foundation for the United States, free enterprise was credited with making the nation "great" through the industrial revolution. The authors wrote that with the use of technology and the "Protestant work ethic," "Men drained swamps and reclaimed land in other ways to make more land available for tilling."[69] Other benefits included increased population and life expectancy. The book also promoted the Republican Party, which was unabashedly the friend of big business followed by a quotation from Calvin Coolidge who reportedly stated, "the business of America is business." The authors further justified the need for a strong economy writing, "Americans realized that prosperity of business meant prosperity for all."[70] In the sections on the twentieth century, the authors labeled FDR's New Deal a "counterproductive deal" because it made people reliant on the government and destroyed incentive. Nevertheless, it is noteworthy that the environmental movement was not categorized along with socialism or big government when exploring events of the twentieth century. In other words, environmentalism was not understood by the conservative evangelical publishers to be at odds with promoting free enterprise.

While consistently supporting the importance of American capitalism and ingenuity, in 1986, A Beka Book published a story for elementary school students warning about the sin of maximizing profits at the expense of the environment. The story featured environmentalist and Sierra Club founder, John Muir titled "Land That I Love." The tale began with the Muir family relocating from Scotland to a farm in the United States. The author explained that John loved the birds, trees, and animals. Over time, almost all the trees on their farm were cut down, as were those on neighboring farms, so that birds that had eaten insects were forced to find new homes, and the streams, once held back by the trees, poured freely onto farms. By the end of the story, only one little grove of trees on the Muir farm remained. Then one morning John's father, who had promised wood to a buyer, requested that his children help chop down the last of the trees. John's reaction was highly emotional: "To one who loved every twig and leaf, it was like killing a friend to cut down a tree." "Suddenly through the chill morning air, the sound of an ax rang out. . . . 'No! No! No, you cannot do that!' John screamed. . . . 'You—you are stripping every tree from the land!'" The story concluded that as an adult, Muir helped preserve forests so that ". . . millions of Americans . . . see the beauty God gave our country."[71] An additional page instructed readers about the necessity of protecting natural resources and offered strategies to wisely conserve what God created.

"The Land that I Love" precisely mirrors key tenets of Schaeffer's understanding of Christian environmental stewardship. Notably, the aspect of humanity "developing" the land into a farm was not portrayed as controversial. People, Schaeffer believed, held the right to use resources because people were God's crowning achievement. However, as Schaeffer argued in his last chapter regarding economics, people must not abuse that right for financial gain.

In the story, John Muir's father sold the oak grove for money, but John rightfully put a stop to the economic transaction by pointing out the unethical action of "stripping every tree from the land." Perhaps most importantly, A Beka Book published the story as late as 1986. This was long after Reagan made environmental protection a partisan issue and employed religious right supporter James Watt who publicly reasoned that natural resources must be used for economic benefit. If the conservative evangelical community by this time agreed with Watt, then why would A Beka Book offer such a controversial story to its readers? This message of stewardship was not unique but freely continued in both BJU Press and A Beka Book publications during the rest of the decade.

History books by A Beka Book's competitor, BJU Press, praised free enterprise just as diligently while simultaneously promoting environmental protection. In 1982 it produced *United States History for Christian Schools*. While advocating strongly for free enterprise, the section discussing the ecology movement evaded bias while others such as FDR's response to the Great Depression did not and the Depression itself was described in part as a positive event in a section titled "Blessings of the Depression." In contrast, the ecology movement was presented in a straightforward manner by stating that the Nixon administration sought to stop pollution by increasing federal regulation of industries. In another neutral statement, the authors noted that rallies and demonstrations pushed for restrictions to control pollution through the implementation of laws.[72] In the conclusion the authors described the present day (1982) as a time of social disintegration and argued that turning to God served as the only way to improve the situation. Notably, one of the social problems the authors pointed to was the failure of businesses to take greater responsibility for their effects on the environment.[73] Thus, the text directly made the point that although business, free enterprise, and prosperity were wonderful aspects of the United States, the health of the environment must also be taken into account. In other words, these nationally distributed conservative evangelical publications allowed for philosophies of nature protection to coexist with capitalism. The message was clear that nature could be used, but not simply for the sake of profits. The authors later concluded that if mankind is not right with God then "problems like pollution, racism, and moral corruption will never be solved."[74]

Later in 1984, after conservative evangelicals had time to read the likes of Lindsey Williams and observe the situation with James Watt on the national stage, the messages produced, especially by BJU Press, changed little. In *Life Science for Christian Schools* (1984), Pinkston maintained a Christian environmental stewardship outlook, encouraging protection of endangered species and warning that not all energy is renewable. He stressed that unwise use of energy can deplete water tables and pointed out the problems associated with strip mining coal and using nonbiodegradable pollutants. "Every year," he wrote, "America alone puts over seventy billion tons of pollution into the air." But he also pointed out the economic cost, writing that because pollution laws are sometimes so expensive, they force some companies to close. In another section dedicated to acid rain, Pinkston explained that the problem was real and was negatively affecting forests, streams, and fish populations. Implementing antipollution laws, however, would be costly. As stewards, he wrote, humans must look at the facts and act responsibility, rather than either exploiting nature for profits or always embracing preservationist views. Thus he concluded, "For this reason, our responsibility as stewards may also include electing lawmakers who will act responsibly on matters of ecology—even when the right action is not the popular one."[75]

In 1989, A Beka Book published a textbook on economics promoting capitalism while also taking a bold stance for resource conservation. Although in other parts of the book, Adam Smith was credited with advocating for freedom of the marketplace, a section titled "Pollution, Waste, and Ugliness" depicted Smith's town of Kirkcaldy, Scotland, as ugly and cheerless because of industry.[76] The author balanced the blame on capitalism however, with the observation that landscapes can suffer just as much in communist nations like the Soviet Union.

Although the author praised American ingenuity and proposed a need to move away from living too frugally, concern for the environment was also validated:

> The short-run costs of pollution prevention, conservation, and urban restoration are high. Yet the long-run costs to humanity of neglecting those economic responsibilities would be far higher. Steps already are being taken, especially in the United States, to preserve mankind's natural and cultural inheritance. An economy that fails to provide for future generations is like a farmer who consumes his own seed-corn intended for next year's planting. Such economic problems must be faced boldly in the future.[77]

This position on nature conservation is also apparent in the book's story about a business named the Gray Iron Fabricating Company of Mortmain, Michigan. The business functioned smoothly, the author explained, until the late 1960s, when unions demanded more money. Later, the Occupational

Safety and Health Administration (OSHA) forced the company to pay a fine for not having the best equipment. Subsequently, management got in trouble for promoting a man instead of a woman and then was sued by an injured employee who ignored safety regulations. By 1980, the company showed a loss. The author concluded by asking the students what they thought the business should do next.[78]

The entire story of the Gray Iron Fabrication Company portrayed the business as the victim of late 1960s progressive philosophies. Although OSHA came about in 1971, one year after the birth of the modern environmental movement and the founding of the EPA, the author validated environmental protection earlier in the text and left it out of the story in which the EPA could have easily been cast with the rest of the villains who tried to ruin American hard work, ingenuity, and economic freedom. In sum, although free enterprise remained important among conservative evangelicals in the 1980s, it did not crush compassionate ideas of Christian environmental stewardship in either A Beka Book or BJU Press publications, which were disseminated and used interchangeably throughout the United States in both home and Christian schools. Like these publishers, Pat Robertson continued his eco-friendly philosophies through to the end of the 1980s as demonstrated in his 1988 presidential campaign.

Robertson's Run for the White House

In 1976, conservative evangelicals who prayed for a spiritual and moral rebirth in the United States were encouraged by Democratic candidate Jimmy Carter, a professed "born-again" evangelical. During Carter's years in office, however, they became disappointed when he did not support their hopes of returning prayer to public school and then invited representatives from the gay community to participate in the White House Conference on Families. Reagan, on the other hand, told them exactly what they wanted to hear by endorsing their movement at the National Affairs Briefing and even utilized their understanding of Christian nationalism claiming, for example, that the United States was, as Puritans envisioned it to be, "a shining 'city upon a hill.'"[79] Nevertheless, like Carter, Reagan put their social concerns on the back burner and focused instead on the economy. He even appointed pro-choice-leaning Sandra Day O'Conner to the Supreme Court, but he was able to retain the religious right's support to a greater degree than Carter. By 1988 Robertson decided he would have to get the job done himself and reported that God had told him to run for the presidency.

Although Robertson traditionally encouraged Christian environmental stewardship, during his campaign he went about choosing his position on the issue cautiously. The environment as a political topic was really an unknown for Robertson. Reagan and Watt had made environmentalism a partisan matter, and Robertson ran under the Republican banner. At the same time, he probably knew that during the 1980s, environmental groups such as the Sierra Club enjoyed a massive membership increase. Instead of making a swift decision or ignoring it altogether, Robertson had his staff compile an information folder on the topic from a wide variety of sources.

Some of the material Robertson's staffers collected included publications from the Sierra Club's conservation campaign of 1987–1988. The issues they pushed were a reauthorization of the Clean Air Act; increased protection for the Arctic National Wildlife Refuge and Bureau of Land Management's wilderness/desert national parks in western states; and keeping a close eye on the U.S. Forest Service.[80] Robertson's staffers accompanied this information with a much larger booklet from the Alaska Coalition titled *Arctic National Wildlife Refuge: Treasure of the North*. Like the Sierra Club's publications, this source argued for the preservation of wilderness in Alaska by demanding a stop to development. It generally presented the reader with a narrative of the timeworn battle between greedy energy developers and the need to save what little wilderness is left.

To balance out arguments from preservationists, Robertson's campaign also compiled information from the business community and right-wing advocacy groups. One anonymous "Acid Rain Background Memorandum" reasoned that the environmental movement produced only knee-jerk arguments based on emotions and concluded that strengthening regulations would result in American corporations losing billions of dollars. Moreover, the author stated, the Clean Air Act of 1970 had already proven effective and cut down pollution caused by the burning of coal.[81] Similar arguments came from Kent Jefferys writing on behalf of the Republican Study Committee, who complained that preservationists wanted to unreasonably lock up resources in Alaska while ignoring the local Inuits who hoped to benefit from energy exploration. In addition to these examples, Robertson received a personal letter in 1988 from the president of the National Coal Association, Richard L. Lawson, asking him to think about the health of American companies in the global market. Depicting his own interests and American businesses in general as barely able to survive under the great strain of regulations, Lawson warned in an attached letter along with co-signers from other industries that environmental regulations would reduce the GDP by $223 billion and cost 862,000 jobs by the year 2000. Some of the other signatories, which compounded the weight of Lawson's view included the American Mining Congress, the Edison Electric Institute, the

National Association of Manufacturers, and the American Iron and Steel Institute.[82]

In addition, a booklet from Paul Weyrich's politically right-wing think tank, the Heritage Foundation, found its way into the Americans for Robertson campaign. Weyrich founded the privately funded organization in 1973, moved on to head the Committee for the Survival of a Free Congress, later known as the Free Congress Foundation, and encouraged Falwell to form the Moral Majority. Edited by Doug Bandow, the booklet was part of a series on "Critical Issues" and was titled "Protecting the Environment: A Free Market Strategy" that featured contributing authors from a variety of similar conservative-leaning think tanks such as the Cato Institute and the Political Economy Research Center. Overall, the booklet stressed the need to relieve the government of environmental responsibility and increase independence on the part of businesses, which would take it upon themselves to ensure a healthy environment. Along with this material, Robertson's campaign gathered a number of general news articles reporting on topics such as toxic waste and global warming.

In addition, Robertson's New Hampshire director of communication, James L. Hofford, played a role in helping Robertson make a decision regarding the environment. Hofford became an ordained Methodist minister in 1960, but in 1983 he joined the English Plymouth Brethren, a conservative evangelical community.[83] As a dedicated member of "Americans for Robertson," Hofford conducted research on a possible environmental position. In December of 1987, he sent Robertson's campaign manager, Connie Snapp, a proposed speech, recommendations for policies, and a press release with the suggestion that Robertson take a solid pro-environmental stand by creating an organization called the Environmental Defense Initiative (EDI) to help carry out such work when Robertson became president. He wrote, "I'm convinced that the Environmental Defense Initiative is Urgent! My prayer is that Pat will build and harness the sense of urgency we need in this nation." The short report described a future speech Robertson might deliver in New Hampshire. After stating that Robertson would ensure U.S. nuclear defense, it added that "the pollution of our precious water supplies are 'self-inflicted wounds in which we all share guilt by using toxic pollutants'" and that "overused landfills are leeching into our country's aquifers and such pollution lasts for centuries."[84] Furthermore, Hofford wrote, Robertson would restrict any disposal of nuclear waste in the Northeast because of its dense population and valuable watershed areas.[85] Nuclear power plants would be allowed to operate only if they all adhered to strict regulations, but Hofford added that the campaign was reasonable and knew that no measure could ever totally guarantee the public's safety.[86]

Upon reading over the speech, Snapp or an assistant edited out the introduction for being overly dramatic because it equated an alien invasion with the ecological crisis. However, what remained was a call for action to address a list of serious environmental problems, including the diminishing ozone layer, a cause of skin cancer; acid rain, the cause of the decline of the maple syrup business in New Hampshire; global deforestation; and overflowing landfills. Hofford insisted that the economy could not be revived until "we restore our environment that supports life itself."[87] He suggested a variety of solutions, the first being recycling and environmentally safe incinerators. The energy derived from the latter process, Hofford wrote, could light every American home.[88] In conclusion the EDI would spearhead regional and local initiatives to save our habitats. Hofford wanted to say that environmental protection was as important as the threat of an imminent nuclear attack but this was reworded by an editor to read, "Just as the development of a strategic defense initiative is necessary to protect us from nuclear attack, so an 'Environmental Defense Initiative' is also needed to protect our natural habitat."[89]

The campaign's response to Hofford's pro-environmental position was initially favorable.[90] Indeed, the proposed speech was edited and prepared but then doubt set in. The combined pressure from the prevalent GOP position toward the environmental movement, the fact that the issue was not regarded as most important among voters, and advice from conservative free enterprise advocates likely dampened Robertson's enthusiasm for adding this new plank to the campaign. Robertson was not writing freely for his followers anymore. Now he was in the political world where allies in business were essential and he needed to pander to a wide voting demographic.

Although Hofford never realized his hope of seeing the EDI become central to the campaign, Robertson was nevertheless open to the proposal. Moreover, the very existence of Hofford supporting the environment as a political issue shows that among Robertson's religious community, a strict utilitarian and/or uncaring view toward nature was not the accepted norm; that is, Hofford thought his pro-environmental platform stood a chance with the campaign supporters. Ultimately however, Robertson listened to the anti-environmentalist rhetoric of the GOP while not adopting their position. At the same time he also passed up the opportunity to embrace an eco-friendly platform. This choice was likely a political move, not a reflection of a long-held understanding that the religious right traditionally opposed environmental protection.

After bowing out of the presidential race, Robertson felt free to once again articulate his views of nature, and he did so at the 1988 Republican National Convention in New Orleans. In tune with Hofford's beliefs, Robertson was unafraid to tell the public his vision for the nation's future.

We see a city set on a hill. A shining light of freedom for all of the nations to see and admire. A city made great by the moral strength and
self-reliance of her people.

A city where husbands and wives love each other and families hold
together.

A city where every child, whether rich or poor, has available to him
the very best education in the world.

A city where the elderly live out their lives with respect and dignity,
and where the unborn child is safe in his mother's womb.

. . .

A city where the water is pure to drink, the air clean to breathe, and
the citizens respect and care for the soil, the forests, and God's other
creatures who *share with us* the earth, the sky, and the water.[91] (emphasis added)

Robertson's GOP address remains, perhaps, the most complete example of
his pre-1990 nature views. First, he underlined the importance of a healthy natural world by including it among other top religious right values such as marriage
defined as a heterosexual union and opposition to abortion. Second, he promoted Christian environmental stewardship. On one level he simply wanted a
healthy environment. He legitimized this view on a theological level by reminding the audience that people shared the Earth with God's other creatures. This
statement echoed his 1980 National Affairs Briefing speech by implying humans
did not own the Earth and were not the only beings that mattered.

By using the term "share" Robertson employed an ecotheology similar to
that of Francis Schaeffer's book *Pollution and Death of Man*. As explained in
chapter 1, Schaeffer believed that humanity was indeed God's crowning
achievement and therefore had dominion over the Earth. As such, humans existed on a spiritual or supernatural level with God. Nevertheless they also
lived as mortals with all living things. Thus, humanity was of the physical world
as well as the spiritual. This dual position, Schaeffer argued, was part of humanity's God-ordained "proper place" and therefore humans should hold dominion over nature, but simultaneously hold nature in reverence because
creation was not only a product of God, but humanity was also a part of creation. In his address to the GOP National Convention Robertson went beyond simply telling people he cared for the Earth; he echoed Schaeffer's
understanding that humans existed *with* the rest of God's creation and that
both therefore deserved health and a promising future. Such environmental
understandings changed in the 1990s as Robertson became more involved with
politics. Nevertheless, as in like his 1980 National Affairs Briefing speech, once

again Robertson communicated an eco-friendly view of Christian environmental stewardship akin to Schaeffer's 1970 stance to a national audience at a politically charged event. Furthermore, his understanding of environmental stewardship ranked among important religious right issues. This is not to say it was as important as abortion, for example, but its addition to Robertson's speech signifies it was not ignored among the conservative evangelicals associated with or within the religious right. Instead, eco-friendly understandings of Christian stewardship existed and were philosophically acceptable within their hopes for a better future.

Conclusion

From roughly 1977 to 1989, eco-friendly Christian environmental stewardship weathered the challenges from beyond and within the conservative evangelical community. For insiders such as Gilbert Turner, Harold Lindsell, James Watt, Lindsay Williams, and E. Calvin Beisner, caring for the natural world posed a threat to American strength and prosperity. Their views during this period, however, were not powerful enough to become the accepted norms or talking points. They were held by individuals who were caught up in the political alliance with the GOP or who on their own (with the help of secular conservatives) targeted the environmental movement as a threat to free enterprise, the latter of which had become a major component in religious right ideology.

Their anti-environmentalist arguments perhaps persuaded a few conservative evangelicals to embrace similar feelings. However, there is no evidence our faithful church member Ferne decided that the need to care for the environment was ridiculous after reading Lindsey Williams promotional pamphlet, *The Non-Energy Crisis*. Years later in 1991, she filled in the answers to a devotional titled "Christian Stewardship of the Environment" by John E. Silvius. Silvius, who presented a basic Christian environmental stewardship argument, encouraged the reader to have compassion for nature because it is God's creation. He asked his reader, "Does the Scripture support 'animal rights'?" Ferne wrote, "No—man rules," but added, "Man has the authority to rule over the creatures but he must not abuse that rule. He is to provide for animals, take care of them."[92] Although this answer is not hard evidence that she rejected the position of people like Williams, it suggests her mind was not closed to the need for compassionate environmental stewardship. Moreover, it is clear that Ferne did not ignore the devotional section on stewardship as unimportant or equate animal's rights with a despised and opposing political position as it would later become for fellow conservative evangelicals.

Indeed, the example of Ferne likely represents the mainstream conservative evangelical community's relationship toward the environment during the late 1970s and into the 1980s. They were exposed to anti-environmentalist ideas from places other than their leadership but did not jump on the bandwagon en masse. Instead eco-friendly environmental stewardship proved a topic they discussed as a community, and it was an accepted Christian position. During the late 1970s, for instance, numerous individual congregations in the Southern Baptist Convention repeatedly justified the reduction of energy use by employing the understanding of stewardship to conserve God's resources. While upholding such views, this community never embraced Reagan and Watt's position that the economy should trump the health of the natural world. Additionally, religious right co-founder Pat Robertson along with the two major fundamentalist education publishers, A Beka Book and BJU Press, happily promoted a strong sense of free enterprise while effectively espousing Schaeffer's and Ford's understanding of Christian environmental stewardship. In short, as demonstrated in this chapter, the common congregant met energy shortages with the ideology of stewardship while Pat Robertson, James Hofford, A Beka Book and BJU Press directly promoted eco-friendly philosophies from the late 1970s to 1989.

Figure 1. Conservative evangelical intellectual Francis Schaeffer articulated the "proper" relationship of God, humanity, and nonhuman nature in *Pollution and the Death of Man* (1970). Photo by Joe Fischetti. Permission to use by English L'Abri.

Figure 2. Liberty University's Chancellor Jerry Falwell Jr. addresses students, faculty, and parents during a ceremony to award President Donald Trump an honorary Doctorate of Laws. In recent decades Liberty University has become an important campaign stop for Republican politicians competing for conservative evangelical support. Permission to use by Redux Pictures.

Figure 3. Robert Dugan addressing the National Association of Evangelicals at the 1990 conference in which resolutions to protect the environment were passed. Later, in 1993, he eagerly joined the Evangelical Environmental Network. Permission to use by the National Association of Evangelicals.

FIGURE 4. The cover to the National Association of Evangelicals' May–June 1990 issue of *A Call to United Evangelical Action* dedicated to Christian environmental stewardship. Permission to use by the National Association of Evangelicals.

Figure 5a and 5b. Two political cartoons produced between 1993 and 1994 in *The Paper*, a Regent University publication. Categorizing caring for the Earth with known positions despised by Christians led to an abandonment of Christian environmental stewardship. Ridicule also played an important role in this process. Cartoons by Chuck Asay. Permission to use by Pikes Peak Library District.

GUESS WHICH SERVICE THE CLINTONS WANT TO REFORM:

FIGURE 5A AND 5B. Continued

FIGURE 6. Richard Land, executive director of the Christian Life Commission, circa 1990. Permission to use by the Southern Baptist Historical Library and Archives, Nashville, Tennessee.

ENDANGERED EARTH

HUMANS ARE CHANGING THE EARTH

• "The world is warming. Climatic zones are shift-ing. Glaciers are melting. Sea level is rising. These are not hypothetical events from a science fiction movie. These changes and others are already taking place, and we expect them to accel-erate over the next years as the amounts of carbon dioxide, methane and other trace gases accumulat-ing in the atmosphere through human activities increase."

- Scientific American, April 1989

• "A United Nations-sponsored panel of experts has concluded that worldwide temperatures will rise an unprecedented 2 degrees within 35 years and more than 6 degrees by the end of the next century, if nothing is done to combat global warming. The new forecast . . . predicts that temperatures will be far greater than any experienced in the last 10,000 years."

- Washington Post, May 26, 1990

BY FOULING THE AIR, WATER AND LAND

• "Emissions from fossil fuels--the oil, coal and gas used to produce energy--are creating environmental havoc everywhere. Unprecedented amounts of their toxic byproducts are clogging the atmosphere with pollution, killing the trees and poisoning water with acid rain and--most ominously of all--threaten-ing to warm the globe's climate and change life on this planet forever."

- Gannett News Service, December 17, 1989

• "Strong evidence of the effect (of chlorofluorocarbons on the ozone layer) emerged in 1985, when British researchers announced the existence of a sea-sonal 'hole' in the ozone layer over Antarctica. That was worrisome: ozone between 10 and 30 miles up absorbs the sun's ultraviolet radiation, which has been linked to cataracts, skin cancers and weakened immune systems in humans and other animals, as well as damage to plants."

- Time, March 13, 1989

• "Researchers have found the first evidence that marine plants in the ocean around Antarctica, the tiny organisms upon which a vast ecosystem depends, are damaged by the ultraviolet light that pours through the seasonal hole in the ozone layer. . . . Laboratory tests at Palmer Station in Antarctica show

FIGURE 7. Information flier for the Christian Life Commission's 1991 annual seminar warns evangelicals of the dangers of anthropogenic global warming. Permission to use by the Southern Baptist Historical Library and Archives, Nashville, Tennessee.

His father lifted his arm. With a squeal of fright, John ducked. He picked up the ax, which lay at his feet, and ran.

Out of sight of his father, he rounded the lake and headed for the untouched forest on the government land beyond.

John fell, panting and sobbing, to the forest floor. Far as he had come from the grove of oaks, the sound of axes carried on the clear air and made him wince. He had known that wild words and the loss of one ax would not stop his father.

Nothing would hold back a man who saw each tree in terms of the dollars it would bring.

John jumped to his feet beside a huge tree and threw his arms as far as he could reach around its great trunk. "Just wait!" he promised. "Just you wait! I'll be grown someday, and *then* I'll take care of you!"

272

FIGURE 8A AND 8B. The final two pages from the story "Land That I Love" about nature preservationist John Muir, published in a fifth and sixth grade reading book by A Beka Book (1986). Such stories taught by Christian School educators reflect mainstream eco-friendly attitudes among conservative evangelicals that lasted from the late 1960s to the early 1990s. Opposition to environmental efforts only became a standard among the religious right beginning in the early 1990s when the community adopted anti-environmentalism from conservative economic advocate groups. Story by Nan Gilbert. Art by W. T. Mars. Adapted from *Widening Horizons*, Golden Rule Series. Copyright © by Houghton Mifflin Harcourt Publishing Company. All rights reserved. Used by permission of the publisher, Houghton Mifflin Harcourt Publishing Company.

As John's eyes followed the mighty trunk up, up to where the branches laced against the sky, his soul stirred with its splendor. And in his heart, the promise took root, never to be forgotten.

This was his land — not by birth, but by love. He would fight all his life to preserve its richness for children yet unborn.

More than any other man of his time, John Muir battled for the preservation of our forests and the development of national parks.

His attempt to have the government set aside beautiful areas has saved, for all of us to enjoy, some of the loveliest places in America. Because of John Muir, millions of Americans have been able to see the beauty God gave to our country.

273

FIGURE 8A AND 8B. Continued

CHAPTER 5

The Struggle between Christian Environmental Stewardship and Anti-Environmentalism in the Religious Right

These final three chapters confirm two important points. First, in 1990, eco-friendly Christian environmental stewardship as understood by Schaeffer and Ford served as the accepted norm within the mainstream of the conservative evangelical community. In response to Earth Day 1990 celebrations, members within individual conservative evangelical churches as well as their leadership in the Southern Baptist Convention (SBC) and the National Association of Evangelicals (NAE) utilized environmental stewardship to advocate for eco-friendly action amongst the wider religious community. Secondly, anti-environmentalist positions from political conservatives eventually crushed calls for environmental action. One of the most effective arguments accused secular environmentalists of being Earth-worshipping extremists and participants in a conspiracy to promote new age religions and a one-world government that would destroy American capitalism. These conspiracy theories were delivered with a strong dose of ridicule aimed at belittling anyone expressing sympathy for the natural world. Such a strategy indirectly vilified Christian environmental stewardship through guilt by association. Additional anti-environmentalist arguments used credentialed experts who rejected the reality of environmental problems (especially anthropogenic global warming) while praising the benefits of a changing climate in combination with equating nature protection with a destroyed economy. All of these tactics proved most effective in shaping anti-environmentalism into a new political position among conservative evangelicals.

As former SBC leader Richard Land concluded during a 2017 interview, anti-environmentalist views held by conservative evangelicals were not "pre-ordained." Although during the interview Land did not admit changing his position, he and others within their religious and political community abandoned eco-friendly views in the face of an onslaught of arguments and social pressure. Indeed, the early 1990s proved to be a missed opportunity thanks to this subsequent struggle, which lasted roughly to 1994. The beginnings of this situation could be witnessed in various locations, including the religious right co-founder's own Thomas Road Baptist Church on Earth Day, 1990.

Pastor Jerry Falwell noticed environmentalism stirring among his own Liberty University students on Earth Day, April 22, 1990, a Sunday. In response to the secular Earth Day observance, the Biology Club at Liberty prepared a hiking trail at the school's picturesque 1950s-style summer camp named Camp Hydaway, located in the green hills of Lynchburg, Virginia.[1] The club members wanted to promote their accomplishments and asked Falwell to make a dedication announcement about their project during the morning service. As Falwell stood at the pulpit, he seemed unsure what to do about the Biology Club's request. Until now he had not officially articulated a position on environmental protection. Perhaps if he simply communicated that a trail had opened, he would demonstrate some degree of pride he typically exhibited when mentioning student activities. He particularly enjoyed giving updates about the school's football team and spoke of the players as hard-working, strong Christians. But on this day, he was asked to make an announcement regarding a student club that had, on its own initiative, acted in parallel with the secular environmental movement.

He stammered, "The new nature trail at Camp Hydaway opens from 2:00 to 4:00 today in keeping with Earth Day, and the Biology Club at LU, they'll sponsor that. Go by and visit with them from 2:00 to 4:00." He felt the need to clarify the situation and with renewed confidence added, "While we will do all we can to keep a good clean environment down here, we need to know it's not going to get better, it's going to get worse, and one day God's going to disband this universe as we presently know it. Dissolve it. Remove it. A new Heaven and a new earth will replace it."[2]

Falwell was grasping at straws. If attempts at improvements here on Earth did not matter because God would return soon, then why had he worked so hard founding and running the Moral Majority? He knew an ecological crisis existed but, overall, thought it was a secondary problem. Falwell did not quite know what to make of his students wanting to participate in the Earth Day observance and chose to downplay its importance with a poorly structured argument. He was later forced to strengthen and restructure his anti-environmentalist approach because others in the conservative evangelical community wanted to help save God's Earth along with the wider population who celebrated Earth Day 1990.

On the national stage, Earth Day 1990 rejuvenated the secular environmental movement. It was twenty years since the first observance when festivities were held across the United States. In New York's Central Park alone, approximately 750,000 people gathered to hear popular tunes from prominent musicians touting the theme of nature protection. The *New York Times* reported that some volunteers wondered if attendees were only there for the concert because they left the ground littered with trash.[3] Although this Earth Day anniversary seemed to lack the purity of the first, its message reached many, including students at Falwell's university as well as the churches of both the SBC and the NAE.

Before the excitement over Earth Day 1990, the SBC was aware of the emerging movement toward eco-friendly policies among moderate evangelical groups active in the 1980s. The SBC collected articles on moderate evangelical and environmental studies professor Calvin DeWitt's Au Sable Institute in Minnesota, which had been promoting Christian-inspired Earth care practices. They also knew of the eco-friendly resolution made by a mainline Baptist denomination known as the American Baptist Churches USA, which in 1988 wrote the "American Baptist Policy Statement on Ecology: An Ecological Situational Analysis." In this spirit and in tandem with Earth Day, SBC moderates such as Robert M. Parham wrote pro-environmental articles to encourage the organization's subgroups to participate in pro-environmental activities..[4]

In getting ready for Earth Day, Gary E. Farley, associate director of the Town and Country Mission Department, an agency of the SBC, sent Robert Parham material for "Stewardship Week," planned for April 29–May 6, 1990. The information for the public featured a letter by sitting president George H. W. Bush in which he endorsed the activity and stated the need to protect America's vast natural beauty, mentioning that new technology and science were helping in the effort. Like the American Baptist "Ecological Resolution," the well-researched and professionally designed booklet explained the theology behind nature protection and listed present-day problems such as the desertification in sub-Saharan Africa and acid rain.[5] The leadership let member congregations know they took their efforts seriously by reporting that the SBC's Home Mission Board started a recycling program and in four months saved almost 150 trees, 2,100 gallons of fuel, and 41 cubic yards of landfill space.[6]

These activities additionally encouraged the theological and political conservatives within the SBC to agree that the religious community must participate as good stewards of the environment.

In response to these environmental efforts by national organizations and simply by virtue of popular interest in Earth Day 1990, a small number of individual conservative evangelical churches joined in across the nation. At Crievewood Baptist Church in Nashville, Tennessee, Pastor Joel Snider stated in a message to the congregation titled, "Celebration of Creation" that at one time the environmental movement seemed like it was all about hippies, but now Christians should get involved. A former church member, Jim Fitch, would be delivering an eco-friendly sermon on the pastor's behalf. Snider concluded, "I hope you will be there to listen to his message and consider a Christian response to saving the environment."[7] Other examples of conservative evangelicals responding to Earth Day included SBC member First Baptist Church in Greensboro, North Carolina, which hosted an event titled "Eden's Earth Day." The church scheduled professional storyteller and environmental advocate Louise Kessel to speak about the relationship between humanity and the natural world.[8] In Loxahatchee, Florida, Barbara O'Malley, a teacher, advisor, and wife of the pastor, reported that students at Southside Educational Ministries were dedicated to environmental protection. Their efforts, she proudly stated, went beyond Earth Day excitement to embracing "a new attitude about our world and we are more aware of what's going on in keeping with Earth conservation and pollution." Furthermore, the school implemented a new recycling program and used the money for supporting missionaries in Grenada.[9] At First Evangelical Free Church in Marietta, Georgia, seventy-five-year-old congregant Willard Sherman took time to teach thirty children how to garden with the reasoning that "along the way [the children] will come to love the Good Earth, which makes all life possible."[10] Sherman believed gardening, teaching, and spirituality were interwoven, which made it seem natural to him to quote Scripture when talking to the gardening club he led. Although sparse in number, these environmental activities demonstrate that a number of conservative evangelicals at the grassroots level were willing and eager to support the eco-friendly efforts like those in leadership positions.

Reasons for little pro-environmental activity among conservative evangelical congregations and schools should not be interpreted as widespread disinterest, but rather as a result of internal conversations taking place within the community at the local and national level. By the early 1990s the conversations were often in the form of a growing struggle between those who were increasingly adopting anti-environmentalist views and those who supported eco-friendly environmental stewardship. Falwell's own church experienced this very situation on Earth Day, 1990, when the Biology Club felt they were doing a good work by observing Earth Day but were then disparaged by their pastor. Elsewhere, a similar situation unfolded at Wilshire Baptist Church in Dallas, Texas, when a new pastor named George Mason received an anonymous anti-environmentalist flier in the mail. An upset Mason accused the religious right of disseminating the material and criticized "secular-minded rightists" for caring only about human progress and profits.[11] He was sarcastically cryptic about the flier's immediate origin, suggesting that maybe it was dropped in his mail by a congregation member. He chided the possible perpetrators, "I know it didn't come from our church because the mail I get from our members is always signed, don't you know?"[12] Mason then read directly from the leaflet. "This is a New Age Extravaganza intended to deceive you! It is designed to get you interested in 'saving the environment.'" The flier explained that Earth Day was a ploy to convert people to worshipping the Earth and advised readers on how they could recognize the malevolent movement by spotting pet phrases like "protecting Mother Earth."[13] Mason thought its message was ridiculous and continued on with a strong Christian environmental stewardship sermon.

The circumstances at Falwell's Thomas Road Baptist Church and Wilshire Baptist Church highlight the activities and impact of growing anti-environmentalism that seeped into conservative evangelical congregations to ultimately douse opportunities for eco-friendly actions that would have made headlines in newspapers. This increasing amount of information circulated via leaflets, pamphlets, and politically conservative magazine articles from conservative think tanks and private advocacy groups such as the well-known John Birch Society. Such material found its way into the hands of conservative evangelical church leaders, congregation members, and ultimately the educational material their children read in Christian schools. Pat Robertson, who once publicly upheld a strong Christian environmental stewardship perspective, was one of the first leaders to reverse his position.

Robertson's increased political activities led to sacrificing environmental views to make an alliance with pro–free enterprise secular conservatives. The same year as the twentieth anniversary of Earth Day, Pat Robertson released *The New Millennium: 10 Trends that Will Impact You and Your Family by the Year 2000*. In it he promoted a conspiracy theory accusing Earth-worshipping environmentalists of trying to realize a "one-world government." Robertson portrayed environmentalists as an army of liberals bent on world domination in hopes of procuring some sort of left-wing utopia. The environmental movement was not the leading force behind the charge, but a method that the conspirators were using to get the job done.

Instead of the traditional compassionate reflections on the health of nature that sat in the background of Robertson's traditional worldviews, the environmental conspiracy took a prominent role in *The New Millennium* as the topic of an entire chapter, titled "Technology and the Environment." He wrote, "The primacy of environmental concerns may hinder technology and prove a front for massive new government spreading intrusion into our lives."[14] "Their [environmentalists'] agenda is control, and it is almost always antibusiness and antigrowth. In fact, this is the very same bunch of radicals who have been wrong so many times before."[15] Robertson seemed surprised at the recent growth of the environmental movement in 1990. He thought environmentalists came out of the "woodwork" to celebrate Earth Day.[16] He gave credit to an uncited *Wall Street Journal* piece which suggested the observance was fueled by nature worship and went on to say that "like the New Agers, these people have lost touch with God Almighty and they are reaching out to nature as their God."[17]

Within the pages of the *New Millennium*, glimmers of Robertson's old sympathies for nature do appear. He endorsed President George H. W. Bush for wanting to plant a billion trees in the United States and hoped that Africa could do the same to control sub-Saharan desertification. Robertson also seemed to contradict his endorsements for free enterprise by recommending that society must limit the use of coal and car exhaust. This latter concern he positioned near an unbiased statement that the EPA was working toward controlling global warming, but he never directly connected the two. Nevertheless, by the end of the chapter he was back to criticizing environmentalists, accusing them of being hypocrites. Environmentalism, he declared, was just a fad led by people yelling about pollution who then took a cigarette break, thus hinting they polluted their bodies. He also criticized them for wanting to save animals while ignoring the fact that society allowed the killing of unborn babies in abortion clinics.[18]

What had happened to Robertson? From at least the later 1970s to 1989, his relationship toward the natural world proved quite stable, and he was unashamed of his conservation and compassionate Christian environmental stewardship views.[19] *The New Millennium* looks like something that the Heritage Foundation would applaud, but in the past Robertson was not a cheerleader for the group and had largely ignored their anti-environmentalist arguments just a few years earlier during his run for the presidency. At the same time, however, Robertson had also chosen to ignore the eco-friendly voices like that of his New Hampshire Director of Communication James Hofford. In this situation, he did not want controversy over the environment to cost him votes and later rearticulated his eco-friendly position once out of the race during the 1988 GOP National Convention. By 1990 Robertson was back in the pollical fray and this time he went along with growing anti-environmentalist arguments of the period. Perhaps he was prepared to turn against the environment if he could gain political capital.

When Robertson ended his bid for the presidency in 1988, he wondered what to do with the leftover campaign funds and infrastructure. He listened to an advisor who suggested he continue energizing and informing his religious supporters who were interested in politics. Thus, he founded the Christian Coalition and anointed a bright up-and-coming Christian named Ralph Reed as its head.[20] The organization picked up where the Moral Majority left off. By the late 1980s, the Moral Majority faced a great degree of opposition. All the efforts Falwell had made to build an ecumenical movement to bring America back to God were being canceled out by an equal if not greater backlash among those who feared a possible theocracy and were repulsed by the negative rhetoric coming from its leaders. By 1987, Falwell realized that the Moral Majority endorsements were actually hurting the candidates they intended to help, so he announced that the group had been successful in its goals and shut it down. But instead of disappearing, support for the Moral Majority, as representative of the religious right movement, merged into Robertson's new Christian Coalition.

Falwell's position as head of a religious and political organization led him to combine secular conservative goals and perspectives with religious worldviews. Similarly, it is not surprising that Robertson cozied up to more right-wing ideologies and the people who peddled them. Although Robertson's name was on the book *The New Millennium*, the man who received "profound appreciation" and whose publishing experience was "responsible for the structure of this work" was an individual named James Black, also known as Dr. Jim Nelson Black.[21] Black was the executive director of the Wilberforce Forum, a private advocacy group that promoted a Christian worldview. As of 2020 Black bills himself as a senior analyst with Sentinel Research Associates and boasts several publications to his name including *When Nations Die: 10 Warning Signs of a Culture in Crisis*. He additionally assisted General Georges Sada in writing *Saddam's Secrets*. His trademark is speculative theories supported by a variety of somewhat dubious information, bringing him to conclusions such as the existence and location of Saddam Hussein's weapons of mass destruction, all communicated in a style of rhetoric not too distant from former Fox News show host and the Blaze channel founder Glenn Beck. Black writes for those who are interested in mixing Judeo-Christian values with geopolitics to help support conservative views in contrast with liberals. Two of Robertson's following books, *The New World Order* (1991) and *The Turning Tide* (1993), intensified the one-world conspiracy theory and further vilified the environmental movement. Robertson was sure to give Black credit for the completion of both volumes.

These books by Robertson represent the beginning of a major shift in the relationship between conservative evangelicals and their perceptions of environmental protection. However, the broader conservative evangelical community was not falling for the conspiracy theories—at least not yet. The pro-environmental efforts within the SBC and to a lesser extent the NAE continued during the early 1990s.

During the NAE's annual conference in May of 1990, participants wanted to protect the Earth even if it meant curbing economic profits. One disseminated position paper titled "Stewardship: All for God's Glory" argued for the basic Christian environmental stewardship message of Francis Schaeffer and other eco-friendly evangelicals. In accord with past environmental stewardship sentiments, the paper began with Psalm 24:1 "The Earth is the Lord's and everything in it, the world, and all who live in it." It acknowledged that modern society is concerned about the health of the Earth, and noted that instead of fulfilling the role of responsible custodians, people were abusing the Earth for economic gain, seeking "selfish and excessive acquisition at the expense of the world's natural wealth." At the same time, the paper did not support total preservation, because humanity is a part of the Earth as well. Thus, humanity should use natural resources but cannot overuse or abuse them especially for "our pursuit of pleasure."[22] These points regarding long-held Christian environmental stewardship views found agreement among the attendees, and they voted the points into becoming convention resolutions. Subsequently, the environment continued as the central topic in the next issue of the NAE's magazine, *United Evangelical Action* (*UEA*).

The May–June 1990 issue of *UEA* featured a variety of contributing authors promoting the traditional position of Christian environmental stewardship. The front cover depicted an ailing cartoon anthropomorphic Earth with an ice pack on its head, cracks under its chin, a black eye, and a dust mask over its nose. Above the picture and in an attempt at sarcasm, a scripture read: "Genesis 1:31. God saw all that he had made . . . and it was very good." The rest of the issue conveyed messages about the Earth needing caretakers and this role fell to Christians who should be responsible stewards. Even big business, the issue reported, agreed with reenergized environmental concerns. Waste Management, Inc., for example, drew praise from environmentalists for their recycling efforts, as did Phillips Petroleum and Amoco who promised to give caring for the Earth a place in corporate decision-making.[23] Another *UEA* report highlighted the new environmental program at the evangelical Taylor University. The knowledge and technical skills learned through the program would enable graduates to "improve the quality of life for all of the world's residents."[24] In addition to reporting on developments and repeating the doctrine of Christian environmental stewardship, the issue listed "Earth Day 1990 Solutions" for readers to implement in their churches and personal lives, telling them to use "public transportation; car pool; bike; walk. Invest in ample insulation, weather stripping and caulking. Use electricity and hot water efficiently." The list went on to similar solutions dealing with food, water, toxins, and pollutants. Within the latter topic evangelical readers were told to "Support legislative initiatives that encourage industry to modify manufacturing processes to eliminate the production of hazardous wastes, and reduce, re-use, recycle what is produced."[25] Overall, these articles and suggestions seem relatively consistent with the mainstream efforts of the secular environmental movement, including possible new controls on profit margins. It should be underscored, however, that the NAE was not promoting preservation, but instead a Christian conservationist/stewardship approach to caring for the Earth. That is, the NAE saw humanity as a part of nature and therefore believed people should use resources within a free enterprise system, but should not abuse the Earth to maximize profits.

NAE 1990

The only aspect of the *UAE* May–June 1990 issue that perhaps compromised the stewardship message was a short piece by the NAE's executive director, Billy A. Melvin, who instead of recording his own views of the environment, deferred to an individual named E. Calvin Beisner who taught at Covenant College and then Knox Theological Seminary. As discussed in chapter 4, during the 1980s, Beisner helped lead the minority voice among evangelicals espousing the importance of industry and economy over that of the environment through the Coalition for Revival's resolution titled, "The Christian World View of Economics." His profile became more prominent throughout the 1990s, and he continues to be a steadfast critic of any eco-friendly argument.

In this particular issue of *UEA*, it was unclear if Melvin understood just what Beisner stood for. Melvin was pleased that evangelicals supported initiatives "aimed at preserving natural resources. Happily today, a growing number of Christians believe a more comprehensive approach to the environment is sorely needed." He then introduced Beisner, who summarized four basic points from his new book, *Prospects for Growth: A Biblical View of Population, Resources and the Future*. These were that God, not creation, should be worshipped; that a cost-benefit analysis should be made regarding the environment on a case by case basis; that instead of looking for solutions from the civil government, private enterprise self-policing may be the best way to stem pollution; and that a stronger economy allows for better environmental solutions. Melvin endorsed Beisner's suggestions, writing that the four points offer "an excellent framework for Christians to explore further environmental concerns."[26] Melvin possibly misunderstood what Beisner was doing. As he read through Beisner's abstract

containing the four points, they sounded like rational, down-to-earth suggestions that seemingly mirrored other recommendations in the UAE issue that
asked people to conserve resources for the sake of the Earth. Upon closer exami-
nation, however, Beisner was cryptically promoting first and foremost a free enterprise system while promising its byproduct would be a healthy environment.
Beisner's anti-environmentalist advocacy continued to mature throughout the
early 1990s and he would play a much larger role later when the NAE went beyond espousing eco-friendly sentiments and came close to taking action.

While Beisner's somewhat obscure anti-environmentalist views percolated
in the background of conversation, at least in 1990, the NAE freely and openly
supported the spirit of Earth Day through their interpretation of Christian
environmental stewardship. It was a very similar tone they had struck twenty
years before in 1971. At both points in time, they felt Christian environmental
stewardship was the right thing to do, but they spoke only about caring for the
Earth; actions were left up to individual Christians and churches. Over in the
SBC, however, by Earth Day 1990 Christian environmental stewardship activity was already underway.

Despite the rise of anti-environmentalism coming from Robertson and Beisner, one of the most important pieces of evidence that conservative evangelicals were making Christian environmental stewardship a top priority was the
work of conservative evangelical and the Christian Life Commission's executive director, Richard D. Land. Land was not a hardy religious right cheerleader
like Falwell, but characterizes himself as a Southern Baptist "movement conservative"[27] In his article "The Southern Baptist Convention 1979–1993: What
Happened and Why?" Land explained that a "movement conservative" inter-
prets the Bible as would a fundamentalist (as the inerrant word of God), but (a
movement conservative) lacks the intense dislike of cooperating with others
with whom they do not share similar political and theological views.[28] During
the time of his hire as executive director of the CLC (since renamed the Ethics
& Religious Liberty Commission), Land was also a political conservative who
actively supported Republican Party positions.[29] As Michael G. Strawser, Matthew Hawkins, and Joe C. Martin note in their book *The Rhetoric of Religious
Freedom in the United States*, Land, whose politically conservative views reflected
the broader SBC membership, was hired to reshape the direction of the
Christian Life Commission, which had, for example, previously supported le-
galized abortion. Upon his hiring, the organization immediately took an
about-face on the issue and has since maintained a pro-life position.[30]

Among the major decisions Land made as the new director of the CLC was
the theme for the annual CLC's 1991 seminar. Although a staunch theological and political conservative, Land resolved this event would be dedicated to

encouraging the Southern Baptist community to switch from holding eco-friendly philosophies to actual environmental advocacy in a spirit similar to that of Schaeffer twenty years before. To achieve this goal, Land drummed up support by personally inviting pastors, church staffs, and congregation members to attend the seminar, as well as publically communicating his Christian environmental stewardship views through the media.

As early as August 1989, Land, with the help of the director of Denominational Relations for the SBC's CLC Lamar E. Cooper Sr., began contacting church pastors and other organizations, asking them to participate as interpreters or attendees at the upcoming seminar. The following are a sampling of individual church pastors and SBC leaders who accepted early invitations to attend the event and function as presenters: Russell Bush, vice-president for Academic Affairs at the Southeastern Baptist Theological Seminary; Rick Irvin, director of the Institute for Environmental Studies at Louisiana State University; Morris Chapman, president of the Southern Baptist Convention; Willard Erickson, academic dean of the Bethal Theological Seminary in St. Paul, Minnesota; Jack Graham, pastor of Prestonwood Baptist Church in Dallas, Texas; and Gary Leaser, director of the Interfaith Witness Department of the Home Mission Board in Atlanta, Georgia.

Building support for the environment among the Southern Baptist Convention was not without problems. Land received letters from individuals who advised him not to get involved with the environmental movement. For example, Southern Baptist congregant Billie Thomas handwrote a letter to Land on March 6, 1990, and warned him about the dangers of supporting such an issue. Thomas stated she agreed with "many of the new programs" Land had brought to people's attention, but she denounced his move to "endorse Earth Day 1990" because environmentalists were part of a nefarious conspiracy plot—a notion that saturated pages of politically conservative private advocacy group material including Pat Robertson's 1990 book, *The New Millennium*. She suggested that if he researched the issue, he would agree that "new agers" and "cult people" were at the heart of the observance.[31] To win him over, Thomas attached a newsletter published by Intercessors for America, a politically motivated religious group whose goal is to inform Christians about current issues. The newsletter quoted Rousas John Rushdoony who reportedly said, "Salvation by means of man's control of the environment is an increasingly militant faith by many. It is, moreover, a very anti-Christian faith. Environmentalism is a false religion."[32] The "evidence" for such an argument included a selection from Francis Schaeffer's book *Pollution and the Death of Man*. Here, Schaeffer was not misrepresented, but the quoted section stressed that humanity was in charge of the environment and should treat it respectfully. It did not explain that environmentalists were a part of a new age cult. The additional attached brief note, like the Rushdoony quotation, reverted the focus back to passing judgment on the environmental movement using guilt by association. The note read, "President George Bush and Communist party leader Mikhail Gorbachev have endorsed it (Earth Day). New Age occultist Jose Argulles, organizer of 1987's World Wide Harmonic Convergence, is one of the masterminds behind it."[33] Although Schaeffer's condensed piece did not warn Christians against the "new age" occultists, the short easy-to-read note is what likely acted as the real evidence that convinced Thomas and led her to advise Land to steer clear of this issue. To Thomas, although President Bush's name was present, anything that Gobachev endorsed along with an occultist "mastermind" who promoted a "World Wide Harmonic Convergence" was something that would leave a very sour taste in the mouth of any conservative evangelical. Land responded to Thomas by clarifying that he did not "endorse" Earth Day and attempted to make that point clearly to her by underlining it in his reply.[34] To further allay her fears, he enclosed several pages from the SBC publication *Light* magazine. Presumably, he sent Thomas the same issue he sent others in the Southern Baptist community to educate them on the CLC's environmental position.[35]

The *Light* magazine issue of April–June 1990 indicated the "right way" Southern Baptists should understand their moral obligation for environmental protection efforts. Land's article in *Light* began by affirming the fact that the industrialized world endangered "Planet Earth" through human ignorance and irresponsibility. He directly cited Schaeffer's *Pollution and the Death of Man* and asserted that "something must and will be done in this decade." He also acknowledged the problem of idolatry within the environmental movement. Land specifically stated, "The pantheistic and idolatrous tendencies exhibited by some elements of the environmentalist movement should be of grave concern to Christians." Here Land echoed the critique of *CT* editor Harold Lindsell and his staff regarding the first Earth Day observance, and likewise, he sought to clarify the Christian position to readers. Citing Psalm 24:1, "The earth is the Lord's and fullness thereof," he elaborated: "Creation belongs to God. As stewards of His property, we are responsible to develop, but not to desecrate or to dissipate, God's Creation. Instead, we are to guard the Creation from such disrespect."[36] In an addendum, he added a plug for the environmentally themed CLC's annual seminar and invited all to attend.[37] In short, Land reiterated classic conservative Christian environmental stewardship sentiments that were clearly outlined by Schaeffer and others over twenty years previous. To Land, the message seemed clear cut and the goal to save God's Earth was a worthy investment for one of his first campaigns as director of the CLC. But for Billie Thomas and many SBC members like her, who were reading increasingly common anti-environmentalist arguments, the environment was an issue too closely connected to liberals and personified the wicked trappings of communism and paganism.

As Cooper and Land worked over the following months organizing the environmental seminar, the tone of their invitations became increasingly desperate and consistently rehashed reasons why the SBC needed to participate in environmental protection efforts. This problem of trying to clarify Christian environmental stewardship in the face of growing preconceived feelings among the membership that connected environmental protection with nature-worshipping environmentalists likely led to a somewhat lackluster response among the Southern Baptist community. Consequently, toward the end of 1990, Land became worried about attendance numbers. He reasoned that if politically and theologically conservative Southern Baptists were securely represented by well-known pastors attending and endorsing his efforts, then the environment might seem more legitimate to the Southern Baptist community over all. Among the many invitations Land sent was one to Dennis Wright, pastor of the First Baptist Church in Meeker, Oklahoma, in which he candidly stated, "We need to have a solid number of people there [at the seminar] and, frankly, this issue does not have the 'sex appeal' some other issues might have. Nevertheless, it is an important issue that Southern Baptists need to hear more about from a conservative Christian perspective." Land enclosed several of the seminar's brochures and concluded that young people should learn the "right way about conservation and the environment" (emphasis in original).[38] The term "right way" meant Christian environmental stewardship in which God owned the earth and people could use judiciously as articulated by Schaeffer in 1970.

In another example reflecting Land's aim to target conservatives, Joel C. Gregory, pastor of Travis Avenue Baptist Church in Fort Worth, Texas, initially said he would participate, but then backed out citing new church responsibilities. Land responded in a letter on December 6, 1990, pleading with Gregory to reconsider. He wrote, "I would not ask this of you if the meeting was not in Ft. Worth and if it wasn't important. . . . To speak at our seminar in Ft. Worth sends all the right signals about bridge building and coalition building in looking toward the future of our Convention. . . . Also, your speaking to the environmental issue gives a conservative imprimatur to that issue which it badly needs and which no one can impart quite so ably as you."[39] Gregory apparently did not reconsider, and Land went on to keep asking pastors to come and, if they could not, to send staff members because it would be "a tremendous boost to us."[40] Although Gregory did not attend, he endorsed the publication of the seminar papers, which were developed into a book published in 1992 by Land and fellow

SBC employee Louis A. Moore. His comments stated on the back cover of the book: "This collection of essays successfully balances contemporary environmental concerns with an evangelical Christian worldview. Every thinking believer will benefit from this work."[41] Fellow conservative evangelical and president of the Baptist Sunday School Board James T. Draper Jr. offered similar comments.

The CLC held its Twenty-Fourth Annual Seminar dedicated to environmental stewardship at the Hyatt Regency Hotel in Fort Worth, Texas, on March 25–27, 1991. For the attendees, Land disseminated printed leaflets or "Fact Sheets" featuring a picture of the Earth in the top right corner encompassed by ideal Christian nature positions supported with Bible verses. These read, "Human Stewardship Gen 1:26, Personal Responsibility Gen 2:15" and in a larger font, "DIVINE OWNERSHIP Ps 24:1."[42]

Like Robertson's position in his 1980 National Affairs Briefing speech, Land's interest in the environment was safely within the zone of traditional eco-friendly Christian environmental stewardship. In addition to citing scriptures supporting respect for the Earth, the fact sheets also utilized alarming statements from mainstream secular media sources. Some examples included: "About 70 percent of all metal products are used one time and then discarded. More than 200 million tons of pesticides are used annually in California alone. . . . The smallest drip of a leaky faucet can waste over 50 gallons a day. Only 3 percent of the world's water is fresh water."[43] One fact sheet validated the reality of human-caused global warming, a position Land would one day reject. The leaflet's title shouted in all capitals, "ENDANGERED EARTH" and "HUMANS ARE CHANGING THE EARTH," followed by a quotation from *Scientific American*, published in April 1989: "The world is warming. Climatic zones are shifting. . . . These changes and others are already taking place, and we expect them to accelerate over the next years as the amounts of carbon dioxide, methane and other trace gases accumulating in the atmosphere through human activities increase."[44] The sheet also quoted other sources making similar claims from various secular publications such as the *Washington Post*, *Gannett News Service*, *Time*, *Newsweek*, and *U.S. News & World Report*. The CLC proudly printed these facts on recycled paper.

By organizing the seminar, Land, a political and theological conservative, publically made the statement that it was acceptable for even the most conservative of evangelicals to collectively take action to save God's Earth. Whereas Robertson had done this somewhat more quietly in the 1980s, by the early 1990s, Land tried to move the most ardent conservative evangelicals to action supported by *scientific facts* published by the mainstream secular media framed in traditional Christian environmental stewardship arguments. Furthermore, he fully embraced the concerns of the environmental movement of the period including, most importantly, the issue of human-caused global warming.

Global warming became the environmental priority of the 1990s and has since become the center of heated debate among the wider American populace. In 1991, Land, representing the conservatively controlled SBC, found nothing controversial about global warming and added it to the list of problems that good Christian environmental stewards must address.

With the help of fellow SBC employee Louis A. Moore, director of Media and Products for the CLC, Land turned the seminar papers into an edited eco-friendly book titled *The Earth Is the Lord's: Christians and the Environment*. Land's paper, presented in chapter 1, gave an overview of the reasons why the SBC community should care about God's creation. Land wrote that he was in full agreement with Francis Schaeffer's *Pollution and the Death of Man* and then listed the environmental problems of air pollution, toxic waste, tropical deforestation, depletion of the ozone layer, and overflowing landfills. Until this time in 1992, conservative evangelicals had not, except for a few instances, denied that any of these problems existed. Land then echoed Harold Lindsell and his staff's early 1970s warning that care for the environment should not be under the monopoly of secular environmentalists who worshipped the Earth via "pantheistic and idolatrous tendencies."[45] He then turned his attention to Lynn White Jr.'s 1967 essay, agreeing that Christians should indeed share in the blame for the ongoing ecological crisis, while emphasizing that the problem was not with the religion per se but with how Christians have misunderstood God's commandment to dominate the Earth, which led to environmental degradation.[46] Thus, Land argued, if Christians simply observed God's intended relationship between people and nonhuman nature, then they would treat nature correctly. Finally, Land explained what the God ordained human/nature relationship entailed by citing a wide variety of verses largely from the book of Genesis. These scriptures supported his overall argument that "creation belongs to God. As stewards of His property, we are responsible for protecting His creation. We come first." He then balanced out the importance of humanity by writing, "We must remember, however, that while human life demands reverence, all life deserves respect." Land understood, as did Schaeffer, that humanity was God's most important creation and therefore had the right to use the environment, but must do so with great reverence.

Indeed, Land was not preaching preservationist ideals, but he was also not making an excuse to ignore environmental problems and was certainly not suggesting that the Earth's resources were infinite as Beisner stated in 1986. Land did not downplay or dismiss the need to respect and protect the Earth. After all, Land had invested a considerable amount of time and energy into organizing this seminar and he had chosen the topic of environmental protection. He knew the issue was not easy to grasp and that it was not a classic "hot button" topic such as the pro-life cause, which had the "sex appeal" to rally Southern Baptists. Nevertheless, he thought it could be successful within his community by understanding the issue not as secular environmentalists, but in terms of Christian environmental stewardship.

Conservative Southern Baptists did attend Land's 1991 annual seminar, but as Land recalled during an interview in 2017, not as many as expected. He felt this problem was a consequence not of disinterest but a repercussion of the disagreements between moderate and conservative factions within the SBC. For the most part, it was conservative evangelicals who attended the seminar and presented papers, not moderates. Even the SBC's conservative evangelical president, Morris Chapman, attended and his paper was included in the edited volume *The Earth Is the Lord's*. During the interview, Land recalled a conversation with a student from Southeastern Seminary at the same time of the event. The student asked when the CLC would get interested in the environment. Land realized as the conference went on that the seminar would have had many more in attendance from the seminary's student body but that they did not know when it was or where. He blamed the problem on the seminary's more "liberal" professors who were upset that the CLC, which was one of their last areas of control in the SBC, had been given to a conservative evangelical such as Land.[47] Regardless of whether Land interpreted the situation correctly or not, this repudiation by the professors did not serve as the single element that explains conservative evangelical rejection of environmental protection efforts.

In contrast to popular assumptions that conservative evangelicals and consequently the religious right movement either perpetually dismissed eco-friendly views in response to theological interpretations or ignored the issue until following political conservatives who favored a strong economy, it must be remembered that until the early 1990s, denial and/or a rejection of environmental problems was not common within conservative evangelical life. As stated previously, for example, the CLC's environmental seminar featured climate change as one of the ways humanity was destroying the Earth. Moreover, Land's co-organizer, Lamar E. Cooper Sr., reiterated the dangers of climate change in his chapter in *The Earth Is the Lord's*, in which he included global warming in his group of "seven serious situations." The first three were acid rain, global warming, and ozone depletion. This position was not an anomaly. There was nothing within the conservative evangelical community at the mainstream level that made them uncomfortable with the issue. Moreover, it must be remembered that Land had just begun his new career as head of the CLC. There would be no reason for him to gamble it on an issue he knew that his own community opposed. He would, however, change his environmental views over the next few years as the conversation within his community became more intense in response to the 1992 Earth Summit in Rio de Janeiro, in which anthropogenic global warming became the predominant environmental issue.

Nineteen ninety-two was a pivotal year for environmental concerns. Then-Senator Al Gore published *Earth in the Balance*, and worry about the depletion of the ozone layer and global warming reached such new heights that the United Nations called for an international summit, the United Nations Conference on Environmental Development (UNCED), to be held in Rio de Janeiro, Brazil, June 3–14, 1992. Representatives from 172 countries attended, with 108 sending their heads of state, in addition to 2,400 delegates from nongovernmental organizations. Solutions to climate change stemming from humanity's burning of fossil fuels proved the top priority for attendees. In hopes of mitigating a possible future of new profit-curbing regulations, economic conservative think tank organizations sprung into action. Paul Weyrich of the Free Congress Foundation, who helped Falwell found the Moral Majority in 1979, found himself on the ground floor of the fiscally conservative response. Senior principal Hilary Sills of the public relations firm Capitoline International Group, LTD, for example, wrote Republican Congressman Tom DeLay and sent a copy to Weyrich: "Congratulations on the good work you are doing [helping to build a bulwark against climate change action] to lend some common sense to the semi-hysterical debate over global warming. I have been working in this area since 1989 and it is only recently that affected industries have come to life to confront the threat to our economy." Sills continued, stating that she felt their approach worked: "The conservative groups' assault on the White House vis-à-vis the UNCED Rio meetings has had a beneficial effect and at least prevented the White House from acceding to a much more damaging climate change convention."[48] Later in the letter, Sills pushed the need for an increase in "correct" scientific information to reach the American public in hopes of debunking environmental efforts. She wrote, "Much of the science has been politicized. In an age of growing scientific illiteracy, distorted risk perceptions, committed advocacy by environmental activists and a sympathetic press, the 'apocalyptic' view gains greater currency than warranted by the facts."[49] Although Sills is only one example among many ardently against possible environmental regulations, it was precisely this strategy of disseminating counterarguments aimed at debunking environmental concerns that was used to build barriers against support for global warming solutions.

Following up on Sills's suggestions, Weyrich took decisive action by supporting Dixy Lee Ray, the former chair of the Atomic Energy Commission under the Nixon administration who later served as the governor of Washington. Ray earned her doctorate in marine biology at Stanford University and taught at the University of Washington. She was given honorary degrees throughout her life, including one from Smith College, Northampton, Massachusetts. To the general populace, her credentials legitimized her conclusions on scientific matters, which she frequently used to authenticate Sills's accusations that the worries over the environment including global warming were just hysterics.

On May 21, 1992, the *Cadillac Evening News* out of Cadillac, Michigan, reported that Ray, whose words were given credibility by listing her scientific background and public service record, criticized environmental worries as "scare tactics." She remarked that acid rain was not killing forests after all and pointed out that other concerns regarding asbestos and dioxin were unfounded. "I'm riled up," she said, and argued that all the hysteria was leading to a "waste of money and the unnecessary disruption of people's lives," which went unchallenged in the media.[50] Ray also published these views in her 1990 *Trashing the Planet: How Science Can Help Us Deal with Acid Rain, Depletion of the Ozone, and Nuclear Waste (among Other Things)*. Her counterarguments that denied the reality of environmental concerns with her position as a credentialed scientist allowed the general public the option to choose what they wanted to believe. Furthermore, she simply did not state that environmentalists and climatologists were incorrect, but framed their concerns as silly antics and hysteria that endangered the economy. Such tactics by Ray and others would play a pivotal role in the environmental conversation developing within the conservative evangelical community throughout the early 1990s.

Paul Weyrich's conservative think tank organization, the Free Congress Foundation, subsequently realized the value of Ray and paid for her to travel to the Earth Summit in Rio de Janeiro, where she stayed at the Copacabana Palace. The group made sure Ray's environmental views reached the public by reserving the Red Room for a press conference.[51] In addition to his organization's own efforts, Weyrich was quite pleased with the cooperation of other conservative groups and congratulated the Competitive Enterprise Institute's president, Fred Smith, on June 11, writing "your expertise and commitment to the truth of the environmentalist agenda was invaluable to this project [called the "Earth Summit Alternatives"]. . . . Hopefully, the movement [conservatives] will begin to get more involved in the environment issue in the future."[52] Weyrich apparently also garnered support from Richard L. Lawson of the National Coal Association (who once lobbied Robertson's presidential campaign in 1988). In his thank-you note to Lawson, Weyrich admitted they were "swimming against the tide," but Ray had spoken on the Rush Limbaugh

Show from the Earth Rio Summit and was contributing to a greater under-standing of environmental extremism.[53]

Around this same time and most likely in response to free enterprise ef-forts to combat "hysterics" as well as to perhaps quell criticisms that the me-dia was biased, mainstream news agencies such as *USA Today* offered opposing viewpoints when running stories on the need for environmental protection. The SBC administration, which was particularly interested in environmental issues since Land's CLC seminar, cut out and added these stories to their files on ecology. The "alternative view" or anti-environmentalist perspective news pieces often featured "experts" who presented their viewpoints as rational, logical, and pragmatic. Some examples included articles titled "Don't Abandon Wetlands" next to the more rational sounding "Use Sense with Wetlands"[54] and "Manage Wild Game Wisely" next to "Don't Kill Wild Animals."[55] Other popular newspapers such as the *Wall Street Journal* also attempted to show both sides of the debate. On April 30, 1992 the paper ran a story titled, "Seen and Heard: Schoolchildren Learn Ecology by Doing—To Alleged Polluters," which reported that children were learning about pollution in school and in response put pressure on their communities to become more eco-friendly. Such activity reportedly upset some parents, including Robert C. Gore, a se-nior partner in the management consulting firm of Towers Perrin, who com-plained that his children "decided the world is not going to be as nice a place when they are adults" and that some teachers are "trying to transfer a sense of guilt to the kids."[56] The idea that schools were brainwashing children likely did not sit well with many readers, who saw it as one more piece of evidence that environmentalists were nonsensical extremists.

Between 1992 and 1993, the arguments by Ray and other credentialed sci-entists who understood rising CO_2 levels as beneficial began finding a home in the conservative evangelical community. At the Institute for Creation Re-search (ICR) the change was especially noticeable, given their position in 1974 that industry was abusing the Earth. In May of 1993, ICR contributor and US government economist Ronald L. Cooper approached current concern for the environment by incorporating a sympathetic free enterprise viewpoint backed by "experts" from the scientific community who argued that climate change is a boon to the Earth. He wrote, "While there is a disagreement among cli-matologists regarding the significance of the 'greenhouse' effect, there seems to be more agreement among other investigators that cutting back significantly on greenhouse gas emissions would have more serious negative worldwide impacts, with large Gross Domestic Product reductions, resulting in lower liv-ing standards in the long run."[57] Cooper furthered his conclusions by citing Dr. Sherwood B. Idso: "Dr. Sherwood B. Idso, a research physicist with the

US Water Conservation Laboratory, Phoenix, Arizona, has found that the 'greenhouse effect' could be beneficial rather than harmful to the planet."[58] More carbon dioxide, he found, would help plants grow. Cooper found these results in the non-peer-reviewed *OPEC Bulletin*. Later, he reassured the reader that if CO_2 levels rose too much, the Earth had built-in global stabilizing factors provided by God. The proof he claimed was that CO_2 levels must have been incredibly high in antediluvian times, but because the Earth was designed so well, they naturally dissipated. This argument of viewing global warming as a benefit echoes others expressed in a film produced by the Western Fuels Association, a supplier of coal to Western utilities. The film documentary, *The Greening of Planet Earth* (1992), was released nationwide and ultimately influenced the political position of members in Congress.[59]

In addition to a more "scientific" attack using experts, the ICR denounced environmentalism as Earth worship. In December of 1992, its founder, Henry M. Morris, connected evolution, the new age movement, and the environmental movement. He argued that evolution stemmed from paganism and quoted Dr. Stanley Jaki, who, Morris was quick to add, held "doctorates in both physics and theology." Morris also cited "Dr. Rupert Sheldrake with a Ph.D. from Cambridge University," who concluded that the green parties in Europe were, at their base, involved in a Gaia religion, which "appeals naturally to scientifically innocent individuals who worry about the environment." Morris continued writing, "This theme is being continually emphasized in public school classrooms today and, with the recent election results, is almost certain to become a major theme in the new federal administration based on the selection of a vice president whose best-selling 1992 book, *Earth in the Balance* . . . is so passionately devoted to such concepts."[60] He also accused the United Nations of trying to take part in Earth worship, a comment made in reference to the Rio de Janeiro Earth Summit.

Beyond organizations like the ICR, concerned church pastors also embraced the message from think tanks featuring credentialed experts such as Dixy Lee Ray. In 1992, Peter J. Leithart of the Reformed Heritage Presbyterian Church in Birmingham, Alabama, wrote a booklet published by the religious right–supporting Coral Ridge Ministries titled "The Green Movement: Its False Claims and Religious Agenda." Although he paid lip service to Christian environmental stewardship, the majority of the booklet was devoted to undermining the general arguments coming from the environmental movement. For evidence, Leithart reproduced anti-environmentalist conservative talking points by citing Dixy Lee Ray as an expert source who debunked environmental extremists and sought the prohibition of DDT. He also used her conclusion that changes in the climate could easily be a consequence of volcanic activity.[61] He went on to inform readers that pollution from volcanoes was likely a punishment from God for violating "some natural law." Such logic paralleled thinking by Rushdoony and Falwell as described in chapter 2.

The debunking of anthropogenic global warming by citing a handful of credentialed scientists associated with conservative think tanks and supported by big business associations not only affected the ICR and individuals like Leithart, but also infiltrated Christian school material beginning in 1993. During the 1980s, A Beka Book textbooks stayed away from heavily delving into the issue of ecology. They strongly promoted forest conservation and cautioned against the overuse of pesticides, but did not speak to the problem as much as Bob Jones University Press publications. However, A Beka Book's *Economics, Work and Prosperity*, published in 1989, took a solid stand in favor of the environment. By 1993, the publisher overturned its previous eco-friendly position in its science textbook for high school students titled *Science: Order & Reality*.

A Beka Book editor Laura Hicks and her co-writers initiated their repudiation of environmental concerns by discrediting the dangers of acid rain. They asked, "Is acid rain really 'poison falling out of the sky?'. . . . Although modern civilization may contribute to the acidity of rainwater, studies indicate that acid rain has existed for up to 350 years, since before there were factories or motor vehicles to introduce acid-causing pollutants into the atmosphere."[62] The book interpreted the 1990 Integrated Assessment Report released by the US National Acid Precipitation Assessment Program to drive home the point that acid rain was not the problem that environmentalists once thought; the coup de grâce was the inferred criticism that the government had spent a ridiculous amount of money on a myth. They wrote that the study took ten years and $500 million of the "taxpayers' money" to find that only 4 percent of lakes were dangerously acidic and the average acidity in lakes was not a consequence of industry.[63] In a tone of disbelief, they followed this information by describing the subsequent illogical government decision to pass the Clean Air Act of 1990, which cost $40 billion targeting acid rain, a nonproblem. The authors advised the reader to stay informed on similar topics so they could voice opinions to representatives in the government.[64] During the 1980s BJU Press also advised their readership to stay abreast of environmental issues so they could voice concerns, but the writers never prefaced the suggestion by marginalizing environmental issues.

Hicks and her fellow writers then took on the issue of global warming for the first time in a separate section. The short poem at the top of the page concisely clarified their position: "Roses are red, violets are blue / They both grow better with more CO_2."[65] The explanation that followed attacked human-caused global warming on two levels. The first, simply denied that it existed with a scientific-sounding approach: "According to records kept over the past 100 years . . . , there has been no significant change in the earth's overall temperature—*there has been no global warming*" (emphasis in the original).[66] This statement somewhat contradicted the following observation by suggesting that even if global warming occurs, it will be beneficial. The authors reasoned, "Scientists generally agree that a rise in atmospheric carbon dioxide would result in a substantial increase in plant productivity; and since plants account for 95% of the earth's food supply, a carbon-dioxide rise would actually benefit all life on earth."[67] The authors paired these viewpoints with discrediting concerns towards the depletion of the ozone layer (presented as a separate issue): "According to some atmospheric scientists, this weakening of the ozone layer is caused predominantly by solar flares, not pollutants, and the ozone layer has undergone a regular trend of thinning and refilling since the hole was first detected, indicating that this cycle is probably a harmless process of nature."[68]

The arguments offered by the authors of *Science: Order & Reality* directly followed the talking point strategies of conservatives as represented by Ray or those featured in the film, *The Greening of Planet Earth*. In the text they clearly told the reader in bold type that there has been no global warming, but if it happens, then humanity will benefit. These points were prefaced by echoing Ray's complaint that investigating the possibility of acid rain was a waste of taxpayer money, which touched on another conservative claim that environmental protection efforts will hurt (or will ruin) the economy. These three basic arguments were identified by sociologists Aarron McCright and Riley E. Dunlap in their study "Challenging Global Warming as a Social Problem: An Analysis of the Conservative Movement's Counter-Claims." As McCright and Dunlap conclude, conservative think tanks were promoting the three messages --namely, denial, treating global warming as beneficial, and foreseeing economic doom as a consequence of environmental action. As demonstrated by the science textbook, the same arguments were successfully received by the conservative evangelical community and taught to students in the Christian school classroom.

Beyond employing these three strategies, A Beka Book's *Science: Order & Reality* comforted the reader with assurance that God would not let environmental problems become dangerous: "As Christians . . . we must remember that God provided certain 'checks and balances' in creation to prevent many of the global upsets that have been predicted by environmentalists. We know from God's promise in Genesis 8:22 that 'while the earth remaineth, seedtime and harvest, and cold and heat, and summer and winter, and day and night shall not cease.'" The authors then validated stewardship while actively minimizing or, in other words, negating any need for it in the first place:

"While it is our responsibility to do all within our power to protect the world God has given us, we must always bear in mind that the fate of the earth rests not in the hands of chance but in the hands of its all-powerful Creator."[69] Therefore, even if the student reader chose to ignore the conservative think tank talking points repeated in the text, the dutiful Christian should take comfort in the theological perspective that it is best not to worry because God will look after the health of the Earth.

Further in the text, the authors returned to denying the reality of environmental concerns by putting the dangers of pesticides into perspective in comparison with other hazards. For instance, the number of accidental deaths per year caused by motor vehicles was listed at 50,000, swimming accidents 3,000, bicycle accidents 1,000, and pesticide use 30.[70] Moreover, the reader was told, pesticides such as DDT were tested on animals in enormous quantities and in the real world no one would ever be exposed to such an amount. The text additionally explained that it is the right of humanity to use pesticides, justified by Genesis 1:28 in which God commanded that humanity exercise dominion.[71] Next, the authors asked students to read directly from chapter 6 of Dixy Lee Ray's *Trashing the Planet*, which explained why environmentalist worries about DDT pushing bird populations to extinction were incorrect.[72]

If Robertson's book the *New Millennium* signifies the beginning of anti-environmentalism knocking on the door of mainstream conservative evangelical culture and the religious right movement, then *Science: Order & Reality* marks its first step across the threshold. Indeed, anti-environmentalist tendencies were visible within the community in previous decades but lingered in the backrooms of individual political thought largely derived from secular conservatives. During the early 1990s, these older views were intensified and augmented by accusations that portrayed environmentalists as hysterical Earth-worshippers, along with arguments for the need to protect free enterprise, a major component of American Christian nationalism. The arguments were strengthened by citing rational-sounding credentialed experts who interpreted scientific studies in such a way as to undercut and deny the largest environmental concerns of the day. These sources offered seemingly legitimate reasons for conservative evangelicals to dismiss the growing environmental support in their own community in response to events like Earth Day 1990 and the 1992 Earth Summit.

Like A Beka Book, which had finally taken a firm partisan position on the environmental debate, in 1992 Jerry Falwell expressed his opinion on the matter using a more effective and interesting strategy than his response to the Biology Club's Earth Day activities. Before delving into the topic, he first praised Senator Jessie Helms for having the courage to stand up and declare that homosexuality was wrong and that it was the cause of the AIDS virus. This comment received applause from the congregation. Falwell then dove into global warming and approached it as a joke combined with a serious topic. "And then there is another subject. Boy, they're talking about global warming. The disappearance of the ozone layer. They got me under convictions putting hairspray on my head."[73] The congregation responded with laughter. Next, he stated that he liked God's Earth: "I think there ought to be national parks and I think we ought to as best we can to preserve the wonderful creations of nature God has provided for us." Falwell then invalidated what he had just said by equating nature preservation with absurdity and hypocrisy, all laced with humor:

> But these tree huggers [laughter] who want to save the snail darter and spotted owl and who want to save the whale and demonstrate outside the fur stores, they don't want any more fur coats and those hypocrites go right across the street to McDonalds and eat a hamburger. Where do you think that hamburger comes from? [little laughter] Some animal sacrificed his life to provide you that Big Mac [the audience chuckled]. Big deal, bring another one.

Falwell's tone then became serious when he brought in the topic of abortion to crush any lingering compassion congregants may have held toward environmental protection. Unlike his supportive and compassionate words about animal rights in the early 1980s, his rhetoric was angry and dismissive. "The question I'd ask these people, how long since you demonstrated outside an abortion clinic? You want to save those snail darters, spotted owls and whales and other furry animals—how about those babies? You hypocrites, shut your mouth [some congregants responded with "amen"]. . . . You call yourself a moral environmentalist. I'm glad our president is not going to the Earth Summit, unless he's going to go down there and preach."[74]

Falwell apparently did not understand global warming at this time. He linked it with the depletion of the ozone layer, his points were disjointed, and he furthermore did not utilize any particular arguments from the scientific community. Instead, he made a joke out of the environmental movement paired with pointing out hypocrisy. His congregation enjoyed laughing at his punch lines, which were then further strengthened by serious outrage and disbelief that environmentalists love a valueless snail over precious babies aborted every day.

Using this strategy, Falwell did not need specific information from think tanks and credentialed experts. Its power and success simply derived from social pressure energized by public ridicule. Although he had to acknowledge that nature was a creation of God, he framed his message in humorous terms and dismissed the environmental movement as a bunch of "tree huggers." Two years earlier, the Biology Club at Falwell's Liberty University was undoubt-edly proud of the trail they blazed when they encouraged fellow students and members of Thomas Road Baptist Church to come by on Earth Day and talk with them about Earth-saving solutions. But now Falwell squelched the op-portunity for anyone in his community to take future proactive environmen-tal measures. He could not accomplish this goal by stating that such efforts were not in accordance to the Scriptures. Indeed, he had to validate the worth of God's creation but negate any efforts at protection by making fun of it and moreover put environmental activity in the same category as prochoice advo-cacy, one of his community's most hated social and political positions. In short, Falwell caustically humiliated anyone who felt sympathy for and wanted to save things that God made, such as spotted owls or trees in the forest. Using humiliation to invalidate nature protection initiatives could be seen elsewhere as in Dixy Lee Ray's characterization that environmentalists were hysterical extremists or the ICR accusing them of being Earth-worshippers. However, in Falwell's case, he seemed to be taking ridicule to a new level.

Public humiliation in any situation has the power to force conforming be-havior within a community by structuring rules combined with enforcement through the punishment of social alienation. Whether it is practiced by children on the playground or adults in a business meeting, ridicule hurts and the de-gree that it stings depends not only on what is said but on the social structure in which it is employed. Mockery is an amazingly effective tool for social con-formity because it demeans or rather devalues the victim often as punishment for breaking a social rule. It can even lead to suicide if the recipient cannot find any avenue back to the realm of acceptance. It is easy to imagine the im-pact of such ridicule on conservative evangelicals, who not only regularly at-tend services together, but often socialize with each other outside of church. The pressure can be greater still for students who attend Christian schools dur-ing the week, play organized sports in the same institution, and then attend the affiliated church on Sundays. Conservative evangelicals build close-knit communities—even if the church is made up of thousands of members as is Thomas Road Baptist Church. Thus, social acceptance for many conservative evangelicals is an important objective.

In 1988, University of Florida political scientists Kenneth D. Wald, Dennis E. Owen, and Samuel S. Hill Jr. published an article titled "Churches and Politi-cal Communities," which explained the surprising conformity of church com-munities. From surveys conducted among 21 church congregations, they found little variation between the political views of individuals. Perhaps the most interesting aspect of this study is that the authors found that although the individual's political attitudes conformed to those of the church they attended, their personal theology did not. Over 40 percent of those in each church had a noticeable discrepancy in religious views.[75] The implications of these findings are quite significant: people go to church for spiritual guidance, but their political views conform to those around them. Falwell was making sure his congregation conformed to his political viewpoints by using an effective strategy.

The tactic of ridiculing environmentalists continued to spring up in other places within the conservative evangelical community, such as in the campus publications of Robertson's Regent University. One 1994 political cartoon in their newspaper read, "Guess which service the Clintons want to reform." Underneath were two boxes—on the left, "The best health care system in the world . . ." and on the right, "or public education?" The health care illustration depicted a serious physician running a brain scan, while the public education image showed an unruly classroom, in which the teacher reads *Sex Ed. News* and students bully each other. On the blackboard is a "Reading test: How many mommies does Heather have?" Another poster in the background encouraged students to "Save the Earth."[76] A year earlier, the newspaper ran a political cartoon in the editorial section featuring a teacher indoctrinating students in stereotypical liberal ideologies while standing between a condom machine and a poster of the Earth encircled by the statement "Love Your Mother."[77]

The accompanying articles in Regent University's publications that discussed the environment took a similar comedic tone and allowed conservative think tank voices to directly address the student readership. The Heritage Foundation's president, Edwin Feulner, for example, wrote an article titled "Compulsive Environmentalism—Only on the Weekends." He demeaned the environmental movement as being the result of America's need to be a part of some "public nuisance" that oddly came around every fifty years.[78] He dismissed the "screwball assertions of global doom" in Al Gore's book *Earth in the Balance* and did the same with concerns over the diminishing ozone layer. Feulner stated that phasing out CFCs to "save" the ozone would cost taxpayers tens of billions of dollars, a waste of money because scientists concluded the depletion was "a natural, temporary phenomenon: gases from the 1991 eruption of a volcano in the Philippines!"[79] In another magazine produced by Regent titled *Focus*, headlines read: "More than Global Warming: One-Worlders May Be Pushing Politics with Disaster."[80]

These last examples from Regent University exhibit the primary challenges to Christian environmental stewardship activity during the early 1990s, which took the form of conflicting scientific truths and old-fashioned mockery. The article by Feulner, for instance, demonstrates that Regent University's newspaper allowed itself to be used as a platform to reiterate chosen scientific "facts" to its student body. Furthermore, the article in combination with the political cartoons, as also seen in Falwell's sermons, simply ridiculed and in turn demeaned environmentalist concerns by portraying them as extremists who fabricated issues to worry about.

Indeed, by 1993, the anti-environmentalist arguments gained firm footing within the conservative evangelical community. As suggested by the experience of Liberty University's Biology Club, Christian environmental stewardship supporters initially thought they were simply enacting philosophies they grew up learning about in their Christian k–12 schools, but now they faced an unexpected barrage of new attacks that increased in intensity starting with Earth Day 1990. In the face of these attacks, individual conservative evangelicals tried to figure out what to do. Their choices consisted of staying silent, embrace anti-environmentalism, or keep fighting for Christian environmental stewardship. As will be demonstrated in the next two chapters, Richard Land of the SBC tried to uphold the latter approach, but like others in his community, including the NAE's Robert Dugan, the pressure from anti-environmentalists proved too great.

CHAPTER 6

The National Association of Evangelicals Turns against the Environment

At Richard Land's 1991 environmental stewardship seminar, the Southern Baptist Convention's (SBC) director of Denominational Relations for the Christian Life Commission, Lamar E. Cooper Sr., clearly argued that Christians must save the Earth. His presentation, which became a chapter in *The Earth Is the Lord's*, demanded immediate action by listing alarming statistics from Diane MacEachern's book, *Save Our Planet*, such as "each year Americans throw away 18 billion disposable diapers, 1.7 billion disposable pens, 2 billion razors and blades, and 220 million tires." Other environmental problems included overflowing landfills, improperly dumped industrial waste, and the fact that "Americans use 270 million pounds of pesticides each year on lawns, gardens, and parks." Although these figures seemed daunting, Cooper felt people could have an impact by recycling and explained how this action at the local level could minimize the major problems of overflowing landfills. Most notably his presentation also highlighted the very real problems of global warming, acid rain, and the depleting ozone layer.[1] Not long after it was published in the subsequent book, Cooper's environmental views changed.

In direct response to the 1992 Earth Summit, Cooper wrote an "Ethics Commentary" titled "Environmental Danger: Chicken Little or little chicken?" In this essay, global warming was not real anymore. He accused secular environmentalists of fabricating the entire problem: "They [environmentalist extremists] point to 'global warming' as an [sic] evidence that we are doomed unless we take immediate, drastic action. This warning is sounded despite the most recent revelations from NASA's ten years of data from its weather satellites which indicate no net global warming this century."[2] He later cautioned Christians not to be alarmists by believing that global warming is real: "When we use overkill to try to motivate people, e.g. global warming is a fact, or overpopulation spells doom for our planet, we lose all credibility when people discover we have misled them."[3] At the same time, he also did not totally abandon his previous environmental view. He advised the reader not to be apathetic toward the Earth or abuse it. People should, he argued, be responsible, and he gave the example of Melissa Poe of Nashville, Tennessee, who started a recycling program that involved fellow children. In this way, Cooper said, we should not be "little chickens" by not taking action. Although Cooper continued encouraging citizens to participate in the environmental cause, this paper marked a sharp turn in his understanding of contemporary environmental problems, most significantly by reversing his position on global warming.

The title, along with his argument, strongly suggests that Cooper bowed to social pressure over concern that his peers would associate him with the secular environmental movement. Similarly to Harold Lindsell's experience in the late 1970s, Cooper's change in attitude was likely in response to reading conservative think tank material that characterized environmentalists as uncredible radical extremists. Beyond the fear of being wrong, Cooper also did not want be the target of public ridicule, of the kind wielded at the pulpit by Falwell or in political cartoons (discussed in Chapter 5). The very purpose of the essay intended to deflect possible embarrassment away from Cooper, who once warned others about the reality of anthropogenic climate change, and instead point the blame on environmentalists who were "Chicken Littles." Indeed, the piece's title and basic message functioned as a warning not to fall for the fake doomsday predictions and thus escape future embarrassment. This example largely embodied the choice fellow conservative evangelicals faced in the early 1990s, when it came to taking a position on the environment. The decision that most conservative evangelicals made, including Cooper, was in reaction to being terrified that others in their own community would categorize them with environmental extremists. This strategy of belittling environmentalists ultimately reduced the evangelical movement to protect the environment to the level of something children might do in their spare time. Cooper's colleague, Richard Land, did not give up the environmental issue as quickly. The more detailed account of Land demonstrates he stayed the eco-friendly course he had set out on for several more years, but like Cooper, even he finally gave up in response to a similar amalgamation of factors.

The same year as the Earth Summit, Land participated in a meeting organized by leaders in science and religion titled "The Joint Appeal by Religion
& Science for the Environment." Some of the notable executive committee
co-chairs included Cornell University professor of astronomy and director of
the Laboratory for Planetary Studies, Carl Sagan, and the moderate evangelical executive director emeritus of the Southern Baptist Convention's Christian Life Commission, Foy Valentine. The organizers reported their efforts in
a statement designated for "Immediate Release," which said, "Despite many
philosophical differences, the 175 religious heads and scientists agreed on a final declaration that urges a joining of forces to resolve the ecological crisis,
and called upon the United States to change habits and activities that made it
'the leading polluter on Earth.'"[4] Although the Bush administration did not find
the time to greet the organizers at the White House, the "meeting was hosted
by a bipartisan committee of U.S. Senators led by Senator Al Gore with Senators Tim Wirth, John Chafee and James Jeffords."[5] Richard Land was one of
the participants who signed the meeting's declaration, which stated, among
other things, that something must be done about human-caused climate
change. These facts, including Land's endorsement, were often cited in subsequent published articles reporting on the event. The *Washington Post*, for instance began an article titled "Denominations Find Common Ground in
Saving the Earth," by highlighting the fact that even Bible literalists such as
Richard Land and "Godless school" professors like Theodore Hiebert of Harvard University can both agree that "the Earth is dying, and only human beings can save it."[6] The piece also cited Land and Cooper's 1991 environmental
seminar as evidence that the SBC took saving the environment seriously.

Land's signature at the bottom of the roughly four-page-long "Declaration of
the 'Mission to Washington'" is perhaps the closest that conservative evangelicals and, by association, the religious right movement, came to actively cooperate with secular environmentalists. Land represented his religious community,
but he likely did not represent their true feelings about wanting to work with
people like Carl Sagan. Sagan who publically promoted evolution was perhaps a
little too uncomfortable of an ally for the regular Southern Baptist congregant.
Beyond this possibility, by 1992, conservative evangelicals were constantly inundated with information from conservative think tanks and private advocacy
groups denouncing the reality of environmental problems as well as consistently
framing environmentalists as a group of extremists and Earth-worshippers.

Due to the large amount of information discrediting environmentalists,
Land found himself continuously defending and clarifying his Christian environmental position. After SBC member Billie Thomas, sent Land a letter saying that Earth Day 1990 was an Earth-worshipping, communist ploy, Land

received another complaint from fellow SBC member, Emily W. Elmone, from North Carolina. Elmone, like Thomas, enclosed information warning that Earth Day was part of a conspiracy working to realize a "World Government." The environment as an issue, Elmone wrote, "is guaranteed to deceive the best of us since we are all interested in our environment."[7] The first piece of information she attached was the John Birch Society's March 26, 1990, publication, the *New American*, featuring an article titled, "Earth Day: The Greatest Sham on Earth." It included a quotation from former Kansas senator James Pearson, who warned that in order to save the Earth, taxes would be raised, profits would be diminished, and sacrifices would have to be made.[8] The article largely discredited ecological concerns as overblown or false and said that the economic cost of curbing global warming would be too great to bear. Another attached article from the same publisher titled "Six 'Crises' All Leading to World Government" stated that volcanoes and ants caused acid rain and not humans.[9]

Elmone's letter and accompanying information exhibit the fact that members of the SBC were reading as well as believing the anti-environmentalist arguments of private advocacy groups like the John Birch Society. The arguments featured in the *New American* are representative of what circulated throughout the 1990s and continues as normal fair unto the present day. Land read other editions of the *New American*, including a June 1, 1992, issue titled "The Resilient Earth," which attacked environmental issues using a mix of arguments similar to that in other material. The editors dedicated this particular issue to dismissing contemporary environmental worries by arguing that the Earth is "designed to flourish under man's innovative stewardship." Several articles pointed to the real reasons or conspiracy behind environmental protection efforts as led by "powerful insiders" who use the ecological crisis as a "pretext for global control" along with accusing environmentalists as being against people, development, and freedom. A hand-written note stapled to Land's copy called attention to page nine, which featured a short article dismissing global warming as only a theory and "nothing more than hot air."[10] Land also received a personally addressed issue of *Citizen Outlook*, a publication from the Committee for a Constructive Tomorrow, which offered the public an "alternative voice on the issues of environment and development."[11] It is unknown if Land subscribed himself to the *Citizen Outlook* newsletter/pamphlet or if someone else did so for him. In any case, it is clear that during the early 1990s, Land compiled a growing personal collection of anti-environmentalist information while he was publicly trying to get Southern Baptists active in Christian stewardship of the environment.

While Land seemingly struggled with Christian environmental stewardship behind closed doors, advocacy for the cause gained a boost from one of the largest conservative Christian organizations, the National Association of Evangelicals (NAE). In response to Earth Day 1990, the NAE endorsed Christian environmental stewardship officially through a resolution and dedicated an entire issue of *United Evangelical Action* to encourage readers to support the topic (see chapter 5). Additionally, in 1993, the organization's vice president of Governmental Affairs and conservative evangelical Robert P. Dugan Jr. accepted an invitation from moderate evangelical and social progressive Ron Sider to join the newly formed Evangelical Environmental Network (EEN).

The EEN was an offshoot of Sagan's open letter inviting scientific and religious communities to fight for the common cause of saving the planet. The call spawned the formation of the National Religious Partnership for the Environment (NRPE), which became an umbrella organization for Sider's EEN. The design of the NRPE seemed perfect for even the most conservative of evangelicals. The group was ecumenical in that it joined a variety of faiths, including Catholics, mainline Protestants, and Jews, to promote the single goal of environmental advocacy. Each group, however, would have complete autonomy in its environmental approach. Thus, cooperation with other faiths was entirely up to individual groups. The EEN could, in other words, save God's Earth through any strategy it wanted.

Sider's invitation to Dugan to join the EEN's advisory council was tactical: Dugan's name, and therefore his politically conservative reputation along with it, would be proudly displayed on the organization's letterhead. Dugan had worked for the NAE since 1978 and was a devout adherent of religious right principles. Previous to his employ, Dugan narrowly lost a bid for Congress in the 1970s. He was, however, able to use his Washington connections to help the NAE lobby government officials throughout the 1980s and 1990s. He was assisted by Richard Cizik, who assumed Dugan's position after Dugan retired in 1997. During a 2019 interview, Cizik recalled that both he and Dugan were "true blue" supporters of religious right positions and even attended hundreds if not thousands of meetings with the likes of Paul Weyrich and Jerry Falwell. Dugan even counted himself a friend of Falwell's, and the two corresponded on occasion. In 1985, Dugan confided to Falwell, "While NAE is more of a politically diverse group than the Moral Majority, my personal voting record and yours would probably be identical." He additionally expressed pride in sharing Falwell's controversial views: "Be assured of my prayers for you and our delight at so often being co-belligerents.[12]

Although Dugan identified as a political conservative, when moderate evangelical Ron Sider invited Dugan to serve on the advisory council of the EEN in March of 1993, Dugan enthusiastically responded, "I am pleased to be invited to serve . . . , and I readily accept."[13] This response was not necessarily out of character at that time. Conservative think tanks and private advocacy groups were only beginning to deny anthropogenic climate change and it is clear that Dugan likely had read little if any of their work. At this early stage, he did not have any reason *not* to support them—which is to say that anti-environmentalism was not an accepted principle among conservative evangelicals. In fact, by 1990, Dugan was fully aware of the NAE's endorsement of environmental stewardship. After witnessing his community's support for the issue during the annual convention, Dugan presented an unbiased report in his weekly bulletin/newsletter the *NAE Washington Insight* writing that the convention's theme of stewardship went far beyond the idea of wisely spending money to discuss humanity's "responsibility for the condition of the earth" and its admonition of those who "err in selfishly acquiring resources at the expense of the world's natural wealth."[14] Additionally, several months previous he wrote a note to himself that he should start a file dedicated to the environment. The topic was not only hot in the secular world; in view of the twentieth anniversary of Earth Day, religious organizations felt it was their theological responsibility to do their part to save the Earth. From 1988–1992, Dugan received invitations from environmentally active religious groups such as the New Creation Institute in cooperation with moderate evangelical Calvin DeWitt's AuSable Trails Environmental Institute (now Au Sable Institue), which asked to help stop the "Greenhouse Effect."[15] Later in 1990, he received invitations from the North American Conference on Religion and Ecology, and he additionally read a variety of articles of religious and secular origins calling for environmental action. All of this information taught Dugan that a consensus existed among religious groups regarding proactively embracing environmental protection. Later, like other conservative evangelicals, he would become increasingly exposed to a rising number of anti-environmentalist arguments, but around 1990, most of the information Dugan collected portrayed environmental concerns in a positive light. In sum, trying to save the Earth from destruction seemed perfectly logical. Over in the SBC, Land initially thought the same thing and consequently made environmental stewardship one of the first initiatives of his career as head of the Christian Life Commission.

After "readily" accepting a position with the EEN, Dugan looked forward to the first meeting as well as being involved in forging the group's official position paper titled the "Evangelical Environmental Declaration." Subsequently, Dugan's support for the environment became increasingly complicated, due largely to the ever-growing amount of mixed research he read in his role as an advisory council member.

The primary problem Dugan faced as he researched environmental issues was trying to figure out what sources to believe. In consequence to this problem combined with his predisposition to lean toward far right political positions, he soon became increasingly confused, and over time, suspicious of the very group he joined. He compiled information from both eco-friendly and anti-environmentalist sources. An example of the former included an article from the December 1992–January 1993 issue of *World Vision* magazine, in which Dugan (or a staff member) highlighted an Al Gore interview advocating for action on climate change. Similar pains were also taken with the accompanying interview of former President Reagan's Secretary of the Interior, Donald Hodel, who felt that people were "almost" worshiping wildlife and that environmentalists consistently "assaulted" the public with "pseudo facts" in the hopes of destroying the economy.[16] During the following months, Dugan read similar articles offering a variety of conflicting views on the subject. Some supported an eco-friendly position, while others like Hodel's interview depicted environmentalists as a blight on society and a threat to Christianity and the United States. Such perceptions came from articles cut from mainstream sources or from NAE publications in addition to secular conservative think tanks and private advocacy groups.

Dugan's first exposure to counterclaims against anthropogenic global warming likely began in October of 1992, when he received a mass-generated letter from biologist Dixy Lee Ray, whom the Free Congress Foundation paid to counteract anthropocentric global warming policies at the Earth Summit and who was later cited by multiple conservative evangelical sources, including A Beka Book educational material. In her letter, Ray claimed global warming was not real. A reader, possibly Dugan, circled the term "global warming" in pen. Ray went on to assert that it was one of many fake doomsday warnings. As evidence, Ray quoted environmental advocate and biologist Stephen Schneider, who she accused of incriminating his own movement by saying they must fabricate environmental problems to gain public support.[17] In addition to Ray's letter, Dugan collected other publications denying global warming and used a red pen or a highlighter to note the most important points.

By September of 1993, Dugan noticed important individuals within the NAE actively dismissing warnings by environmentalists, which pressured him to do the same. The president of the NAE, David A. Noebel, told his community that environmental experts were enamored not with facts, with but "junk" science. For evidence, he cited Walter E. Williams, presumably a professor of economics from George Mason University, who claimed that lies from the scientists were aimed at controlling people and that scientists were fixated on using global warming to shape economic policy. To further his point, Noebel subsequently listed a series of supporting articles from mainstream newspapers including the *New York Times*, which stated that during the industrial age (implying since the nineteenth century, but not specifying) "there has been no increase in temperatures."[18] This particular report in Dugan's collection was important enough to be highlighted in blue.

With prominent individuals like the president of his own organization denouncing the motives of environmentalists as well as the reality of the problems they sought to rectify, Dugan started wondering if promoting environmental protection was the wrong decision, especially when weighing his reputation within the NAE. What hung in the balance was God's Earth, but more important to Dugan was his job and his life-long social position in his religious community. Why should he fight for a cause if his own organization's president thought it was a sham? Like the SBC's Lamar E. Cooper Sr., Dugan began worrying about being labeled an environmental extremist himself.

On October 20, 1993, Sider sent Dugan a draft of the Theological Declaration of the Evangelical Environmental Network for review. Beyond reading it over, Dugan secretly sent a copy to an "expert" to help him decide what to do. By this time, he had procured a connection with outspoken evangelical anti-environmentalist E. Calvin Beisner, who during the mid-1980s praised unfettered resource use. As the profile of environmental issues expanded during the 1990s, so did Beisner's personal crusade of fighting any eco-friendly sentiment or argument.

It is unclear how Dugan got in contact with Beisner. He was apparently unaware of Beisner's anti-environmentalist arguments before he joined the EEN in 1993. Possibly, Billy Melvin, who worked closely with Dugan as executive director of the NAE, may have linked the two. Three years earlier, Melvin allowed Beisner to speak for him in the Earth Day 1990 issue of *United Evangelical Action*. Melvin's possible role notwithstanding, Dugan relied on Beisner as an expert in environmental matters. Thus, Dugan sent the draft of the EEN's declaration to Beisner in trust that he would receive back a definitive answer about whether it was something he should support.

Perhaps the most important point regarding Dugan's action in pushing the issue to Beisner in October of 1993, is the fact that Dugan had not come to any hard conclusion about the reality of popular environmental concerns. He knew he was not an expert and therefore deferred to someone he felt knew the real story. Over the preceding months, he read a variety of conflicting reports on the issue including those from political conservatives, but delayed in making up his own mind. This fact illustrates that even Dugan, an ardent political conservative, was not preordained to reject calls for Christian environmental stewardship nor was he simply playing along with Sider to show the wider community that he was impartial. Rather, he sought out a trusted "expert" to help him decide.

Beisner's response was a simplistic rejection of the EEN, all but sealing Dugan's absolute distrust of Sider and the organization. On October 25, 1993,

Beisner presented his evaluation as if he were an academic climatologist peer-reviewing a piece from a colleague who strayed far from legitimate research. The evaluation began by rejecting the whole declaration, stating that it was so fundamentally flawed that it could not be salvaged or redeemed.[19] Thereafter, Beisner took Dugan through the myriad of reasons—most being that the environmental problems raised by the declaration were fake. Beisner began his long list saying that the ozone layer was not in danger because no one knew what normal ozone levels were. He cited Dr. Jim Angell of the National Oceanic and Atmospheric Administration who, Beisner said, never talked about a "normal" level and "no good scientist would." He continued with the following views: concerns for declining ocean fish stocks are ridiculous because there is no evidence for such declines; forests are not being depleted because evidence shows forests are improving; acid rain does not damage human health and it even fertilizes forests and crops; soil degradation in "advanced countries" is not a problem simply because the problem does not exist.

In addition to his evaluation of the declaration, Beisner specifically asked Dugan and his assistant Richard Cizik, to sabotage the document by strongly advising them not to send his critique to Sider and EEN. He wrote, "I would appreciate your *not* passing these on to the organizers, because frankly, I don't want them to know in advance what sorts of criticisms I'm going to level if the Lord gives me the time to prepare a review for publication" (emphasis in original).[20] In other words, Beisner hoped to keep his views quiet, so he could launch the strongest critique possible against the unsuspecting NRPE and EEN. Beisner looked forward to publishing these critiques in Christian magazines, which he did in November. His claims in *World* magazine mirrored those he made privately to Dugan and Cizik.

After Beisner's critique, Dugan, fatigued by the environmental issue, moved toward abandoning the whole thing because the controversy was simply not worth it. Apparently, he and Cizik complied with Beisner's request to keep secret the plans to undermine Sider and the EEN. In his response to Sider regarding his review of the declaration, Dugan did not repeat any of Beisner's critique. Instead, he told Sider, "I have been trying to increase my awareness and knowledge of environmental issues in recent day, but it seems the more I study the less certain I am about the Declaration." Dugan was in a difficult spot. He had agreed to be on the EEN's advisory council, but now distrusted everything it stood for. Regarding signing the declaration, he told Sider that he would pray about his final decision.[21]

While Dugan became partial to Beisner's argument between October and November 1993, Richard Land of the SBC also began second-guessing his dedication to the cause of Christian environmental stewardship. In an article by

Beisner titled "Are God's Resources Finite?: A Group of Christian Leaders Claim They Are, but Does the Claim Square with the Evidence?" he noted that Land had considered endorsing the EEN's declaration but reported, that upon further reflection, he would be going over the document with a "fine-tooth comb."[22]

Land's reevaluation was likely due to direct advice from Beisner. In addition to sending Beisner a copy of the declaration, Dugan also enclosed a copy of plans devised by members of the EEN who wrote that Land's endorsement of the declaration would be a boon to their efforts.[23] Upon reading this, Beisner expressed concern saying that the EEN intended to "exploit" Land's conservative reputation. Furthermore Beisner warned, "He's a pawn in this game, and shouldn't be allowed to be used in this way."[24] In hopes of saving Land embarrassment as well as destroying the possibility for the public to witness a political and theological evangelical conservative stand with the EEN, Beisner advised that Land pull away from the Christian environmental push that he led since he became the head of the CLC. This suggestion is exactly what Land decided upon. Like Dugan, Land came to trust Beisner as an environmental expert. During an interview twenty-four years later, Land suggested that if one wants to know what Southern Baptists think about the environment, they should read Beisner's long list of publications.[25]

By November of 1993, Dugan's rejection of environmental protection was complete save for officially resigning from the EEN. On the 24th, he received an article from a group called Evangelicals for Social Action requesting an immediate review so that it could be published in the evangelical periodical *Light*. The article reported on the declining number of climate scientists skeptical of global warming and on the agreement of groups such as the Intergovernmental Panel on Climate Change and the National Academy of Scientists that action must be taken to reduce the impact of anthropogenic climate change. The article noted that some uncertainly surrounded the issue such as just how the changes would manifest, but that this possibility was "no excuse for complacency." In congruence with past conservative evangelical environmental solutions, the article ended by listing a variety of environmentally friendly actions Christians could implement such as cut back on using fossil fuels, plant trees, install energy-efficient light bulbs, and support renewable forms of energy.[26] In his review Dugan said that the article offered nothing but an "alarmist approach" and as evidence cited the mainstream periodical *U.S. News and World Report* as "regard[ing] it as a myth that there is anything approaching unanimity on this issue [global warming]."[27] As Dugan claimed, the article did say that there was no scientific consensus about global warming—it cited MIT physicist Richard Lindzen, Harvard planetary scientist Michael

McElroy and University of Virginia atmospheric chemistry professor Fred Singer as saying as much—but it also made the point that "none of the global environmental issues now under attack is a hoax." Thus even Singer, who was often cited as a climate change skeptic, promoted a variety of actions humans could and should take to cut back on energy consumption because over the long term, the solutions would benefit the environment and science.[28] Dugan overlooked these critical points. For him, the apparent lack of consensus meant there was no point in taking action. In other words, a once unsure Dugan now totally rejected anything to do with pro-environmental activity. At the same time however, he also did not want to take the blame for officially supporting or rejecting calls to protect the environment and instead quietly remained a member of the EEN for a short time longer.

The final decision regarding the EEN's declaration weighed heavily on Dugan. He spoke extensively with Executive Director Billy Melvin, who in 1990, deferred to Beisner to represent his environmental views. In addition, the Trinity Evangelical Divinity School's president, Kenneth Meyer wrote a disapproving letter to Dugan demanding to know what he was doing associating with the likes of Ron Sider by agreeing to be a member of the Evangelicals for Social Action (ESA, another organization founded by Sider). A careful Dugan responded that he was a member of the EEN not the ESA. He also distanced himself from the EEN's declaration saying its fate was uncertain.

When it came to the deadline for signing the EEN's declaration, the social pressure proved too great causing Dugan to leave it up to the NAE as a group. In December, Dugan sent a final letter to Melvin listing his thoughts and enclosing memos, the final draft of the EEN's declaration along with Beisner's evaluation, the first page of the *U.S. News and World Reports* article "Doomsday Myths," and even a copy of the angry letter he received from Meyer of the Trinity Evangelical Divinity School. The inclusion of that letter is quite interesting, in that it has less to do with the environmental issue than with Dugan's concern over what Meyer thought of him. If he received such a letter from a president of a divinity school, what might other NAE members be thinking? In his letter to Melvin, Dugan did not note that Meyer had been mistaken about his being connected with the ESA, but instead wrote that Meyer expressed his "concern about the NAE linkage with the EEN."[29] As reflected by his report to Melvin regarding Meyer, Dugan was not focused on making a decision that was ethically right or wrong. Instead, he was worried about what members in his religious community thought of him. Meyer said nothing about whether environmental issues were real or not, he only pressured Dugan not to associate with the ESA and Ron Sider. By Dugan adding Meyer's letter and the accompanying material, he all but asked Melvin and ultimately the NAE to reject the EEN.

In March of 1994, Dugan formally resigned from the EEN. He listed "personal" and "organizational" reasons for his decision. Both were intertwined. Since the beginning of his tenure at the EEN, Dugan was more interested in being on the socially acceptable side of the environmental political debate. He initially found nothing wrong with joining the EEN, but once he realized that political conservatives were mounting a "backlash," as reported in various publications, Dugan became increasingly wary about what that meant for him and especially his reputation. As noted, Dugan was a firmly established conservative within the religious right movement. Initially, his serving on the advisory council of the eco-friendly EEN was in line with the fact that anti-environmentalism among his community had not become a hardened position as of 1993. However, as he immersed himself in the national environmental conversation, he became more uncomfortable with the issue while watching the view of the subject change. Ultimately, he leaned toward the far right conclusions supported by Beisner and Noebel while officially leaving the decision about the declaration to the wider NAE membership, thinking that disapproval for the EEN would likely be the general consensus as reflected by Meyer's letter. Thus, around November 1993, to his resignation in 1994, Dugan decided he had enough of the environmental controversy and chose to separate himself from it.

The environment was not an issue that he was willing to fight for and in the process possibly alienate himself from the community that he socialized with and paid his salary. This latter point particularly worried Dugan who in November of 1993 expressed to Sider that he did not want to be on the wrong side of the truth when the science, which he thought was divided at the time, finally became settled. He believed choosing the wrong side could mean being fired. In a letter he told Sider about his insecurities: "I am not eager to have NAE board members asking, in effect, 'Not counting tomorrow, Bob, how long did you serve with NAE?'"[30] In other words, he would rather keep his name off the declaration and know his job was secure. Still, Dugan was not worried they would fire him for *not* signing the Declaration and thereby miss out on an opportunity to be a good Christian environmental steward as Schaeffer once hoped the evangelical community would be even before it became a popular issue in 1970.

Richard Land of the Southern Baptist Convention underwent a similar experience as Dugan. The difference between their journeys was that Land initiated and led the cause of Christian environmental stewardship since 1989, whereas the EEN invited Dugan along and therefore he had an easier time dropping out. As previously stated, Land signed his name to the very progressive environmental document the "Declaration of the 'Mission to Washington,'" in 1992 along with E. O. Wilson, Al Gore, and Carl Sagan, and was close to also signing the EEN's declaration in December of 1993. He paused on the issue at the same time that Beisner suggested to Dugan and Cizik that they save Land's reputation from being linked to the EEN. Richard Land's signature on the declaration may have helped normalize Christian environmental stewardship among conservative evangelicals, or perhaps as Beisner thought, it might have instead destroyed Land's career. In any case, it was at this time in 1994, that Land finally let go his attempt to energize the over 15-million-member SBC into supporting the environment along with the EEN.

Indeed, from 1993 to early 1994, anti-environmentalism grew into an accepted social norm for conservative evangelicals. The story of Richard Land and Robert Dugan reflects the struggle many within the conservative evangelical community faced. Until this time, they did not have reason to ignore Christian environmental stewardship and their eco-friendly messages can easily be found in their national conversations, including educational textbooks for Christian schools. However, as the pressure mounted in response to the 1992 Earth Summit from venues such as conservative think tanks and private advocacy groups, conservative evangelical resolve for their eco-friendly philosophies crumbled. As covered in chapter 5, by 1993, A Beka Book abandoned previous nature-friendly views by citing environmentalist critic Dixy Lee Ray, and followed the classic conservative think tank strategies for dealing with environmental problems, including global warming—namely, by asserting that it did not exist, but that if it did, the outcome would be positive for humanity and finally, any pro-environmental action would ruin the economy. Moreover, the incessant accusations pairing environmental protection with earth worshippers and conspiracy theories wore down remaining advocacy for Christian environmental stewardship. Richard Land and Robert Dugan are two examples of a larger story in which they became willing casualties of a war within their religious and political community. By 1994, the anti-environmentalist supporters all but claimed absolute victory over the conservative evangelical eco-friendly philosophies held since the late 1960s.

politics → faith convictions

CHAPTER 7

"It Could Have Taken a Very Different Path"

Upon reflection during an interview in 2017, Richard Land denied any personal responsibility for the failure to energize the Southern Baptist Convention (SBC) into adopting Christian environmental stewardship as a theological and social matter. Instead, he blamed secular environmentalists. He believed the issue would have gone down a "very different path, had environmentalists not gone completely wacko . . . and they have." By "going wacko" he meant that they worship the Earth goddess, Gaia.

Land is wrong about where to place the blame. It was his and his community's choice to abandon the call for environmental action. Schaeffer's, Ford's and at one time Land's understanding of Christian environmental stewardship was not secular environmentalism and/or nature worship. Land repeatedly made this very point in the early 1990s and encouraged others to join in to support their unique faith-based position on nature protection. Ultimately however, he and others dropped the cause out of fear that they might be equated with environmentalists. Indeed, of all the different arguments that impacted the conservative evangelical decision to abandon the issue, perhaps the most effective was the stereotype that environmentalists worshipped the Earth, which was presented through public ridicule as exemplified by Land who, like Jerry Falwell, chose to separate themselves from their own cause because they feared being associated with an image they held toward another movement.

The Conspiracy Theories

Conspiracy theories connected with environmentalism and evangelicals date back to the beginning of the environmental movement. In their reading of *The Environmental Handbook*, conservative evangelicals thought that environmentalists were not only blaming Christianity for the ecological crisis, but also trying to destroy the Christian faith by advocating the adoption of all other religions that elevated the Earth and its creatures to a higher plane above mankind. In a sense, such an interpretation was not unfounded. The *Handbook*'s editor reprinted Lynn White Jr.'s article blaming Christianity along with several other authors who promoted what they felt were more eco-friendly faiths than Christianity. As for the accusation that environmentalists worship the Earth, such a portrayal was not far from the mark as some environmentalists describe their connection with wilderness in spiritual terms. Earth First! co-founder Dave Foreman, for example, sees the nonhuman natural world, and in particular the pristine wilderness, as sacred. To Forman, wilderness is the environment where he viscerally communes with nature on a spiritual level to feel his connection with the living landscape as well as the wildlife. Humanity, he additionally believes, is a disease on the Earth that destroys the purity of wilderness. Environmental historian, William Cronon famously criticized this religious human/nature understanding in "The Trouble with Wilderness; or, Getting Back to the Wrong Nature." Fellow environmental historian, Thomas Dunlap later expanded upon Cronon's observation in his book, *Faith and Nature: Environmentalism as Religious Quest*. In short, both authors explored the ways that environmentalists elevate wilderness to the level of the sacred. Indeed, conservative evangelicals such as Harold Lindsell quickly recognized this connection in 1970 after being exposed to environmentalist rhetoric. Thus, subsequent editorials in *Christianity Today* vehemently criticized environmentalism as tantamount to pantheism, yet at the same time they consistently supported eco-friendly Christian environmental stewardship throughout most of the 1970s. Although Lindsell abandoned these views by the late 1970s, others continued to uphold them throughout the 1980s.

In 1986, aspersions toward idolatrous Earth worshippers combined with further accusations of subversion and intrigue in Constance Cumbey's bestselling book *The Hidden Dangers of the Rainbow: The New Age Movement and Our Coming Age of Barbarism*. In it Cumbey explained how left-leaning occultists and Earth-worshippers were trying to gain converts to destroy traditional beliefs held by Christians, Jews, and Muslims. New age faith would be human-centered and create a "new-world order" that aimed to dissolve the nation-state; humanity would become one and value all living creatures equally; war, poverty, and all other ills including the ecological crisis would theoretically disappear. Such a message linking environmentalists to the new age movement, and the new world order as described by Cumbey did little to keep Land, Dugan, Robertson or A Beka Book publications away from the eco-friendly philosophies held by conservative evangelicals since the late 1960s. However, as noted with Robertson, his early 1990s books, *The New Millennium* and *The New World Order* continued and expanded the legitimacy of the different conspiracy theories, which plagued the attempts of people like Richard Land who strove to spark environmental action among conservative evangelicals.

The new age movement and new world order conspiracies were not well defined by conservative evangelicals except for a few examples. Most often they mentioned the subjects only in name as something that evangelicals knew they did not want to be associated with. The most prominent action mainstream conservative evangelicals took to seriously explain the conspiracies were either through Robertson's early 1990s books or notably a resolution passed in 1990 by the National Association of Evangelicals (NAE) that formally defined and denounced the new age movement. Even in the latter instance, however, the new age movement was largely described as a competing faith to Christianity and not in terms of being a tool connected to a new-world order. Other than these instances, the conspiracy theories were utilized mostly in name only by congregants, publications, or sometimes by pastors in sermons. In the early 1990s, for example, the Intercessors for America, a private advocacy group, warned readers to stay away from environmental causes because the movement was led by a "New Age Messiah" fueled by "militant New Age environmentalism."[1] The authors neglected to define the new age movement and only paired the labels of "environmentalists" with "New Age" perhaps thinking that association was enough to sway readers to reject calls to protect the natural world. In the case of SBC member Billie Thomas, the tactic worked. She read the information and then informed Richard Land of her disappointment when she realized he was trying to support the environment via Christian environmental stewardship. Likewise at Robertson's Regent University, the new age movement was often used in passing such as in the school's newspaper review of the eco-friendly 1992 children's cartoon film *FernGully*. The review mentioned the new age movement in the article's title, "FernGully Fairies Proclaim New Age Salvation." The reader was otherwise left without any explanation to guess why the movie was "new age" except for telling parents the film disparaged how humans treat the Earth. Thus, the details of the theories themselves more or less played a background role albeit an important one in expanding the much broader accusation that environmentalists worshipped the Earth and therefore invalidated all eco-friendly initiatives. At Thomas Road Baptist Church, Falwell also utilized the conspiracies largely in name only. From 1994 onward, he consistently labeled environmentalists as "new agers" while additionally describing them as comically emotional radicals who kissed and worshipped the Earth, "and like our dear vice president, hug(s) the trees."[2] Such sarcasm often sparked approving laughter from his congregation. It was these more informal venues where the conspiracies lurked perhaps due to the lack of evidence. They may have known that some environmentalists felt a sacred bond with the Earth, but exactly who and how they were planning to realize a one-world or new-world order existed simply as an ominous theory.

Neither the NAE nor the SBC officially used the new age movement or one-world government conspiracies to destroy environmental efforts, but nevertheless, they complicated the issue. As exemplified by Land's correspondence with Billie Thomas and Emily Elmone, who read conspiracy pieces by Intercessors for America and the John Birch Society, Land was forced to spend time trying to clarify and reframe his environmental position. At the NAE, Dugan also read articles describing conspiracy theories as published by the *EP News Service* titled "New Analysis: Al Gore's Environmentalism Has Troubling New Age Spiritual Overtones." The theories could also be observed in everyday secular newspapers. In Eugene, Oregon's, *Register-Guard*, for instance, an October 3, 1993, article on scientists cataloguing the health of ecosystems in order to determine what environments and species needed protecting reported that some people thought the program was an excuse for government to increase its power. The critics stated, "it is a mammoth government power grab in disguise." Dugan underlined and highlighted these words in the article clipping he collected.[3]

As the 1990s progressed, the conspiracy theories became so salient among common congregants that those trying to motivate the community into environmental action felt compelled to continuously clarify their views and reframe the issue. Even years after nature protection advocates such as Land gave up on the cause, their own nuanced arguments for Christian environmental stewardship were used against them to bolster the anti-environmentalist cause. In 1996, *Crisis* magazine used a 1994 *New York Times* quote from Richard Land to suggest he always rejected environmentalists and in turn any type of environmental protection. They cited Land as saying, "We make it very clear we do not worship creation, we worship the God of creation." Land's quote continued, "For us to join with other groups that don't speak expressly in biblical terms dilutes our message."[4] The writers of the *Crisis* article deftly omitted the middle portion of Land's remarks, in which he said, "What we're trying to do is combat what is a real bad image among rank-and-file Southern Baptists about the environmental movement, while at the same time speak to our concern for the environment."[5] Thus, Land specifically addressed the problem that Southern Baptists see the environmental movement as a bad thing while saying that caring for the environment was nevertheless an important and worthy concern for all Christians. In this 1994 instance, Land attempted to clarify his Christian environmental stewardship views in the face of Earth-worshipping conspiracy theories, and even long after Land had given up on his eco-friendly philosophies, those supporting the conspiracies continued their message that protecting the Earth meant worshipping it, and they misquoted Land to help them do it.

For the Evangelical Environmental Network (EEN), which continued its crusade without the help of conservatives like Land or Dugan, the problem of fighting the conspiracy theories continued to dog the organization's leadership, who felt forced to reiterate that they did not worship creation and that they had no political agendas. In April of 1994, one month after Dugan's resignation (although his name was still listed as a member of the advisory council), the EEN distributed 20,000 professionally designed booklets printed on recycled paper using soy-based inks to churches nationwide.[6] The booklet's first point clearly stated that the organization worshipped the "Creator, not the creation." The very next line read: "Christian environmental commitment is not New Age."[7] Subsequent statements continued the attempt at dismantling the conspiracy rumors. The EEN also tried convincing readers that the organization was committed to protecting human life—this argument targeted an audience that connected the new age environmentalists with an anti-human agenda. It also attempted to combat the one-world order theory by stating the EEN was "not driven by the world's political agendas." The following paragraphs explained that its members were not extremists looking to jump on political bandwagons, but instead wanted to simply follow biblical commandments that mandated environmental responsibilities. Thus, Sider and the EEN's first publication intended for 20,000 congregations presented their purpose in a reactive or defensive posture in order to combat the tide of previously formed perceptions linked to conspiracy theories. In other words, the EEN could not simply state what they stood for in hopes of gaining support. They had to oppose preconceived images that they worshipped the Earth and were in league with plots for global political power.

Although the EEN tried to correct misconceptions, suspicions continued to circulate. In 1997, a private advocacy group called the Institute on Religion and Democracy published an article titled "Gore's God," which accused the EEN's umbrella group, the National Religious Partnership for the Environment (NRPE) of politicizing the environmental issue and endorsing neo-paganism as well as being influenced by new-age philosophies. Specifically, the article revealed that Al Gore, who worked with the NRPE, attended a 1991 feast day of St. Francis at St. John the Divine Cathedral in New York City where the participants listened to "the taped cry of a timber wolf and the aquatic grunts of a humpback whale" before praying to the Egyptian god Ra and other "ecologically safe deities."[8] Other publications elaborated. An article in the June 1996 issue of the *Metro Voice* titled "Pagan Howl-Le-Lu-Ia Chorus" reported that religious groups supporting Earth care initiatives attended an event at St. John of the Divine Cathedral, and were invited by Paul Winter, the musician-in-residence, to howl with him. "At that," the article continued, "nearly 300 mostly Episcopalians began howling at the moon, expressing their oneness with the wolf." In the following paragraphs, the author connected environmentalism with communism, world socialism, and paganism and stated that the New Age Journal Source Book advertised the NRPE.[9]

Although there were too many accusations for the EEN to respond to, at least in the case of the article "Gore's God" the group's president Ron Sider angrily contacted Diane Knippers, the president of the organization that produced the article. He demanded, "Where is the evidence, Diane? Reading totally undocumented conclusions into a perfectly legitimate general purpose statement is not the kind of argument I would expect from you."[10] To help deal with the attack, Sider assured Knippers that he would be sharing the article with all members of the NRPE.

Although Knippers sent Sider an apology, "Gore's God" was one of a mountain of articles published by different sources throughout the 1990s that wore away at the fledgling attempts to launch the evangelical community into Christian environmental action. They claimed that caring for the environment was really worshipping the Earth—an obvious breach of Christian monotheism—and then the one-world order theory simultaneously upset American-loving religious patriots by suggesting environmental supporters would rather be loyal to a global government. These tactics were mixed with a heavy dose of public ridicule, which made Christian support for the environment something a congregant would not want to touch lest they be singled out by their peers as tree hugging, Earth-worshipping, and anti-American traitors.

Although Dugan had left the EEN in 1994, he continued collecting articles accusing the organization of being in league with Earth-worshippers and even received a letter in 1996 thanking him and the NAE for not taking an environmental position. The praise came from Professor Emeritus of Geology Edwin Olson who reassured Dugan that "scientifically qualified evangelical Christians among whom I consider myself" did not support the efforts of environmental advocates like Ron Sider. Olson included reading material for Dugan in case he ever needed to refute eco-friendly arguments in the future. Instead of using scientific reasons for rejecting the aims of the EEN, the enclosed information focused on the conspiracy that the EEN was actually a "front group for the Clinton/Gore reelection committee and the Democrat Party's Congressional Campaign Committees." More nefariously it proposed that the EEN received money from "extreme environmentalist foundations and federal government agencies with a direct interest in expanding their power and increasing their budgets."[11] Olson assured Dugan that more Christians would hear about these shady dealings by promising he would send a copy of the material to *Christianity Today* for possible publication.

Dugan was likely thankful he did not need to defend a decision to support environmental protection to people like Olson and was probably relieved that readers of think tank and private advocacy articles did not see his name as among those attending meetings where people howled at the moon. To him, as well as Land, dropping the cause of Christian environmental stewardship was comparable to dodging a bullet that might well have killed their professional careers and social lives. Perhaps they would not have been fired from their positions at the NAE or the SBC for sticking with Christian environmental stewardship, but they would have likely crippled their credibility among their friends and would have had to repeatedly deal with the headache of clarifying and legitimizing their eco-friendly efforts as Sider was still doing through the end of the 1990s.

In sum, conservative evangelicals including Land abandoned Christian environmental stewardship out of fear they would be associated with a variety of conspiracy theories combined with the potential threat of being ridiculed by fellow evangelicals. In a similar spirit, Jerry Falwell once told his congregation to stay away from environmentalists because they are "not with Christ," but added, "I do recycle, but I do it after dark so they won't know I'm doing it."[12] His congregation erupted into laughter and applause. What Falwell was really saying was that he did not have a problem with the idea of caring for the environment. Instead, his problem, was that his community had vilified environmentalists to the level that he was ashamed or frightened his neighbors might label him an environmentalist because he participated in an activity they were known to endorse.

After abandoning Christian environmental stewardship in 1994, Land restructured his understanding and position regarding how humanity should treat the Earth. His new view stressed a different interpretation of the biblical scripture Genesis 2:15 in which God commanded Adam to cultivate or till the soil in the Garden of Eden. Tilling the soil, Land said, means that we are to "improve" the Earth and not let it sit as environmentalists want as pristine wilderness. Every decision, he continued, must have humanity's interests as the number one priority. Humans, for example, could develop land even if it destroys the spotted owl habitat because humanity is more important and that is a right given by God. People should, he added, nevertheless "keep some around" in case we need them for some reason in the future. Such a view that placed humans at the forefront of all environmental decisions was not what Schaeffer explained in *Pollution and the Death of Man*, nor was it a message in Land's 1991 seminar or his subsequent book *The Earth Is the Lord's*. In his chapter, Land indeed covered God's command to develop the Earth, but he described a balanced relationship. Schaeffer likewise argued that humanity was a part of God's created order and therefore must respect nonhuman creatures as we do our own species. In *The Earth is the Lord's*, Land followed this value system writing, "We (humans) come first. We must remember, however, that while human life demands reverence, all life deserves respect. We have a right to use animals and plants for human good. We do not have the right to disregard living things or to treat them as inanimate objects." When covering developing or tilling the Earth, Land stated, "we are responsible to develop, but not to desecrate or dissipate, God's creation. We are required to develop God's creation and to bring forth its fruit and increase."[13] Thus, he believed that *all* of God's creation should be developed and increased, not just humanity's. His post-1994 philosophy regarding the development of land to the point that there maybe only "some" spotted owls left for future human use is not what Land was thinking in the early 1990s and not by any means Schaeffer's view in *Pollution and Death of Man*. Nature, said Schaeffer, had value unto itself, beyond that of being a resource for humanity.

Quiet but Sustained Growth

By 1994, conservative evangelical interest in Christian environmental stewardship seemed virtually dead, but by the end of the decade it proved a thorn in the side of those who tried to kill it. As previously stated, at this point, Dugan and Land had turned their backs on Christian environmental stewardship and only the EEN remained to carry on its mantle. The remaining EEN members were additionally hobbled by having to continuously fend off accusations that they were Earth-worshipping new agers. Although the organization seemed doomed and ineffective, their very existence allowed for the idea of Christian environmental stewardship to survive on a low level throughout the 1990s. It's simple presence provided a small opportunity that accomplished two things. First, their message of Christian environmental stewardship proved strong enough to attract an eventual level of interest around the evangelical community. Second, although the EEN was led and supported largely by more moderate evangelicals concerned with social action, their identification as "evangelical" garnered curiosity from secular Americans at every Earth Day observance because the newspapers in part suggested that maybe even political conservative evangelicals were warming up to the idea of protecting the environment. This annual attention became an annoyance for political conservative evangelicals, who continuously tried to set the matter straight.

Indeed, the idea that the environmental movement might receive help from the entire evangelical community proved attractive to wider America. In 1994, the EEN made news across the country in regional newspapers like the *Long Beach Press Telegram*, the *Miami Herald*, and the *San Antonio Express*. Each proclaimed that evangelicals are "beginning to be concerned with the human habitat as well." Although the viewpoints representing the dissenters such as Dugan warned the group's goals were "over-dramatized" and promoted "destructive policies," the articles nevertheless gained interest because at least to the public, it suggested surprising changes may be taking place within the entire evangelical community.[14]

In each newspaper article, the EEN clearly communicated its Christian environmental stewardship messages that the "Earth is the Lord's," that a healthy environment equals healthy people, and that being eco-friendly is neither Earth worship nor extremist. The EEN kept pushing these messages and by 1996 they reported interest from individual churches nationwide. Chattanooga's *Times Free Press* interviewed the director of Philadelphia's EEN chapter, Stan LeQuire, who reiterated the organization's common talking points that "the Earth is the Lord's" and stated that during the past two years, 30,000 congregations received in the mail creation care information, and among that number, 1,200, churches responded with requests for further material. The article interpreted this development as meaning that mainstream environmentalists had found an ally among all evangelicals. LeQuire continued to drum up a positive outlook saying that they would hold a two-day seminar at Chattanooga State Technical Community College. Jerry Faulkner, the organizer of the event, was also sure to clarify his distance from "New-Agers and Eastern Mysticism."[15] In 1998, LeQuire's efforts were featured farther afield in the *Fort Worth Star-Telegram*, Texas, and in Ontario, Canada's, *Waterloo Region Record*. "Evangelicals," LeQuire stated, without distinguishing between moderates and conservatives, were increasingly supporting environmental protection efforts as a way to rightly honor "God by caring for creation." The newspapers linked this thought with other religious denominations such the U.S. Catholic Conference, the National Council of Churches, and the Coalition on the Environment and Jewish Life.[16] By the following year, the EEN's movement appeared even larger when the executive director of the NRPE, Paul Gorman, reflected, "What started as a trickle is now a river with an ever-increasing number of tributaries. . . . The current of that river is now irreversible." His understanding appeared to have merit as the previously inactive NAE sponsored an environmental conference in which William A. Dyrness, of the traditionally conservative Fuller Theological Seminary, called for "an ecology of hope." The event began with a skit clarifying that evangelicals who care for creation are not new agers.[17] Indeed, at least in the secular media and with the help of the EEN, evangelicals were portrayed as becoming more and more comfortable with the idea of actively participating in Christian environmental stewardship initiatives.

Although the EEN worked year round to motivate evangelical congregations at the grassroots level, the mainstream press generally featured their efforts only once a year, around April's Earth Day. This national attention likely irked Falwell, Land, and Robertson, who felt they needed to make a firm policy regarding where politically and theologically conservative evangelicals should stand on the environmental issue. In April of 2000, the president of the Christian Coalition, Roberta Combs, Falwell, and Land, along with a handful of others, drafted and signed an official statement regarding environmental issues titled "A Faith Community Commitment to the Environment and Our Children's Future."[18] The need to protect the environment amounted to lip service by the authors and was overshadowed by stronger concern for the US economy as a source of people's well-being—a theme heightening the importance of capitalism, a central element by this date in their understanding of American nationalism. They promised "to never forget that America was founded on the principle of expanding economic opportunity and economic justice for all citizens, especially for the economically disadvantaged. To this end, environmental policies must not close doors to opportunity for our poorest citizens, but open and expand their opportunities to share in the American Dream" and "to implement policies that protect the future job opportunities for our children and grandchildren and to protect their right to enjoy the natural resources and beauty of America that is your heritage."[19]

Beyond supporting the paramount importance of the economy, the authors tried to discredit those from the scientific community who warn of environmental crises by using the example of the 1989 ALAR scare,[20] brought about by a story on the television news magazine *60 Minutes* regarding the carcinogens in the growth-regulating chemical ALAR with which apples were treated. The response set off a nationwide controversy among different groups that looked to scientists to find answers. As Kerry E. Rodgers explains in "Multiple Meanings of ALAR after the Scare: Implications for Closure," the health dangers of ALAR was in reality slight. However, Rogers argued, even after the product was no longer used, the public employed the issue to support their personal viewpoints. Some, for example, maintained the chemical was indeed too dangerous, while others used the controversy as an example of people overreacting. Accordingly, the writers of "A Faith Community Commitment" used the ALAR controversy to plant seeds of distrust among followers toward eco-friendly media and scientists who, they believed, were coming to incorrect conclusions spurred on by biased political motivations. Moreover, the authors specifically used the example to protect industry and blame whistleblowers who used "bad" science to destroy capitalism.

The example of the ALAR scare was not a major point consistently raised by the religious right throughout the 1990s or 2000s. But rather than seeing the debate over the chemical as an isolated event, the authors of the Faith Community Commitment employed the story to dismiss future health concerns by pointing out the fallibility of the science community. Furthermore, and most importantly, the ALAR example signifies that Falwell and his ilk tended to believe industry over consumer advocate groups. In other words, there was less concern about their follower's physical wellbeing than the health of American industry. Evidence of this conclusion can be found in various other areas within the religious right.

Conservative evangelical trust in industry within the area of pesticides illuminates the close relationship between these two groups, particularly since the mid-1990s. For example, in 1993, A Beka Book's *Science: Order & Reality* accused environmentalists of incorrectly warning that DDT would lead bird populations to extinction and cited the Audubon Society's annual accounts as evidence that no concern was necessary. Pesticides, the authors wrote, were, in effect, God-ordained: "Because environmentalists do not recognize that God appointed man to be superior to the rest of creation, they often attack pesticides as cruel disruptions of nature rather than praising them as remarkable developments in human progress."[21]

In contrast, back in 1986, A Beka Book's *Biology: God's Living Creation* presented the reader with a balanced approach to the use of pesticides. The authors even promoted more "natural" ways to control pests, such as releasing a large population of sterile male insects into a given area to reduce the number of insects in the next generation.[22] Rachel Carson suggested this method in her 1962 book *Silent Spring* as an alternative to using pesticides such as DDT. The 1986 textbook also cited other harmful results of using potent chemicals, warning they may kill helpful insects along with the pests.

In addition to now backing pesticides, the authors of the 1997 edition of *Biology: God's Living Creation* extolled the food additives, BHT, coloring agents, aspartame, sorbitol, and saccharin, as more than fine for human consumption. The text assured the reader that "food additives and preservatives are tested for safety by high-dose rodent tests, in which a group of laboratory rats are fed extraordinary doses of the additive being tested." When the rats eventually die of old age, they are autopsied and searched for tumors. "Because the doses used in the rodent tests are so high, any additive that passes these tests is almost certainly completely harmless at normal doses."[23]

Beyond describing additives and preservatives as "almost certainly completely harmless," the book encouraged readers to become comfortable with pesticides, writing, "(1) most synthetic pesticides are designed to be less toxic to humans than many natural pesticides, and (2) synthetic pesticides can be washed off the food after the food is harvested because they are applied to the outside of the plant; natural pesticides, on the other hand, remain inside the plant and are consumed when the food is eaten."[24] Furthermore, the authors wrote that by the time the synthetic pesticide reaches the consumer, only 1/10,000 of the residue remains on food. The science book went so far as to say that God intended for humans to consume artificial products along with the natural: "Neither the natural residues nor the synthetic residues are cause for concern because God has designed our bodies to easily break down these substances (a job performed by special cells in the liver). In fact, studies have shown that *eating large amounts of fresh fruits and vegetables—pesticide residues and all—can cut your risk of cancer in half*" (emphasis in original).[25] Thus, readers were meant to feel comforted knowing that God intended for business to further human progress almost as a joint venture. The Christian consumer could therefore fully trust corporations that offered humanity safe and amazing products.

The biology textbook went so far as to accuse those who advocated for foods without the pesticides of endangering the health of the consumer:

> Unfortunately, these insect-resistant plants are also more toxic to *people*. For example, one insect-resistant variety of celery sold as a "pesticide free" food has nearly eight times the toxic psoralens of normal food celery, making it so toxic that some people break out in rashes just from touching it. (In addition, psoralens have caused genetic mutations and cancer in high-dose rodent tests.) In another case, a "pesticide-free" potato was pulled from the market because its high levels of nerve poisons made it toxic to humans.[26]

Among the conservative evangelical community as demonstrated by the 1986 edition of *Biology: God's Living Creation*, the environment was not yet a politicized issue. The authors thought nothing of promoting the same approach to control pests as Rachel Carson advocated when warning the reader about synthetic pesticides. However, for the 1997 edition of the same book, the editors switched to promote a strong pro-industry position along with their products including pesticides. The Faith Community Commitment document likewise reflected a similar trust and love for industry while denouncing concerns by environmentalists and climatologists who argued for action to reverse anthropogenic climate change.

The Faith Community Commitment drafted in 2000 stands out as an official statement signed by co-founder of the religious right, Jerry Falwell, and a representative of fellow co-founder Pat Robertson's Christian Coalition. The document also confirmed a change in environmental views of the other notable signer, Richard Land. As previously described, during the early 1990s Land went well beyond simply promoting Christian environmental stewardship to incorporating top environmental issues including global warming into the CLC's environmentally themed annual seminar and then signed the Joint Appeal By Religion & Science for the Environment's "Declaration of the 'Mission to Washington'"—a document that may be easily categorized as within the secular environmentalist cause. By 2000, it was apparent that he had bowed to Christian climate-change deniers and stepped in line with his politically conservative peers.

Land signed not only the Faith Community Commitment statement in 2000, but also a similar and more popular resolution created the same year called "The Cornwall Declaration on Environmental Stewardship." This document, spearheaded by longtime environmentalist opponent E. Calvin Beisner, directly denied anthropogenic global warming. It stated: "Some unfounded or undue concerns include fears of destructive manmade global warming, overpopulation, and rampant species loss." These "fake" problems were contrasted with those that were "real": "While some environmental concerns are well founded and serious, others are without foundation or greatly exaggerated. Some well-founded concerns focus on human health problems in the developing world arising from inadequate sanitation, widespread use of primitive biomass fuels like wood and dung, and primitive agricultural, industrial and commercial practices," and "distorted resource consumption patterns driven by perverse economic incentives." It is interesting that these problems were thought to originate in developing countries; therefore, corrective solutions would not directly threaten the US economy. Global warming, however, a problem that demanded action by all, was thought to be "unfounded."

The Faith Community Commitment and the Cornwall Declaration served as official statements to the wider conservative evangelical community as well as the secular world who might have confused the EEN's goals with those of the religious right. Through these documents Falwell, Land, Beisner, and the Christian Coalition attempted to set the record straight since every past year newspapers ran the story regarding evangelicals as budding environmentalists under the guidance of the EEN. These official documents, however, did not silence the problem but allowed both sides to publically promote their views. Two years later, for instance, CNN featured both Sider and Falwell in a segment concerning the environment. Sider and EEN's new tagline, which received a great deal of attention, ran "What would Jesus drive?"[27] The host asked Falwell if getting into the environmental debate was appropriate for Christians. Falwell replied that Jesus walked everywhere so he never had a view on such philosophical questions. However, Falwell minimized any effort to change one's lifestyle for environmental reasons, saying that he loved his GMC Suburban. "My wife drives one and I drive one. I have a lot of people piled in with me at all times." Sider responded by citing the scientific community, who he said advised consumers not to purchase such polluting commodities. Falwell turned his attention from the host to attacking Sider's environmental and religious argument: "It was global cooling 30 years ago Ron, and it's global warming now and neither one of us will be here in 100 years to know what it is. . . . I don't believe a moment of it and the whole thing is created to destroy America's free enterprise system . . . and our economic stability. I'm so glad that President Bush and 99 of the 100 senators refused to sign the Kyoto Treaty."[28] Later Sider tried explaining that humanity should care for the Earth using the best scientific knowledge. In response Falwell equated the theory of evolution to global warming, asking Sider if he believed the book of Genesis. Sider ignored Falwell and repeated Genesis 2:15. Falwell then said that he loved the Earth too but did not worship it, nor did he observe Earth Day. Sider began talking over Falwell, assuring viewers that he did not worship the Earth either but that there were thousands of evangelicals who are orthodox and because of that they will watch over the Earth. Just before the host ended the debate Falwell recommended that viewers "go out and buy an SUV today."[29]

The same year as the debate on CNN, Robert Dugan's friend and onetime assistant, Richard Cizik, became a believer in anthropogenic climate change; a conversion he later recalled during an interview in 2019 was only second to his conversion to Jesus Christ in 1972. This life-changing moment occurred during a conference at Blenheim Palace, England after listening to a presentation by co-chair of the Intergovernmental Panel on Climate Change, Sir John Houghton. Cizik attributed the conversion to his familiarity with the academic community, which became strengthened while he was earning masters degrees in divinity and public affairs. He reflected that the combination of the fact that climate change is real and his religious beliefs meant that action was not a choice but a moral imperative. He knew, however, what the social consequences would be if he publically took a stand on the issue. During the conference he told Houghton that environmental action might cost him his job. Hougton simply replied, "You'll just have to decide." Cizik knew his conservative evangelical community. He was well entrenched in the religious right at the organizational level and knew the culture. Supporting causes connected to environmentalism was by this time off limits and breaking ranks would make peers view him as a "traitor." Cizik was correct. After publically advocating that evangelicals confront the reality of anthropogenic climate change, Cizik was roundly excoriated by the religious right leadership including James Dobson on his radio show, *Family Talk*. Specifically, Dobson warned that focusing on the environment would be divisive for evangelicals, it would marginalize more pressing matters, and furthermore taking action on climate change would be dangerous to capitalism as well as the American way of life. After the conference and making his pro-environmental remarks, Cizik returned to the United States. He visited the NAE's president, Ted Haggard at his office in Colorado Springs who reported that both James Dobson and Chuck Colson had called earlier that day complaining about Cizik's new environmental cause. Instead of reprimanding or firing Cizik, Haggard advised him not to talk about global warming for three months. After the time passed, a sympathetic Haggard telephoned and gave Cizik permission to speak on the issue again.

To a certain degree Dobson's critique of Cizik proved correct. Global warming was and continues to be a divisive issue among the evangelical community, but on the other hand, announcing a pro-environmental position was not grounds for immediate professional expulsion either, at least not in 2002. With Haggard's support, Cizik kept his job with the NAE. He was criticized but not excommunicated. This level of acceptance continued with conservative evangelicals throughout the 2000s and was thrust into the spotlight again in 2006, when a number within the leadership including Cizik, developed and signed a document titled the "Evangelical Climate Initiative (ECI)." Jonathan Merritt, a seminary student and son of former SBC president James Merritt, produced the declaration. After releasing the ECI, Merritt told the media he was inspired to take action during a class in which the professor said, "When we destroy creation, which is God's revelation, it is no different than tearing a page out of the Bible."[30] As with Cizik's first public announcement in favor of environmental action, a storm of controversy erupted in response to the ECI. Land who was working for the SBC's Ethics & Religious Liberty Commission (ERLC; formally the CLC) immediately received a series of angry calls asking why the ERLC supported the document. This claim he quickly denied and then publically reassured the membership that the SBC had nothing to do with it.[31]

The ECI led to a much louder conversation amongst evangelicals than Cizik's public announcement in 2002. Falwell, for example, worried that the outside world would think he agreed with those who signed the eco-friendly document. His apprehension was not unmerited. Later that same year, the president of the

Union for Reform Judaism, Rabbi Eric H. Yoffie, came to speak at Liberty University's convocation on April 26, 2006—a few days after the secular Earth Day observance and a few months after the drafting of the ECI. Yoffie praised what he thought Falwell and the students supported: "And now you're turning your attention to world poverty, debt relief and global warming. In these battles we are your allies. I hope we can strengthen and expand that alliance." Afterward, Falwell thanked him and let his audience know that what Yoffie said was not in keeping with his and in turn, Liberty University's beliefs. Falwell reminded the audience that he had spoken at many synagogues and that "nobody ever booed me in a synagogue when I said things totally opposite of what they believe." Yoffie sat politely smiling, probably wondering what he had said that was against the beliefs of the conservative evangelical religious right audience.[32]

To clarify his environmental position, Falwell vented his frustration with the ECI in his "private" newsletter, *Falwell Confidential*. He lamented, "Many of the people who signed this document are my friends—some are dear friends. Nevertheless, I have felt compelled to oppose their efforts because I believe that global warming is an unproven phenomenon and may actually just be junk science being passed off as fact."[33] He then utilized a variety of other arguments, such as reminding readers that in the 1970s some scientists thought the world was cooling. Another argument was that since other countries refuse to cut down on fuel emissions, doing so would weaken the United States. Additionally, he hypocritically wrote, "Alan Wisdom, president of the Institute on Religion and Democracy, stated this week, 'Churches should be reluctant to attach the name of the Gospel of Christ to contemporary political agendas to things that lack a clear and scriptural mandate and consensus among the faithful.'" However, in this newsletter, Falwell also suggested government regulation on emissions: "At most, I recommend asking the U.S. government to take reasonable measures to establish limits on emission at the federal level and 'to pass and implement national legislation requiring sufficient economy-wide reductions in carbon dioxide emissions through cost effective, market-based mechanisms.' I stop right there for fear . . . that [taking action will] diminish our nation and likely injure our children and children's children."[34] This concession was the closest he ever came to suggesting that CO_2 may need regulation, and he never expressed the thought again.

By November 2006, Falwell, like Dobson had done several years before, acknowledged climate change was a divisive issue among his religious community: "there is a developing cultural divide occurring within the evangelical community over an unlikely subject: global warming." He specifically cited the ECI and went on the offensive, accusing the resolution of having been initiated by Al Gore and declaring that it was linked with "abortion-on-demand

and population control organizations that are touting global warming as genuine science."[35] He reported that a conservative private advocacy group called the Interfaith Stewardship (which later became the Cornwall Alliance led by E. Calvin Beisner) was gathering a group of scholars and pastors who believed evangelicals should be wary of the politicization and bad science of global warming alarmism. If such warnings went unheeded and secular environmentalists got their way, he wrote, the economy would suffer.[36]

Finally, by February 21, 2007, Falwell, fed up with the whole situation, decided to dedicate an entire sermon to climate change. In an email to church members and his television audience, he drummed up interest:

> Spend Sunday Morning and Evening, February 25, at Thomas Road Baptist Church. 11:00 a.m.—Pastor Jerry Falwell will confront one of the World's most controversial issues in his message entitled: THE MYTH OF GLOBAL WARMING * Is there incontrovertible scientific evidence of global warming? * Will the curbing of greenhouse emission affect the global climate? * Do Christians have a moral responsibility to commit time and resources to the so-called "green evangelical movement?" * Should America submit to the international Kyoto Protocol even though China, India, and most of the third world have refused to do so?

The answers to such questions were clear in the next paragraph: "Pastor Falwell will expose, from a Biblical perspective, this international global warming fraud."[37]

Falwell continued to promote his upcoming sermon in subsequent emails explaining why he, who was not a scientist, would be taking on such an unusual topic. He told his congregation and television audience that climate change was not real and criticized those who signed the ECI, which he interpreted as tantamount to environmental extremism. "Some members of the evangelical community have recently aligned themselves with radical voices within the global warming movement. I see this as unnecessary and, worse, dangerous."[38] "Never mind that in November, for the second consecutive month, temperatures across the continental U.S. were cooler-than-average, according to scientists at the National Oceanic and Atmospheric Administration's National Data Center."[39]

In February of 2007, Falwell filmed promotional shorts for his "Myth of Global Warming" sermon. In the scene, Falwell stood leaning on a chair. He stated, "Today's message may be the most important one I've delivered this year. I'm speaking on the myth of global warming. . . . I mean it really has become a hysteria. It has become an alarmist state today."[40] A few days later, he delivered his message using conclusions of "true scientists" and citing the

Bible. He first quoted Psalm 24:1–2, which states that the Earth is the Lord's. He then recited Genesis 8:22 to assure his congregation and television audience that global warming speculations suggesting that humans are upsetting natural temperature changes could never happen because God promised that while the Earth remained, heat and cold, harvests and seasons would continue. Next he turned his argument to information provided by conservative think tanks and public ridicule. He acknowledged that temperatures fluctuate, but that such things are only cyclical and that only thirty years ago scientists were warning of cooling temperatures. He humorously concluded these remarks saying, "This goes back farther than when Al Gore invented the internet," to which the congregation responded with laughter. Falwell blamed the hysteria on the United Nations, liberal politicians, radical environmentalists, liberal clergymen, Hollywood, and pseudo-scientists. He uploaded "A Skeptic's Guide Debunking Global Warming" to the church's website, which he promised would be updated on a regular basis. Falwell went on to say that "some good evangelical men, some who preached right here at this pulpit and friends of mine had joined the ECI. And they put their name on a document along with the people who are left of everything." He had asked them why they are doing this. They responded that they must uphold the biblical mandate to exercise prudent dominion over the Earth. Falwell agreed with this to a point. "We oughtta keep the streams clean. I love the mountains best. Others love the coast better. But-ah we should certainly work—this is my father's world. We should work to keep it clean, healthy and reseed the forest and all the things that go along with responsible citizenship, but we shouldn't be hugging trees and worshiping the creation more than we worship the creator. [Here the camera broke to a man nodding in agreement and saying "amen."]. And that is what global warming's all about." He went on to say that last year sixty prominent "real scientists" said that global warming is problematic. He ended with ridiculing environmentalists and Al Gore again calling them "tree huggers" and redirecting his congregation to the more important goal of gospel preaching.[41]

Beyond Falwell, other powerful voices in the conservative evangelical community countered the ECI. They included megachurch pastor James Kennedy's Coral Ridge Ministries, who produced a DVD in 2007 titled *Global Warming: The Science and the Solutions*. As one of those interviewed, Richard Land reflected on Al Gore's "croc-u-mentary" [ridiculing Gore's *An Inconvenient Truth*], saying it featured "doomsday" environmental crisis scenarios that had "no evidence" and no "reputable scientist is talking about a twenty foot increase in the oceans." The film furthermore countered environmentalist predictions by featuring an interview of E. Calvin Beisner who stated that action to curb global warming would endanger the lives of millions of those living in developing nations because environmental solutions destroy economies that would otherwise lead to healthier living conditions. In this vein, he warned Christians not to endorse a policy they knew little about because it would hurt the development of people who are trying to move above poverty. Land followed Beisner by citing Genesis 2 and saying that "Adam was put into the garden to keep it and to till it. To keep it means to guard it and to protect it. To till it, means to cause it to bring forth its fruit, to develop it, for what purpose? For human good." Once again, Land reiterated his new understanding that only humans mattered.

Evangelical Environmental Approaches

Three months after his sermon attacking the reality of global warming, Falwell died in his office at Liberty University. He once told his supporters: "When I breathe my last breath, I will have a smile on my face for two reasons: 1. I will know that I will awaken in the presence of my Savior. 2. I will be confident that I will have left a legion of Liberty alumni who will collectively take up the mantle, carried by Senator Helms, myself and many others of my generation, to defend biblical values in our one nation, under God. And I hope they give the liberal politicians and the ACLU more trouble than I ever did."[42]

Falwell indeed left legions to carry on his work, including his anti-environmentalist views. Long after his death in 2011, his church's website accused the environmental movement of attempting "(1) To Create Major Economic Damage to America. (2) The Desire To Change the Subject Concerning the World's Moral Bankruptcy [and] (3) Most Importantly, it is Satan's Attempt to Re-direct the Church's Primary Focus."[43] Somewhat more recently the list was taken down, and why is unclear. It is doubtful that there was any change in the church's environmental views. Perhaps it was too controversial for Jonathan Falwell, who took over as pastor of Thomas Road Baptist Church after his father's death. Jonathan continued sending out *Falwell Confidential* but does not seem the dogmatic, politically-charged general of the religious right like his father. He steps into the political realm when it comes to more secure topics like abortion, but often presents his arguments in compassionate terms rather than raging sarcasm and disbelief. Jerry Falwell's other son, Jerry Falwell Jr., assumed the role of chancellor of Liberty University. Before resigning in 2020 in response to scandal, Falwell Jr. portrayed himself to the student body as a cool and relaxed kind of guy and addressed the school community with a swagger and cocky demeanor.

Unlike his quiet brother, Falwell Jr. continued his father's habit of actively rejecting and demeaning concern for the environment. In 2010, Falwell Jr. and

Liberty University's director of communication appeared on Fox's *Glenn Beck Show*. Beck had his chalkboard out with a list of terms. In descending order it read, "God, morals, global warming, environmental justice, socialism, R/W (redistribution of wealth), and Marxism."[44] Beck explained that social justice and environmental justice had nothing to do with the Bible or God. Later he asked Falwell Jr. his view on the matter; he responded with a recounting of Jesus' parable of the talents in which a servant is praised for succeeding in the market place. Beck laughed, "Are you saying Jesus was a capitalist?" Falwell Jr. replied, "That one parable sure sounds like it." In accordance with his father, Glenn Beck, and other conservative evangelicals, Falwell Jr. championed an unrestricted market place at the expense of the environment if necessary. He was clear that government control was not the answer to environmental matters and that individuals through charitable actions could make environmentally friendly decisions.[45] Later that year, he invited climate change denier Lord Christopher Monckton to address Liberty University and explain the science behind why humans are not causing global warming.

Falwell Jr. introduced Monckton and applause followed when it was noted that Al Gore refused to debate the guest speaker. Monckton greeted the crowd and asked them to return his salutation by addressing him as "my Lord." The response was not good enough and the audience was asked to repeat the title louder, which they did begrudgingly. The awkward beginning quickly dissipated as Monckton delved into an argument explaining why anthropogenic global warming was a host of lies with dire consequences.

Monckton delivered a well-rehearsed presentation, backed up with numerous statistics communicated in a public-friendly format generously buttressed with comedy. The crowd laughed and applauded in response to the description that Gore's Oscar winning pro-environmental documentary *An Inconvenient Truth* was a "horror comedy." Monckton also took on the disturbing popular perception that because of higher temperatures and melting arctic ice, polar bears were drowning. Not to worry, he comforted, such things were simply not true. "Just four were found dead because of a storm . . . because as we scientists say, 'shit happens.'"[46] The auditorium erupted in a fit of laughter followed by thunderous applause. The response lasted half a minute before the presentation could continue. Beyond simple denial, Monckton offered a variety of other reasons why efforts to stem climate change were a fool's errand. He discredited warnings regarding increased levels of CO_2, repeating old arguments from the 1990s: more of the gas is good for plants. Instead of reshaping the US economy, the best thing to do is to wait and adapt. He asked the rhetorical question why the United States and Britain were asked to make the most environmental concessions when countries like China were not although they emit pollutants in far greater amounts. He ended by telling the audience that fortunately the United Nations could not force countries such as the United States to be eco-friendly "And I hope it stays that way." Applause followed.[47]

When it comes to the environment, the conservative evangelical world is divided, as Jerry Falwell pointed out years ago, but one side is winning. Falwell Jr. refused to admit global warming is real, as did his father, but in the recent past Liberty University jumped whole-heartedly into campus recycling. Ridiculing environmentalists, however, continues at Thomas Road Baptist Church. In 2011, longtime religious right supporter Elmer Towns told the audience there that he wished for the Northeast to get hit by as much snow as possible because that is where people live who believe in global warming (although he recanted moments later, saying that he only wanted Al Gore to get hit).[48] Likewise, the dean of Liberty University's seminary, Dr. Ergun Caner, disparaged worries over the subject in 2008. Caner was upset that some Christians spoke to him privately about concern for climate change. He told the congregation that such worries were unnecessary because the problem is insignificant, as is concern for animal rights.[49] His approach to the environment, like Falwell's, was couched in derisive humor, saying his church blesses animals—before they eat them. Caner would later step down from his position after it was found that he and his brother fabricated their personal stories as "former Islamic terrorists" depicted in their 2002 best selling book *Unveiling Islam*.

A Beka Book material also continues arguing the same anti-environmentalist points as it has promoted since the early 1990s. Bob Jones University Press, on the other hand, always advocated that readers should care for nature and presented these sentiments in a compassionate manner. In 2012 however, the publisher promoted the view that Christians should approach current issues such as global warming with a "wait, see and study" attitude. In other words, the jury was still out, and in the meantime capitalism should continue to "wisely" use resources—although what "wise" means was never defined. BJU Press's 2012 *Earth Science* textbook described the science community as very divided on a host of environmental issues, writing "some scientists say" that global warming may be helpful, while "other scientists say" that humans may be causing climate change through pollution. The authors mostly left the decision up to the reader, but in a leading way touching on the argument that environmental protection efforts would do more harm than good. "If global warming is happening," they wrote, "we have three choices. We could do nothing and assume that we can handle problems if they develop. Or we could immediately try to change features of the earth's systems in ways that might have major unintended impacts on global weather, air pollution, and our ability to grow food. Or we could attempt to refine our understanding of the problem and take appropriate actions."

Taking action that might lead to "major unintended impacts" seems scary. The authors further helped the reader reason through the predicament: "Which is more likely to succeed: predicting and responding to problems like rising sea levels, or attempting untested ways to control global climate?"[50] Responding to individual problems produced by climate change sounded much more reasonable than trying untested ways to control the climate.

Such environmental views from those like Falwell, Monckton, Caner, and Christian school publishers reflect the fact that opposition to environmental action is presently alive and well within the conservative evangelical religious right community. There is, however, a small movement within the group and beyond the EEN intent on structuring, what they feel, would be the most effective strategy to gain evangelical support for the environment. The primary tactic is to focus on how pro-environmental action would benefit humanity.

In 2009, Texas Tech climatologist and evangelical Katherine Hayhoe published a book with her husband and pastor, Andrew Farley, titled *A Climate For Change: Global Warming Facts for Faith–Based Decisions*. In their book, the authors clearly and concisely dispel a long list of anti-environmentalist arguments that existed within their community for years. They explained that evangelicals do not worship the Earth; environmental care is not intended to ruin the economy; acid rain is real as are problems with the ozone layer, and the consensus among scientists is that global warming's principle cause is humans and not volcanoes. In addition to overturning well-worn beliefs, Hayhoe and Farley attempted to sway the evangelical reader primarily through the argument that humanity will suffer if anthropogenic climate change continues. Conversely, the health of non-human nature was only lightly touched upon. The book featured a few paragraphs about global warming's threat to polar bears and biodiversity, but overall, it stated that Christianity is about the call to help humans. The authors reasoned, "In the end, it comes down to loving real people who may be in real danger."[51] In addition to this quasi-anthropocentric approach, the authors also admitted that the Bible does not have a clear mandate about taking environmental action. Nevertheless, they concluded that the Earth is all we have and until the Lord returns we need to take care of it for ourselves and for others.

Such was also the approach of a short booklet titled *Loving the Least of These*, published in 2011 by the NAE. Like Hayhoe and Farley's approach, this booklet focused primarily on pro-environmental action to benefit humans and particularly the poor. The booklet, however, clarifies that its message is not a resolution from the NAE, but only a discussion piece. In short, the "call to care" is only a suggestion, asking the reader to think about the issues in an effort not to cause controversy. After clarifying that they do not worship creation, the booklet's authors tried countering conspiracy theories while connecting environmental action to the hottest topics among conservative evangelicals, which is that climate change will endanger what they want to preserve the most such as the sanctity of human life, the integrity of the family, and the government's ability to guarantee peace and individual freedom.

Although the human-centered argument in both publications is wisely constructed, in retrospect, the approach has not made a noticeable impact. Former NAE employee and Dugan associate Richard Cizik, who today heads his own organization called the New Evangelical Partnership for the Common Good, hopes that maybe Hayhoe's approach will help "flip a switch" among evangelicals, but knows it has not worked yet. Instead of asking Republicans and their evangelical religious right allies to act on the environment, Cizik directly challenges them on the issue, saying that caring for creation will help both the Earth and humanity, that it is what God calls followers to do, and that it is simply "the Christian thing to do."

Cizik's strategy, like Hayhoe's, is well meaning, but it is not likely to bring about change in the future. Challenging evangelicals using Christian principles is something Ron Sider has done throughout his career. His strategy uses biblical understandings of Jesus' ministry of love, forgiveness and charity to try and motivate evangelicals who pride themselves on an inerrant understanding of the Bible to live and practice what Jesus actually taught. Sider's crusade has certainly grown over time, but he is easily ignored and dismissed by conservative evangelicals who do not consider him one of their own. Cizik experienced something similar once he took up the environment as an issue, when he became thought of, as he feared, a traitor to their cause.

While reflecting on his firing during a 2019 interview, Cizik pointed out that even a national group made up of millions of members like the NAE is weary of controversy and that problem, he believes, was the key that finally led to his being dismissed from the NAE in 2008. The NAE only functions on donations and therefore cannot lead on issues that are controversial. The SBC functions nearly the same way. Individual churches are not beholden to the SBC and are only asked to donate money to help run the organization including the seminaries. Thus, fear of losing support was likely one of the reasons why Land kept the ERLC aloof from the 2006 ECI issue saying such a position was "out of respect for the Southern Baptists' autonomy."[52] Similarly, Dugan's final decision regarding the EEN's declaration in 1994 hinged on the fact that he felt it too controversial and therefore feared for his job and social status. As a consequence, he abandoned the topic and let others decide what to do. Land, however, has in the past stood his ground on other controversial issues. In particular, around the same time that he promoted Christian environmental stewardship in the early 1990s, he also made racial equality a primary goal for the SBC. This is one of the primary reasons, he speculated, why he was hired to lead the Christian Life Commission in the first place. While being considered for the position of executive director, Land expressed that as a baby boomer growing up in the 1950s and 1960s, he knew that racial equality was simply the right position to take and that the SBC traditionally had been woefully lacking in that area. Therefore, once hired, he became heavily involved with the issue and remains proud of his work, which he stated, led to an increase in African-American evangelical membership from 300 to roughly one million. To accomplish this goal, Land worked with moderate evangelical Foy Valentine. He determined that this cooperation led to conservative friends yelling at him over the phone and not speaking to him for months. "But" he recalled, "it was the right thing to do." These recollections are partly corroborated by the SBC's first African-American president, the Rev. Fred Luter, who said that he personally worked with Land to produce a 1995 resolution in which the SBC formally apologized for supporting slavery during the Civil War. The level of Land's commitment to racial equality, however, is suspect, especially when considering that Luter shared these remarks during Land's 2012 retirement dinner, likely to diminish speculation that Land was pressured to resign after making racist remarks in response to the Trayvon Martin case.[53]

Despite some SBC churches presently practicing Christian environmental stewardship independently, the community apparently does not consider it an issue they want to incorporate into their political agenda. In the 2016 election, over 80 percent of evangelicals, and about the same number in the 2020 election, voted for climate-change denier, Donald Trump, who appointed like-minded evangelicals Scott Pruitt as his first head of the Environmental Protection Agency and Mike Pence as his vice president. Although the EEN, Cizik and Hayhoe continue waving the banner for the long-established understanding of Christian environmental stewardship, their calls seem drowned out by the din of votes supporting free enterprise over the Earth. The fact, however, that theologically based eco-friendly views existed within the conservative evangelical community as late as 1994 offers the possibility that their current position could change again.

Conclusion

Just prior to and directly after Earth Day 1970, conservative evangelicals discussed the issue of ecology with an interest in forming a parallel movement defined by the term "stewardship." Consequently, a variety of moderate and conservative religious leaders promoted what became Christian environmental stewardship, including Francis Schaeffer, Harold Lindsell, and a host of authors from *Christianity Today*, *Moody Monthly*, *Eternity*, and *United Evangelical Action*. During Billy Graham's radio show, *Hour of Decision*, Leighton Ford also promoted the eco-friendly understanding of stewardship steeped in "born again" rhetoric. Others in agreement included hundreds of Southern Baptist pastors and Sunday school teachers who specifically advocated that air and water pollution problems should be addressed at the local church level. The Earth Day excitement, however, did not last long.

There were two major reasons why interest towards Christian environmental stewardship did not translate into action after Earth Day 1970. The first was a consequence of the secular environmental movement. Those leading the secular cause encouraged what they considered more "Earth- friendly" faiths and blatantly blamed Christianity for the poor state of the environment. This situation pushed the willing conservative evangelicals away, worsening a schism that never healed and marginalized future attempts by those who advised fellow believers that God wanted them to protect the natural world. The second is that conservative evangelicals became preoccupied with other contemporary issues, most notably the Equal Rights Amendment, abortion, and gay rights. Despite the diversion, conservative evangelicals on the whole did not dismiss or turn against Christian environmental stewardship throughout the 1970s and 1980s. Instead it remained as an accepted but quiet philosophy. [11]

Beyond maintaining eco-friendly philosophies, the community developed other ways to understand the natural world beyond the aims of preserving God's Earth. One approach is somewhat abstract and deals with how conservative evangelicals and in consequence the religious right, understood humanity's proper place in God's created order. To fight the women's and gay rights movements, religious leaders framed opposition in terms of what is natural versus the unnatural; they believed God created humans to act out preordained roles, which could not be deviated from. Falwell, for example, repeatedly cited the Genesis creation story to support heterosexual marriage and extended it to include traditional gender norms. In other words, feminism and gay rights were, according to this religious community, unnatural deviations from God's original formula. Furthermore, it was believed God could communicate his evaluations of human actions through earthly signs. The natural world, for instance, could be used by God as a tool to punish the perversions of people who appropriated his position through artificial insemination, abortion or ignoring separate gender spheres, as in women choosing careers over the home. In the mindset of those who later made up the religious right, the health of the family, church, and nation all depended on humanity functioning within its proper roles as originally created by God.

Another way conservative evangelicals understood the natural world could be witnessed within Christian education material bought and utilized in the ever-increasing number of Christian and homeschools throughout the 1970s. The first priority for these institutions was the production of educational information written for Christians by Christians. Their next order of business, especially when it came to writing history textbooks, involved developing a Christian American nationalist ideology which they used to teach the next generation of conservative evangelicals what the United States should represent and be. As future voting citizens, students would one day fight for a "correct" understanding of the American family and take the nation back from the unnatural aspirations of progressives who ignored God's intended order and fabricated their own "human-centered" social agendas.

Christian American nationalism centered on an idea of a historic relationship between God and the "traditional" family. Writers of Christian educational material credited the family for building the United States and making it prosper. To legitimize such views, the authors cited handpicked episodes from early American history. The Pilgrims, for example, were praised as the founders of what became the United States. Within this narrative the physical environment played a vital role. Stories frequently portrayed primitive frontier lifestyles and early settler struggles with wilderness as the blueprint thought to keep people strong, God-fearing, and well within their naturally separate gender roles. This frequently touted "'proper" lifestyle offered a feel-good imagined past, which suggested that the nation might one day return to its more wholesome roots rather than being led to ruin by the artificial modern-day alternatives. This interpretation led thousands of students to the doors of "safe" Christian k–12 schools and to the campuses of Bob Jones University, Pensacola Christian College, Regent University, and Liberty University in the 1970s and beyond. Perhaps most importantly, the development of the Christian American nationalist narrative gave a sense of identity for the religious right, which officially formed in 1979.

While Christian American nationalism developed throughout the 1980s, eco-friendly philosophies and a love for capitalism coexisted within the religious right. Falwell, for one, stayed mostly silent on the issue of the ecological crisis, while others, including Pat Robertson, voluntarily and always in a sympathetic tone, brought up the need for Christian environmental stewardship. Robertson did this most notably at the politically charged National Affairs Briefing in Dallas, Texas, in 1980, when he spoke in front of his religious right peers and future president, Ronald Reagan. He continued with these views throughout the 1980s and even at the Republican National Convention in 1988. This latter appearance was well after Reagan proved in rhetoric and actions that he favored economic prosperity over the environment.

During his presidency, Reagan set his secretary of the interior, James Watt, to support a healthier economy at the expense of nature if necessary. Watt understood stewardship to mean that nature was an economic resource for humanity. In the 1980s, Robertson never expressed similar thoughts nor did he come to the aid of Watt who was under continuous attack by environmental groups. Even Falwell, who spoke out in favor of the beleaguered secretary of the interior, did not to any real extent endorse Watt's understanding of the natural world. If the religious right had emphatically chosen free enterprise over the environment, they would have flocked to support Watt and pressured Robertson to abandon his eco-friendly position.

Running parallel to these developments and in partnership with Robertson's views, compassionate Christian environmental stewardship periodically appeared in Christian educational material throughout the 1980s. Bob Jones University Press produced sympathetic portrayals of God's world and at the very least promoted a balanced understanding of environmental issues. When it came to pesticides for instance, no direct stand was taken but the dangers and benefits were stated with simply a cautionary note to readers not to become environmental extremists or to destroy God's creation. More often than not, BJU Press agreed with contemporary environmental concerns about contaminated water, acid rain, deforestation, and endangered species. A Beka Book stood a little farther back from the debate, but nevertheless praised environmental preservationist John Muir as late as 1986. A Beka Book publications also did not vilify the environmental movement and in 1989 released an economics textbook taking a strong stand for a sustainable environment. Throughout the 1970s and 1980s, A Beka Book as well as BJU Press portrayed the health of the environment as being just as important as economic stability. Such an approach remained directly in line with Schaeffer's teachings that humanity could use nature but must never maximize economic profits at its expense.

Amongst these larger developments, traces of anti-environmentalism emerged during the 1980s within the conservative evangelical community. The most prominent example is Harold Lindsell, who as late as 1976 promoted resource and energy conservation in the spirit of Christian environmental stewardship. A few years later however, Lindsell accepted the arguments offered by politically charged conservative reading material that accused the environmental movement of hindering American business and moving the nation toward socialism and regulation. Such views helped Lindsell develop the premise for his 1982 book, *Free Enterprise: A Judeo-Christian Defense*, in which he stated it was the right of Americans to use resources to any extent they wished to support a strong economy. Other lesser-known figures in the community shared similar feelings and spun conspiracy theories blaming environmentalists for trying to convert Christians to new age faiths. Nevertheless, anti-environmentalism did not break into the mainstream rhetoric of the conservative evangelical religious right until the early 1990s.

In response to growing popular interest surrounding the twentieth anniversary of Earth Day in 1990, conservative evangelicals attempted to turn Christian environmental stewardship into action. The conversation, however, quickly descended into an argument. To combat wide support for climate change solutions connected with the 1992 Earth Summit, conservative think tanks launched an information campaign that attracted converts within the religious right. The easy-to-access information featured handpicked credentialed experts who denied environmental problems existed, suggested higher CO_2 levels would be beneficial, and warned that any nature protection efforts would ruin the economy. These arguments were effectively reinforced by ridiculing environmentalists for worshipping nature and being in league with anti-American plots. In consequence, people like Richard Land who supported

Christian environmental stewardship felt forced to keep correcting accusations that they were working with Earth-worshipping environmentalists. In the end, he like Dugan, ultimately asked if the cause was worth fighting for and after thinking about the risk to career and social standing, the answer was a resounding "no." Dugan's longtime assistant, Richard Cizik, on the other hand, refused to compromise his religious principles and publicly supported the issue at the late date of 2002. This decision cost Cizik his job and credibility within his religious community.

When considering these factors, including Cizik's story, it is important to note that Christian environmental stewardship itself was faith-based. It was founded on Christian theological principles in which God created and owned the Earth. Therefore it was humanity's responsibility to treat it as custodians and not to maximize profits to line one's pocketbook. Conversely, the main argument to reject stewardship was first and foremost its apparent threat to the economy made effective through conspiracy theories and mockery.

To most observers, the idea that conservative evangelicals choose economic prosperity over the health of the environment may appear insensitive and frankly unchristian especially when considering the more compassionate message of being stewards of God's creation. Such a contradiction however, is more complex. As sociologist Arlie Russell Hochschild explains in her book, *Strangers in Their Own Land: Anger and Mourning on the American Right*, the faithful greatly value nature and desire a clean and healthy environment, but remain opposed to environmental protection largely due to economic reasons. She explains this conflict by noting that so called red states are often where major industry employers are located. Thus, their employees have come to the "pragmatic" conclusion that they must sacrifice the environment and even their own health for virtually the only type of work that is available to them. Additionally, Hochschild touches on the fact that these same conservative evangelicals know that in American culture one's success and value as a person are often judged by how much money one has. In this vein, conservative evangelicals see the federal government giving away money and benefits to people who, they feel, did not earn it. For them the free market is their only ally and helps them "get ahead." Consequently, the wages that buy material goods eclipses the wish for a clean and healthy environment. As Hochschild quotes one individual, "Pollution is the sacrifice we make for capitalism."[1] In this sense, although the environment matters for conservative evangelicals, it does not matter enough. This way of reasoning is likewise reflected in the examples of Dugan and Land. In one of his final letters to Ron Sider, Dugan blatantly stated that he feared for his job if he signed the EEN's declaration. Years later, Richard Cizik faced the same quandary and knew his decision was attached to being employed. Unlike his former colleague Robert Dugan, Cizik chose to publicly take a stand for environmental protection and credits that decision as the determining factor which led to his firing years later.

Woven in with economic arguments was and is the threat of social ridicule with the possibility of total alienation. Katherine Hayhoe, climatologist, professor, and author of *A Climate For Change*, is well aware that environmental support is socially untouchable within her evangelical community. She highlighted such a point in her 2014 PBS video, in which she told a personal story about attending church and being confronted by members who thought she could help debunk anthropogenic climate change. In the clip, Hayhoe said she responded by reluctantly and awkwardly saying, "I'm afraid that that's true (regarding the reality of anthropogenic climate change)." Within her community, she explains that publicly admitting the reality of anthropogenic climate change is a little like "coming out of the closet." It is, in other words, a breaking of social ranks, which possibly puts one in the enemy's camp and therefore in social peril. Her efforts have indeed made her a target as she was featured in several articles on anti-environmentalist and evangelical E. Calvin Beisner's Cornwall Alliance's website, which functions as one the most popular anti-environmentalist evangelical information hubs. In one article published in 2020, Beisner reprinted personal correspondence from Dr. Judith Curry, a professor emeritus at Georgia Tech, who directly denigrated Hayhoe's research, and in short personally attacked her by saying among other things, "She (Hayhoe) is a faculty member at Texas Tech (a 2nd rate univ at best) in the political science department. Apparently none of the nearby universities in TX (her husband is a pastor there) would hire her in the atmospheric science dept." Earlier in the article, Beiser was sure to note that Dr. Curry did not include Hayhoe on a list with "real scientists" and further demeaned her credibility by stating "is anyone concerned about her outsized Kardashian Index?" (the comments in parenthesis are Curry's words as quoted by Beisner).[2] In this case, Beisner did not use the traditional accusations that caring for the environment was Earth worship, but freely used someone else's words to belittle Hayhoe's credibility.

Environmental concerns being eclipsed by the more important factors of financial and/or social status should not pinpoint conservative evangelicals as the sole perpetrators of environmental indifference. Since the birth of the modern environmental movement in 1970, the environment has barely registered as a top-five election issue for either Republicans or Democrats. For Democrats, who are known to be more environmentally sympathetic, during the 2020 election, climate change ranked behind healthcare, the economy, the coronavirus outbreak, and the issue of race and ethic inequality.[3] Those who traditionally support environmentalism itself have come to question just why the movement seems ineffective. As previously discussed, environmental historians William Cronon and Richard White explained that environmentalists often understand humanity as separate from rather than connected to the natural world and therefore make wilderness into a sacred object, which in turn alienates people who have financial problems to worry about. In 2004 Ted Nordhaus and Michael Shellenberger made similar points in the essay "The Death of Environmentalism: Global Warming Politics in a Post-Environmental World." In this piece, they argued that the old guard environmentalists represented by large lobbyist groups such as the Sierra Club are misdirected in their polarized portrayal of wilderness as good and human impact as bad. Consequently, these environmental groups make enemies of working Americans as they employ a strategy to save wilderness areas through government regulations, which may be at the expense of employers and employees. Richard White's chapter in *Uncommon Ground* titled, "'Are You an Environmentalist or Do You Work for a Living?': Work and Nature" speaks to this very point. Perhaps in this way, conservative evangelicals may have been onto something ever since Schaeffer promoted Christian environmental stewardship in the late 1960s. He and other conservative evangelicals understood humanity as a part of and not separate from the natural world. Within this perspective, humans were indeed thought of as God's pinnacle of creation, but nevertheless believed that nonhuman nature should not be abused, because as Schaeffer articulated, humans share a plane with the Creator (albeit in a lower status) as well as with the created order as its stewards. Accordingly, God made both humans and nonhumans, and thus, as Land wrote, echoing Schaeffer, both should increase and multiply. Therefore, the environmental strategy people should pursue, as Nordhaus and Shellenberger also argue, ought to be one that benefits both. This way everyday people, industrial wage-earners included, will see the worth of having a healthy environment rather than perhaps feeling that they have to choose between a prosperous economy or a pristine environment.

Roughly between 1993 and 1994, conservative evangelicals left behind their more balanced philosophy of Christian environmental stewardship. Their new view was similar to the traditional environmentalist approach by perceiving choices in stark black and white terms. Gone was the eco and people friendly view they once promoted, but nevertheless it quietly survives by the efforts of a minority of evangelical individuals and small organizations (such as the Evangelical Environmental Network).

Today it might seem improbable that Christian environmental stewardship could once again become an accepted view among the conservative evangelical mainstream. However, Richard Land is correct that conservative evangelical support for the environment "could have taken a very different path." In the early 1990s, he was so certain that protecting God's Earth was uncontroversial and theologically defensible that he virtually staked his newly accepted job on it. Like others, including Lamar Cooper Sr. who helped him organize the Christian Life Commission's 1991 environmental seminar, he eventually changed his mind in response to intensifying social pressure made possible by the anti-environmentalist arguments disseminated by think tanks and private advocacy groups. Such a development is not astonishing. Conservative evangelicals live, like everyone else, in a very real world where being estranged from their close-knit community is an extremely unwanted prospect as is the threat of being financially poorer. Nevertheless, evangelicals should at least acknowledge and remember their own community's history, in which those including Francis Schaeffer, Pat Robertson, Richard Land, and their children's trusted educational publishers promoted the nuanced philosophy of Christian environmental stewardship that strove to respect God as creator and to protect both humanity and the nonhuman environment. This is an approach that even some in the environmental movement believe is the way forward. Perhaps remembering this past might help build future bridges between environmentalists and conservative evangelicals. There would, however, need to be a relinquishing of categorizing and ridiculing anyone who promotes eco-friendly views as simply Earth-worshipping tree-huggers who are trying to realize a one-world government. In other words, a re-embracement of Christian environmental stewardship would need to become socially safe. Additionally, the intense prioritizing of money may need some dampening. After all, during the 1970s and 1980s, support for the economy and a healthy environment coexisted within the worldviews of conservative evangelicals. Christian environmental stewardship was, at least during this period, understood as the right thing to do. When considering this past, it is possible that among conservative evangelicals, Christian environmental stewardship could again "take a different path."

Notes

Introduction

1. Elaine Howard Ecklund, "Religion vs. Science," interview by Leith Anderson, February 15, 2018, audio, 33:50, https://www.nae.net/ecklundpodcast/.

2. For more on this scholarship, see Douglas Eckberg and T. Jean Blocker, "Varieties of Religious Involvement and Environmental Concerns: Testing the Lynn White Thesis," *Journal for the Scientific Study of Religion* 28, no.4 (December 1989), 509–517; James Guth, John C. Green, Lyman A. Kellstedt, and Corwin E. Smidt, "Faith and the Environment: Religious Beliefs and Attitudes on Environmental Policy," *American Journal of Political Science* 39, no.2 (May 1995), 364–382; Darren E. Sherkat and Christopher G. Ellison, "Structuring the Religion-Environment Connection: Identifying Religious Influences on Environmental Concern and Activism," *Journal for the Scientific Study of Religion* 46, no. 1 (March 2007), 71–85; and John Evans and Justin Feng, "Conservative Protestantism and Skepticism of Scientists Studying Climate Change," *Climate Change* 121, no. 4 (December 2013), 595–608.

Brian McCammack's article "Hot Damned America: Evangelicalism and the Climate Change Policy Debate" leaned toward the conclusion that politically conservative evangelicals refuse to support environmental protection efforts, primarily those intended to address global warming, because they feel a strong economy is more important in that it offers opportunities for those in poverty. Such arguments were indeed made by the leadership of the religious right in one of their first official environmental statements titled "A Faith Community Commitment to the Environment and Our Children's Future" (2000). Additionally, religious studies scholar Robin Globus Veldman clearly demonstrates antipathy conservative evangelicals hold toward anthropogenic climate change in her book *The Gospel of Climate Skepticism: Why Evangelical Christian Oppose Action on Climate Change*. She argues that conservative evangelical leaders pressured and taught parishioners to reject calls to support global warming initiatives.

3. Political scientist Robert Booth Fowler's *The Greening of Protestant Thought* (1995), chronicled environmental perspectives held specifically by Protestants in general since the birth of the environmental movement in 1970. He found that although the community initially wanted to participate, they ended up not taking cooperative action until the 1980s when evangelicals like Calvin DeWitt founded the Au Sable Institute to teach fellow believers how to care for the earth. Fowler, however, largely ignored perhaps the most politically important group, the conservative evangelicals, or as he refers to them as fundamentalists, who to this day make up the religious right, the fervently dedicated

political allies of today's Republican Party. Fowler devoted eleven pages analyzing this group and concluded that they either dismissed or opposed environmental efforts because of the premillennialist belief that Christ would return soon so protecting nature was unnecessary. The other argument he used rested on the idea that fundamentalists interpreted Genesis 1:26—28 to mean that God gave the earth to mankind with the commandment to "dominate" or in other words, attain a mastery over nature. Fowler wrote that these "fundamentalists" understood these verses to mean that the earth is a simple resource to be used for the benefit of people. He singled out religious right cofounder and popular Charismatic televangelist Pat Robertson who, he argued, endorsed the latter belief. Several years later, English Professor Linda Kintz in her book *Between Jesus and the Market Place* (1997) cited analogous rhetoric by Robertson and mirrored Fowler's conclusion, as did David Larsen in "God's Gardeners" (2003).

Laurel Kearns, in "Cooking the Truth: Faith, Science, the Market and Global Warming," takes the view that conservative evangelicals believe that Christians should be saving souls rather than the environment, as well as pointing to their lack of faith in the science.

In her book *Between God & Green*, Katharine Wilkinson covers the 1970s to 1990s in a brief overview. She concludes that environmentalism amongst the conservative evangelical community was "limited" and "waned as the decade wore on." The socially liberal evangelicals, however, receive most of the focus in the overview and first chapters until the conservative evangelicals are reintroduced as those who led the "backlash" in the later 1990s and 2000s against the Rev. Jim Ball and others who created the Evangelical Environmental Network.

Similarly to Wilkinson, Kearns in her explanation of Fundamentalism in the *Berkshire Encyclopedia of Sustainability*, remarks that some Southern Baptists are beginning to support environmental protection but notes "(not the Southern Baptist Convention)." Indeed, the SBC today opposes anthropogenic climate change, but as will be shown in *The Nature of the Religious Right*, the SBC initially tried leading the community into becoming eco-friendly, which included accepting anthropogenic climate change and arguing that Southern Baptists should take action. This position, however, changed in the early 1990s and largely remains in the present.

Overall, McCammack, Kearns and Wilkinson offer excellent explanations regarding the recent situation regarding environmental views of socially liberal and conservative evangelicals. *The Nature of the Religious Right*, however, fills in the background that took conservative evangelicals from holding eco-friendly philosophies during the 1970s and 1980s to environmental opposition in the present. By approaching the topic in this manner, a more nuanced and complex story emerges that shows how nature mattered in different ways and changed over time within the conservative evangelical community.

Finally, *The Nature of the Religious Right* complements Stephen Ellingson's *To Care for Creation: The Emergence of the Religious Environmental Movement* (2016). Ellingson follows the rise of environmental friendly evangelicals attempting to grow Religious Environmental Movement Organizations (REMOs). Like McCammack, Kearns and Wilkinson, Ellingson's book spends most of its time in the 1990s and 2000s, telling the story from the perspective of those who support REMOs. For instance, Ellingson writes in chapter 3, "Like David facing Goliath, Jonathan Merritt (a REMO organizer) faced a set of seemingly insurmountable challenges as he hoped to start the Southern Baptist Climate Initiative (SBCI)." It is explained that Merritt knew the Southern Baptist Convention believed nature should be protected but would not support pro-environmental action. Merritt cites, for example, statements from Richard Land's book, *The Earth is the Lord's*. Merritt explained that the book offered environmental views similar to his own, but Land's "orthodoxy" led him to reject nature protection efforts. Merritt also believed that Southern Baptist opposition stemmed from environmentalism being too closely associated with political liberalism. In furthering Ellingson's work, *The Nature of the Religious Right* explores the origins of *The Earth is the Lords* and demonstrates that Land's views and actions in the early 1990s were actually pro-environmental until 1993/1994. The problem, as discussed by Merritt, was not simply Land's "orthodoxy" but rather that Land and others in the SBC changed their position on the issue. The reasons for this change are addressed in the introduction and chapters 5, 6 and 7.

4. Nan Gilbert, "Land That I Love," in *Widening Horizons: The Modern McGuffey Readers*, ed. Ullin Whitney Leavell, Mary Louise Friebele, and Tracie Cushman (Pensacola, FL: A Beka Book Publication, 1986), 273.

5. Laurel Hicks et al. *Science: Order & Reality,* 2nd ed. (Pensacola, FL: A Beka Books, 1993), 167.

6. Dugan also went by the title Director of Public Affairs.

7. The Christian community had discussed the issue not only as a reaction to looming environmental problems, but also largely in response to medieval historian Lynn White Jr.'s article "The Historical Roots of Our Ecologic Crisis" published in 1967. This situation is addressed in chapter 1.

8. As religious historian Matt Sutton explains in *American Apocalypse: A History of Modern Evangelicalism*, the religious community that became the fundamentalists of the later twentieth century had a history of being politically conservative and a friend of the Republican Party since the 1920s. Bethany Moreton also shows in *To Serve God and Wal-Mart* that the relationship began flourishing in the mid-twentieth century in combination with a love for free enterprise. See also Darren Dochuk, *Anointed with Oil*.

9. Conservative evangelicals championed capitalism long before Earth Day 1970. *The Nature of the Religious Right*, however, demonstrates that the community's eco-friendly philosophies did not become secondary to their love of free enterprise until the 1990s.

10. The "exceptions" may explain the lower levels of environmental concern amongst conservative Protestants as noted by Eckberg and Blocker when they analyzed their study of 300 individuals from Tulsa, Oklahoma. In contrast to the study, documents from the politically conservative evangelical community throughout the 1970s and 1980s shows that anti-environmentalism was not this group's mainstream and accepted position.

11. This statement is not to suggest that the group's pro-life stance was taken without discussion. The pastor of the First Baptist Church of Dallas, W. A. Criswell, for example, initially voiced support for abortion, but then reversed his view.

12. Brian McCammack, "Hot Damned America: Evangelicalism and the Climate Change Policy Debate," *American Quarterly*, 59, no. 3 (September 2007), 664; quoted from Mark A. Noll, *The Scandal of the Evangelical Mind* (Grand Rapids, MI: William B. Eerdmans, 1994), 8.

13. Michael J. McVicar, *Christian Reconstruction: R.J. Rushdoony and American Religious Conservatism* (Chapel Hill: The University of North Carolina Press, 2016), 112.

14. Think tanks will be defined as organizations that produce research to support certain conclusions. Private advocacy groups, on the other hand, are slightly more informal and largely disseminate information that would be considered opinion pieces.

15. Jerry Falwell, Old Time Gospel Hour #627, "A Biblical Perspective on Church/State Relations," 16, Falwell Ministries 3–4—Series Folder, Old-Time Gospel Hour Series 5 Unit, Liberty University Archives and Special Collections, Liberty University, Lynchburg, VA (hereafter LUASC).

16. Judith Vecchione, "Awakenings," *Eyes on the Prize* interview of Amzie Moore, Public Broadcasting Station, 1986.

17. CBS News, "CBS Reports: The Homosexuals," 1967, in CBS Evening News, "Evolution of gay rights from 1967 to today," 2015, YouTube, https://www.youtube.com/watch?v=NY7Lh8cD2e8.

18. Eric Marcus, *Making Gay History: The Half-Century Fight for Lesbian and Gay Equal Rights* (New York: Perennial, 2002), 121.

19. "Most Powerful Protest Song Ever, 'Eve of Destruction' by Barry McGuire to Be Performed at Fundraising Library Concert on Sept. 1" by Steve Fieldsted, City of South Pasadena, https://www.southpasadenaca.gov/Home/Components/News/News/707/714?arch=1&npage=21.

20. John Warchol, e-mail to author, August 12, 2019.

21. Robert Rudd, "Pesticides and the Living Landscape," in *DDT, Silent Spring and the Rise of Environmentalism*, ed. Thomas R. Dunlap (Seattle: University of Washington Press, 2008), 78.

22. Little exists in the Liberty University archives dating before the early 1970s. Thus it is difficult to validate Falwell's claim that before 1973 he did not think Christians should get involved in politics. However, after *Roe v. Wade* Falwell began actively building the foundations that led to the religious right and the attempt to realize America as a Christian nation. Jerry Falwell, *Falwell: An Autobiography* (Lynchburg, VA: Liberty House, 1997), 362–365, 368.

23. Asset ID: 223671, Tape No: F1-LHF-026.mov, Tape Name: LBC Graduation 1983–James Watt Line (Reel 2 of 2), Rec Date: 05-09-1983, Tape Series, LU Historical Footage, Liberty University Communication Department.

24. Kellstedt et al., "Has Godot Finally Arrived? Religion and Realignment." *Public Perspective* 6 (1995): 18–22.

25. Matthew J. Wilson, *From Pews to Polling Places: Faith and Politics in the American Religious Mosaic* (Washington, DC: Georgetown University Press, 2007), 17.

26. Mark J. Rozell and Gleaves Whitney, eds. *Religion and Bush Presidency* (New York: Palgrave Macmillan, 2007), 17.

27. David E. Campbell, ed. *A Matter of Faith: Religion in the 2004 Presidential Election* (Washington, DC: Brookings Institution Press, 2007), 5.

28. "Jerry Falwell Jr. Asked to Lead Trump Higher Education Task Force," NBC News, January 31, 2017, http://www.nbcnews.com/news/us-news/jerry-falwell-jr-asked-lead-trump-education-task-force-n715116.)

29. Tom Gjelten, "2020 Faith Vote Reflects 2016 Patterns," National Public Radio, November 8, 2020, https://www.npr.org/2020/11/08/932263516/2020-faith-vote-reflects-2016-patterns.

30. Jessica Martínez and Gregory A. Smith, "How the Faithful Voted: A Preliminary 2016 Analysis," Pew Research Center, November 9, 2016, http://www.pewresearch.org/fact-tank/2016/11/09/how-the-faithful-voted-a-preliminary-2016-analysis/.

31. Putnam, *Bowling Alone*, 72.

32. Putnam, *Bowling Alone*, 76.

33. Putnam, *Bowling Alone*, 162.

34. Leege and Kellstedt, *Rediscovering the Religious Factor in American Politics*, 126.

1. Conservative Evangelicals Respond to the Founding of Earth Day

1. White, "The Historical Roots of Our Ecologic Crisis," 1205.

2. Francis Schaeffer firmly believed in the inerrancy of the Bible, which allowed him to mesh with fundamentalists theologically. However, he enjoyed associating with anyone to discuss God and therefore could also be understood as an evangelical. Nevertheless, the very important works he produced, such as *How Should We Then Live*, were thoroughly embraced by politically conservative evangelicals. Falwell, for example, highly respected Schaeffer's work and felt it articulated and supported the philosophies of the Moral Majority.

3. Jean to Jim Nyquist, June 28, 1976, Francis and Edith Schaeffer Papers, Schaeffer/Tapes/Miscellaneous (part 4 of 5—Correspondence, 1972–1986, box 3, folder 11), Archives of Wheaton College (hereafter AWC).

4. Francis Schaeffer, "The Christian and Nature," St. Louis 1968, 22, Book on Ecology, ed. David Winter, manuscript with editions, Francis and Edith Schaeffer Papers, box 1, folder 6, AWC.

5. Francis Schaeffer, lecture given in April 1968, 46–47, Book on Ecology, ed. David Winter, "The Christian Ecology" April 1968, manuscript with editions, Francis and Edith Schaeffer Papers, box 1, folder 5, AWC.

6. Francis Schaeffer, "The Christian and Nature," 3, Book on Ecology, ed. David Winter, manuscript with editions,. Francis and Edith Schaeffer Papers, box 1, folder 6, AWC.

7. Schaeffer, *Pollution and the Death of Man*, 54.

8. Schaeffer, *Pollution and the Death of Man*, 82.

9. Schaeffer, *Pollution and the Death of Man*, 87.

10. Schaeffer, *Pollution and the Death of Man*, 88.

11. In Schaeffer's other books, such as *Escape from Reason*, nature makes an appearance in his diagrams and explanations of the proper God-human or supernatural-natural relationship. It once again appeared in his very popular book and film documentary *How Should We Then Live*, released in the later 1970s. But again, in these publications the natural world only merited a mention.

12. *Eternity* and *Christianity Today* represent the most popular of these magazines. McVicar writes of the latter publication, "No single national Christian publication was more prominent in the mid-twentieth-century struggle to create a coalition of theologically conservative, socially aware Protestants than *Christianity Today*." He goes on to cite

George Marsden by writing, "Billy Graham and a group of financial supporters founded the magazine in 1956 to 'plant the evangelical flag in the middle of the road, taking a conservative theological position but a definite liberal approach to social problems. It would combine the best in liberalism and the best in fundamentalism without compromising theologically'" *Christian Reconstruction*, 111. In contrast to this statement regarding *Christianity Today's* "liberal approach," it must be noted that politically conservative positions were not absent from its pages especially since its editor for much of the 1970s was Harold Lindsell. Lindsell was not only theologically conservative as demonstrated in George Marsden's *Reforming Fundamentalism: Fuller Seminary and New Evangelicalism* (1987), but proved politically conservative as well. During the 1970s, as will be shown, *Christianity Today* spoke out against abortion and homosexuality and during the late 1970s Lindsell began researching for his politically conservative book *Free Enterprise: A Judeo-Christian Defense*, published in 1982. Furthermore, the publications, *Moody Monthly* and *Evangelical Action* communicated a more politically conservative stance than *Christianity Today* or *Eternity* and yet they initially featured eco-friendly articles. Some examples include Fred P. Thompson, Jr., "Culture in Crisis," *United Evangelical Action* 29, no. 4 (Winter 1970); Harold Lindsell, "Suicide Ahead?," *United Evangelical Action* 29, no. 1 (1970): 13–17; James Hefley, "Christians and the Pollution Crisis" *Moody Monthly* 71, no. 9 (1970): 21.

13. Ron Widman, "When You've Seen One Beer Can You've Seen Them All," *Eternity* 21, no. 5 (May 1970): 16.

14. Widman, "When You've Seen One Beer Can," 16.

15. Widman, "When You've Seen One Beer Can," 29.

16. The *Hour of Decision* was a thirty-minute Christian radio show begun in 1950 by Billy Graham. Since 1934, the Federal Communications Commission (FCC) had asked radio stations to set aside a few hours each week for public service broadcasting, and many pastors took advantage of this free radio time to put their sermons on the radio.

17. Leighton Ford, "Good Earth or Polluted Planet?" *Hour of Decision*, April 26, 1970 (audiocassette), Billy Graham Evangelistic Association: Records of the Hour of Decision Radio Program, Collection 191, T1059a, b, Wheaton College Billy Graham Center Archives (hereafter WCBGCA). In 2019 the Billy Gram Evangelistic Association moved this collection to their headquarters in Charlotte, NC.

18. Ford, "Good Earth."

19. Ford, "Good Earth."

20. Ford, "Good Earth."

21. Editorial, "The Defilement of the Earth," *Decision*, September 1970. From Sherwood Eliot Wirt, *The Social Conscience of the Evangelical* (New York: Harper & Row, 1968).

22. Adam Rome, *The Genius of Earth Day: How a 1970 Teach-In Unexpectedly Made the First Green Generation* (New York: Hill and Wang, 2013), 56.

23. Garrett Hardin, "The Tragedy of the Commons," in De Bell, *The Environmental Handbook*, 42. The pressure of zero population growth angered some conservative Christians who believed that people have a right to choose how many children they want.

24. Hardin, "The Tragedy of the Commons," 49.

25. Keith Murray, "Suggestions Toward an Ecological Platform," in De Bell, *The Environmental Handbook*, 318.

26. Murray, "Suggestions Toward an Ecological Platform," 331.

27. Marsden, *Reforming Fundamentalism*, 260. Marsden also writes that in response to the national cultural revolution of the 1960s, especially over Vietnam, evangelicals became split. He cites Lindsell as supporting the conservatives. "Conservatives, such as Lindsell, now fused militancy on both cultural and biblical questions."

28. Harold Lindsell, "Suicide Ahead?," *United Evangelical Action* 29, no. 1 (1970): 14.

29. "Ecologism: A New Paganism," *Christianity Today*, April 10, 1970, 33.

30. "Ecologism," 34.

31. Harold Lindsell, "De-Polluting Ecology Theology," *Christianity Today*, May 8, 1970, 26.

32. James M. Houston, "The Environmental Movement: Five Causes of Confusion," *Christianity Today*, September 15, 1972, 8–10.

33. "The New Pantheism," *Eternity*, June 1970, 11; Fred P. Thomson, untitled editorial, *United Evangelical Action*, Fall 1970, 35.

34. "In the *Saturday Review* of December 2, 1967, Richard L. Means, who is associate professor of sociology at the College of Kalamazoo, Michigan, quoted White and extended White's concept and asked: 'Why not begin to find a solution to this [the ecological crisis] in the direction of Pantheism?'"(Schaeffer, *Pollution and the Death of Man*, 14).

35. Carl McIntire, "Ecology Anti-Christian," *Christian Beacon*, June 17, 1971, 1–2.

36. Kenneth Hayes, "Baptist Leaders Speak Out on Pollution Problems," *California Southern Baptist*, January 7, 1971, 9.

37. Dan L. Thrapp, "Christian Leaders Join Ecology Drive," *L.A. Times*, April 20, 1970, D12.

38. Arthur Everett, "Earth Day Sweeps County: Students, and Aged Join in Demonstration," *Dallas Morning News*, April 23, 1970, 1.

39. The Associated Press, "Students in Texas to Note 'Earth Day,'" *Dallas Morning News*, April 14, 1970, 13.

40. Walter B. Moore, "Harris County's Cleanup," *Dallas Morning News*, January 14, 1971.

41. "Another TACT Finalist: Youth Lives Busy, Useful Life," *Dallas Morning News*, April 3, 1971, 14A.

42. "Wheeler Opposes Tax Hikes," *Dallas Morning News*, April 22, 1972, 11A.

43. Sam Kinch Jr., "Steelman Doesn't Look Republican," *Dallas Morning News*, October 24, 1976, 12A.

44. Billy Graham, "The Generation Gap." Billy Graham, as heard on the *Hour of Decision*, 1972, loose pamphlets, WCBGCA.

45. Richard Nixon, "The Energy Emergency," in Merrill, *The Oil Crisis of 1973–1974*, 66–71.

46. John Shanks, "Responses of First Baptist Church of Dallas, Texas," in The Energy Crisis and the Churches: Proceedings of a Consultation, Sponsored by The Christian Life Commission of the Southern Baptist Convention, Nashville, Tennessee, August 22–23, 1977, 20, Inventory of Christian Life Commission Resources Files AR 138-2, box 63, folder 1 Energy, 1983, Southern Baptist Historical Library & Archives (Hereafter SBHLA).

47. "Energy Crisis: Bleakness or Blessing? *Christianity Today*, December 21, 1973, 33, 34.

48. Harold Lindsell, "Waste as a Wrong," *Christianity Today* 19, April 11, 1975, 26.

49. Richard Nixon, "Address to the Nation About Policies to Deal With the Energy Shortages," November 7, 1973, https://energyhistory.yale.edu/library-item/richard-nixon-address-nation-about-policies-deal-energy-shortages-november-7-1973.

50. Addison H. Leitch, "Without Natural Affection," *Christianity Today*, May 11, 1973, 50.

51. "Energy Crisis: Bleakness or Blessing? *Christianity Today*, December 21, 1973, 34.

52. Lindsell, "Waste as a Wrong," 26.

53. Lydia Saad, "Americans Believe Religion Is Losing Clout," Gallup, December 23, 2008, http://www.gallup.com/poll/113533/Americans-Believe-Religion-Losing-Clout.aspx.

54. As David Larsen notes in his dissertation, "God's Gardeners: American Protestant Evangelicals Confront Environmentalism 1967–2000" under the subsection "The Failure to 'Take the Lead,'" articles continued to be published, although in smaller numbers throughout the 1970s. The authors continued promoting action and questioned why little to nothing was being done to save God's Earth.

2. Humanity's Proper Place between God and Nature

1. Ann Vileisis, *Kitchen Literacy: How We Lost Knowledge of Where Food Comes From and Why We Need to Get It Back* (Washington DC: Island Press/Shearwater Books, 2006), 209.

2. "In a moment, in the twinkling of an eye, at the last trump: for the trumpet shall sound, and the dead shall be raised incorruptible, and we shall be changed. (1 Corinthians 15:52, King James Version).

3. The term "fundamentalist" is used here because it was not until around the 1940s that the modern definition of evangelical evolved into existence. As stated in the introduction, both evangelicals and fundamentalists share basic theology, but at this point, fundamentalists decided they wanted to remain separate, while evangelicals followed leaders such as Billy Graham who wanted to connect with others religiously as well as on social issues.

4. Matthew Sutton writes that Los Angeles pastor and fundamentalist leader Louis Bauman "boasted that he had first identified Mussolini in 1922 as the problem Antichrist. A few years later he warned, 'if Mussolini does not prove to be Antichrist he is certainly a magnificent fore-shadow of Antichrist!'" (*American Apocalypse*, 213, 214).

5. Lindsey and Carlson, *The Late Great Planet Earth*, front cover of the 1981 eighty-seventh printing.

6. Lindsey and Carlson, *The Late Great Planet Earth*, 93, 146–47, 169.

7. Lindsey and Carlson, *The Late Great Planet Earth*, 179.

8. Lindsey and Carlson, *The Late Great Planet Earth*, 188.

9. Rushdoony, *The Institutes of Biblical Law*, 448.

10. Jerry Falwell, "Characteristics of a Christian Home," August 29, 1976, 2, Falwell Ministries, record group 3: Old-Time Gospel Hour, sub-group 4, series 3: OTGH Transcripts 200s, unit 1: OTGH #204, LUASC.

11. Falwell, "Characteristics," 12.

12. Jerry Falwell, "Strengthening Families in the Nation," speech delivered at the Christian Life Commission in Atlanta, 1982, 3, Falwell Family Papers, record group 4, Speeches and Sermons, FAL 4:1–3 box 1, sub-group 1: Speeches, series 1: 1980s, unit 1, LUA.

13. Jerry Falwell, "Learning to Do The Right Things," August 15, 1976, 9 and 10, FM, record group 3: Old-Time Gospel Hour, sub-group 4, box 1, series 3, unit 1: OTGH #202, LUA.

14. Jerry Falwell, "Battle Hymn of the Republic," September 21, 1980, 17, FM, record group 3: Old-Time Gospel Hour, sub-group 4, box 2, series 5: OTGH Transcripts 400s, unit 2: OTGH #418: 17, LUA.

15. Phyllis Schlafly, untitled, 1980, 11, FM, record group 3: Old-Time Gospel Hour, sub-group 4, series 4, box 2, unit 6: OTGH 370–379, OTGH #377, LUA.

16. Mona Charen, "The Feminist Mistake," *Christian Activist*, Summer 1984, 20, Francis and Edith Schaeffer Papers, 1968–1999, series 3: Frankie Schaeffer, sub-series 5: Secondary, box 5, folder 3: The Christian Activist, Buswell Library Special Collections, Wheaton College, Wheaton, Illinois (hereafter BLSC).

17. Mary Pride, "The Way Home Part 2: Beyond Feminism, Divorce, and Selfishness: Back to Marriage," *Christian Activist* 1, no. 4 (1985): 30, Francis and Edith Schaeffer Papers, 1968–1999, series 3: Frankie Schaeffer, sub-series 5: Secondary, box 5, folder 3: The Christian Activist, WCA.

18. Jerry Falwell, "Let's Rise Up and Build (Easter Sunrise Service on the Mountain)," March 23, 1977, 3–4, FM, record group 3: Old-Time Gospel Hour, sub-group 4, series 3: OTGH Transcripts 200, unit 4: OTGH #234, LUA.

19. Jerry Falwell, untitled sermon, June 1, 1977, 16, FM, record group 3: Old-Time Gospel Hour, sub-group 4, box 8, series 10: Mid-Week (MW) Transcripts, unit 1, 102: 16, LUA.

20. Falwell, "Strengthening Families in the Nation," 3.

21. Schaeffer was aware that Jefferson was not a traditional Christian. However, Schaeffer still felt Jefferson's ideas were molded by the Christian culture that surrounded him.

22. Francis Schaeffer to James Sires, August 22, 1977, Francis and Edith Schaeffer Papers, 1968–1999, sub-series 5: Secondary, box 3, folder 11, WCA.

23. Franky Schaeffer, *Crazy for God* (Cambridge, MA: Da Capo Press, 2007), 260.

24. Franky Schaeffer writes in his biography *Crazy For God* that after the publication of *How Should We Then Live*, he and his father traveled a lecture circuit speaking to conservative Protestant audiences and showing the film. Overall Franky speculates they presented the film to forty thousand people (269).

25. Jerry Falwell, untitled sermon, 3 and 4, Falwell Ministries, record group 3: sub-group 4, box 5, unit 17: 490–494, OTGH Transcripts #491, LUA.

26. Jerry Falwell, "The Law of Sowing and Reaping," 21, Falwell Ministries, record group 3, Old-Time Gospel Hour, sub-group 4, box: 6, unit 11, OTGH 561, LUA.

27. Adrian Rogers, "The God of Creation," 5, Adrian Rogers Legacy Library.

28. *How Should We Then Live?*, directed by John Gonser and Mel White, FilmRise, 1977, episode 10.

29. Jerry Falwell, "An Agenda for the '80's," December 29, 1980, Fal 4-3, series 1, folder 1, Dr. Falwell's Notes for Speaking with Ronald Reagan, 1980, LUA.

30. Harold Lindsell, "Suicide Ahead?," *Evangelical Action* 29, no. 1 (1970): 13–14.

31. Lindsell, "Suicide Ahead?," 14.

32. Pat Robertson, *Pat Robertson's Perspective*, May 1981, 7, Christian Broadcasting Network Info File, Pat's Perspective 1977–1982, 1 of 2, Regent University Library, Special Collections & Archives (hereafter RULSCA).

33. Robertson, *Pat Robertson's Perspective*, Fall 1981, 5.

34. Robertson, *Pat Robertson's Perspective*, Fall 1981, 5.

35. Robertson, *Pat Robertson's Perspective*, November–December 1990, 8.

36. Guest Pastor Jerry Johnson, untitled sermon. 11, record group 3: Old-Time Gospel Hour, sub-group 4, box 5, series 6: OTGH Transcripts 500s, unit 5, 520, LUA.

37. Jerry Falwell, "America Back to God," 10, Falwell Family Papers, record group 4: Jerry Falwell Sr. Speeches and Sermons, sub-group 2, series 1, folder 1, LUA. Although no date accompanies this sermon, Falwell discusses the bicentennial and the upcoming election. Thus, it was likely delivered in 1976.

38. Jerry Falwell, "I am Not Ashamed of the Gospel of Christ—Romans 1," Rec Date: 08-19-1979, 11:30:26:21, asset ID: 254560, tape no: FB-POT-0362.mov, tape series: Old Time Gospel Hour, Communications Department, Liberty University.

39. Rushdoony, *The Institutes of Biblical Law: Law and Society*, 274.

40. Rushdoony, *Institutes of Biblical Law: Law and Society*, 274.

3. Nature in a Religious Right Perspective

1. Although calls for environmental action indeed disappeared from the pages of magazines such as *Christianity Today*, the message remained in the conservative evangelical community. It continued, however, in rhetoric only and on a philosophical level. In short, conservative evangelicals throughout the 1970s maintained eco-friendly philosophies, but the topic did not have the energy it held before, during, and after Earth Day 1970. Nevertheless, as will be demonstrated, it was prevalent.

2. Thomas Road Baptist Church services were recorded live and televised in the United States and Canada at a later date. The television program was called *The Old Time Gospel Hour*—a slight change from the older Charles Fuller show titled *The Old Fashioned Revival Hour*, a radio show that Falwell listened to as a child and that led him to become a pastor.

3. Lynchburg Baptist College changed its name in 1976 to Liberty Baptist College. "These other schools" refers to the k–12 Christian schools that operated in association with Thomas Road Baptist Church.

4. It should be noted that Falwell was not a "Bible thumper" who typically shouted during sermons. While delivering this message, he was calm, collected, and communicated with a comforting and friendly demeanor. At the same time however, it was clear he was speaking passionately about a serious issue.

5. Jerry Falwell, "America Must Come Back to God," April 4, 1975, Falwell Ministries, record group 3: Old-Time Gospel Hour # 133, sub-group 4, unit 2, box 1, CAS 1:1, Liberty University Archive (hereafter LUA).

6. Paul F. Parsons, *Inside America's Christian Schools* (Macon, GA: Mercer University Press, 1987), x, quoted in Adam Laats, "Forging a Fundamentalist 'One Best System': Struggles Over Curriculum and Educaitonal Philosophy for Christian Day Schools, 1970–1989," *History of Education Quarterly* 50, no. 1 (2010): 57.

7. Rose. *Keeping Them Out of the Hands of Satan*, 34–36.

8. Laats, "Forging a Fundamentalist," 83.

9. Laats, "Forging a Fundamentalist," 67.

10. Laats, "Forging a Fundamentalist," 67–68. BJU Press released some material in the 1970s similar to A Beka Book, such as reprints of older stories. However, its impact on Christian nationalism largely came in the 1980s with fresh material, which will be discussed in chapter 4. Their first history textbook, for example, was published in 1981. The third major Christian publisher since the early 1970s is Accelerated Christian Education (ACE). This publisher produces material primarily for homeschool students who lack a trained instructor. Finding ACE's surviving older products has proven extremely difficult owing to the fact they were published in paperback spiral ring binders and many were intended for use as workbooks. Nevertheless, messages regarding the environment from A Beka Book and BJU Press did not conflict throughout the 1970s to the present, which strongly suggests ACE was in agreement on the issue as well. The information provided in these textbooks was intended to be accepted truths and not conflict with the views of those who purchased the material including religious leaders, educators, and parents.

11. Using older textbooks that complemented the Christian view for understanding the world were commonly used during the early years of the Christian school movement. See Laats, "Forging a Fundamentalist," 68.

12. Much of the Christian educational material used in this chapter was found in a former Christian school by the author. The school was run by a conservative evangelical church and operated between 1975 and 1987. Upon closing, the classrooms were subsequently used for vacation Bible school and Sunday school classes. The bookshelves, however, remained untouched, making them virtual time capsules. The books were issued to the students in the late 1970s and early 1980s. This school's educational material is not unique. A Beka Books and BJU Press were two of the most popular Christian school publishing companies in the United States. Beyond the educational material found at this school, the author located all other Christian school editions and titles, which span from the early 1970s to the 2000s, in piecemeal fashion.

13. "The years following World War II saw the kind of rapid industrialization and urbanization other regions had experienced earlier. In the 1940s, the South was nearly two-thirds rural; by 1960, that percentage had dropped to under fifty. In the 1940s, one third of the South's workers were in agricultural occupations; by 1960, only 10 percent worked on farms" (Ammerman, *Baptist Battles*, 54). Religious historian Darren Dochuck cited a similar statistic: "Between the late 1930s and late 1960s, . . . over six million southerners relocated from the South's small towns and farms to industrial centers like Detroit and Los Angeles. . . . By 1970 11 million southerners—7.5 million whites, 3.5 million blacks—lived outside their home states" (*From Bible Belt to Sun Belt*, xv).

14. Beverly Rainey, ed., *OF AMERICA Vol. II* (Pensacola, FL: A Beka Books Publications, 1975), first page before the table of contents.

15. Felicia Hemans, "The Landing of the Pilgrim Fathers," in Rainey, *OF AMERICA Vol. II*, 63.

16. Caroline Sherwin Bailey, "The First Fight," in *Flags Unfurled*, ed. Laurel Hicks (Pensacola, FL: A Beka Book Publications, 1974), 36.

17. Alberta Walking and Mary R. Parkman, "Pioneers," in Hicks, *Flags Unfurled*, 58–63.

18. Rainey, *OF AMERICA Vol. II*, front cover.

19. Hicks, *Flags Unfurled*, front cover.

20. Laurel Hicks, ed., *Liberty Tree* (Pensacola, FL: A Beka Book, 1974), front cover.

21. McVicar, *Christian Reconstruction*, 133.

22. Walking and Parkman, "Pioneers," 58, 59.

23. Margaret Rhodes Peattie, "Dangers of Pioneer Life," in Hicks, *Flags Unfurled*, 74, 75.

24. Bob Jones University Press INC. Textbooks for Christian Schools, 1978. Promotional emailed to author from The Archives Research Center at Bob Jones University, Mack Library, Bob Jones University, Greenville, SC.

25. Burton Egbert Stevenson, *American History in Verse* (Greenville, SC: BJU Press, 1975), v.

26. Stevenson, *American History in Verse*.

27. In the 1922 version by Stevenson, this remark preceeded William Bradford's "New England's Growth." The BJU Press editors took this preface and placed it in front of Howe's poem and added the comment about the wilderness.

28. Peter Marshall and David Manuel, *The Light And the Glory: Did God Have a Plan for America?* (Grand Rapids, MI: Fleming H. Revell, 1977), 13–15.

29. Marshall, *The Light and Glory*, 153.

30. Marshall, *The Light and Glory*, 134.

31. Jerry Falwell, "Back to School Special," 1979, 17–21, Falwell Ministries, record group 3: Old-Time Gospel Hour, sub-group 4, box 2, unit 5: OTGH #360, LUA.

32. Anonymous. 1974. The Proud Oak Tree. In *Footprints*, ed. Laurel Hicks, 61–62. Pensacola, FL: A Beka Book.; An Aesop Fable. 1974. The Fly and the Moth. In *Footprints*, ed. Laurel Hicks, 62–63. Pensacola, FL: A Beka Book; Hans Christian Andersen. 1974. The Flax. In *Footprints*, ed. Laurel Hicks, 64–66. Pensacola, FL: A Beka Book; Gertrude E. McVenn. 1974. Catching the Colt. In *Footprints*, ed. Laurel Hicks, 78–79. Pensacola, FL: A Beka Book.

33. Billy Graham, "Our Bicentennial: America at the Crossroads," *Hour of Decision* (Minneapolis, MN: Billy Graham Evangelistic Association, 1976), 5–13; *Hour of Decision* Tracts, Wheaton College Billy Graham Center Archives, Wheaton, IL.

34. Although the environmental movement experienced criticism in the past, Cronon's "The Trouble with Wilderness; or Getting Back to the Wrong Nature" was the first academic challenge to the traditional understanding of environmentalist wilderness preservation efforts. Wilderness supporters initially criticized the essay, but it soon became an important work that impacted the environmental movement and how environmental historians approached their work. "The Trouble with Wilderness" directly challenged the popular environmentalist view that wilderness should be devoid of humans and staunchly protected in contrast to "developed" areas. The essay, however, did not "fix" the environmental movement, but forced people to at least rethink how they understood the relationship between humanity and nature. The essay is also a featured chapter in Cronon's edited volume *Uncommon Ground: Rethinking the Human Place in Nature*.

35. This idea led to environmental historian Thomas Dunlap's *Faith and Nature*.

36. "For many Americans wilderness stands as the last remaining place where civilization, that all too human disease, has not fully infected the earth" William Cronon, "The Trouble with Wilderness; or, Getting Back to the Wrong Nature," in William Cronon, ed., *Uncommon Ground: Rethinking the Human Place in Nature* (New York: W. W.

Norton &Co., 1995), 69–90. Cronon furthermore uses Earth First! cofounder Dave Foreman as evidence that some environmentalists understand humanity as a disease or the destroyer of wilderness. For more see Dave Foreman's *Confessions of an Eco-Warrior* (New York: Crown, 1991).

37. William Cronon, "The Trouble with Wilderness; or, Getting Back to the Wrong Nature" in William Cronon, ed., *Uncommon Ground: Rethinking the Human Place in Nature* (New York: W. W. Norton &Co., 1995), 69 http://www.williamcronon.net/writing/Cronon_Trouble_with_Wilderness_1995.pdf.

38. Emmett L. Williams and George Mulfinger, *Physical Science for Christian Schools* (Greenville, SC: Bob Jones University Press, 1974), 294.

39. Williams and Mulfinger, *Physical Science for Christian Schools*, 295.

40. This example, at least in spirit, is supported by William Cronon in his book *Changes In the Land*. Cronon wrote that Native Americans in New England cleared land through controlled burning, which sometimes could get out of control and have "deleterious effects for trees and Indians alike. *Changes in the Land*, 13.

41. Williams and Mulfinger, *Physical Science for Christian Schools*, 299.

42. Williams and Mulfinger, *Physical Science for Christian Schools*, 308.

43. John Burroughs, "The Bluebird" in *Liberty Tree,* ed. Laura Hicks (Pensacola, FL: A Beka Books, 1974), 52.

44. Judy Hull Moore and Stan Shimmin, *Exploring God's World*, Laurel Hicks, ed. (Pensacola, FL: A Beka Books, 1976), 122, 123.

45. Judy Hull and Stan Shimmin, Enjoying God's World, (Pensacola, FL: A Beka Book): 122: "The Bible says, 'he hath made everything beautiful and in his time' Ecclesiastes 3:11." A short chapter followed describing how the food chain and ecosystem function.

46. Henry M. Morris, "Creation and the Environment," *ICR Impact Series* no. 13 (April 1974), I, box 62–3, HH 1079, 76.62, Hall-Hoag Collection, Brown University Library Special Collections Department Manuscripts Division (hereafter BUL).

47. Morris, "Creation and Environment," ii.

48. Morris, "Creation and Environment," iii. Additionally he wrote that in large quantities, these pollutants are too much for the environment and "initiate various abnormal reactions which accelerate and accentuate environmental decay."

49. Henry M. Morris, "Evolution and the Population Problem," *ICR Impact Series* no. 25 (December 1974), 2, HH1079, 76.62, Hall-Hoag Collection, BUL.

50. Mark 12:41–43 (King James version).

4. The Moral Majority Finds Favor in the Republican Party

1. Ronald Reagan, Republican National Convention Acceptance Speech, July 7, 1980, Ronald Reagan Presidential Library & Museum, https://www.reaganlibrary.gov/7-17-80.

2. The Sunday School Board was founded in 1891 and now operates under the name of LifeWay.

3. Jerry A. Privette, "Resource Conservation in Southern Baptist Churches," 28, Inventory of the Christian Life Commission Resource Files, AR 138-2, box 48, folder 1 Energy: 1978–1979, Southern Baptist Historical Library & Archives (hereafter SBHLA).

4. Privette, "Resource Conservation in Southen Baptist Churches," 26.

5. Privette, "Resource Conservation in Southen Baptist Churches," 29.

6. Mike Bush, "Energy Crisis/Cost Prompts Varied Response," *Baptist Standard*, 1977, 3, Inventory of the Christian Life Commission Resource Files, AR 138-2, box 48, folder 10 Energy Crisis, SBCLA.

7. Jim Lowry, "Conservation: Serious Business for North Carolina Baptists," August 8, 1979. *Baptist Press*, August, 8, 1979, 2, Inventory of the Christian Life Commission Resource Files, AR 138-2, box 48, folder 1 Energy: 1978–1979, SBCLA.

8. W. A. Criswell to church members, April 21, 1977, Poster/mailing, "What have we paid for Utilities in 1972 thru 1976?," Inventory of Christian Life Commission Resources Files, AR 138-2, box 48, folder 4 Energy: 1982, SBHLA.

9. John Starks, "Responses of First Baptist Church of Dallas, Texas," in *The Energy Crisis and the Churches: Proceedings of a Consultation*, sponsored by the Christian Life Commission of the Southern Baptist Convention, 20, Inventory of Christian Life Commission Resources Files, AR 138-2, box 63, folder 1 Energy, 1983, SBHLA.

10. Cecil A. Ray, "What Baptist Churches Can Do," in *The Energy Crisis and the Churches*.

11. Gilbert Turner, "Responses of a Baptist Businessman," in *The Energy Crisis and the Churches: Proceedings of a Consultation*.

12. Pat Robertson, *Pat Robertson's Perspective*, May 1977, 2. CBN Info File, Pat's Perspective 1977–1982, 1 of 2, Regent University Library Special Collections & Archives (hereafter RULSPCA).

13. Robertson, *Pat Robertson's Perspective*, May 1977, 3.

14. These conclusions regarding Robertson's conservation views are additionally found in an article by this author dedicated specifically to Pat Robertson's environmental rhetoric. See Neall Pogue, "The Religious Right's Compassionate Steward and Conservationist: The Lost Environmental Philosophies of Pat Robertson, 1977–1989," *Environmental Ethics* 38, no. 4 (2016): 483–97.

15. *America's Future* 21, no. 8, April 20, 1979. 1, Harold Lindsell, CN 192, box 1, folder: America's Future, 1978–1981, Archives of Wheaton College (hereafter AWC).

16. *America's Future* 21, no. 10, May 18, 1979, 1, Harold Lindsell, CN 192, box 1, folder: America's Future, 1978–1981, WCA.

17. *America's Future* 21 no. 25 December 1979, 3, Harold Lindsell, CN 192, box 1, folder: America's Future, 1978–1981, WCA.

18. *America's Future* 22 no. 20, October 17, 1980, 6, book review of *Power Grab: The Conserver Cult and the Coming Energy Catastrophe* by James A. Weber, Harold Lindsell, CN 192, box 1, folder: America's Future, 1978–1981, WCA.

19. *America's Future*, 6.

20. Harold Lindsell, "The Lord's Day and Natural Resources," *Christianity Today* 20, no 16 (1976): 816–20.

21. The Lindsell collection at Wheaton College, Illinois, does not offer much more in the way of what other elements affected Lindsell's position toward nature. Lindsell felt his opinion on current matters was important and thought himself somewhat of an intellectual elite. For example, he felt the need to sway the conservative Protestant conversation regarding the topic of the infallibility of the Bible and wrote *The Battle for the Bible* in 1976. During the same year, he joined a social organization that allowed

him to converse with other well-to-do and highly educated Americans by purchasing membership to the Cosmo Club in Washington, DC.

22. Harold Lindsell to the Library of Congress, February 16, 1980, attached: reply from the Library of Congress, Harold Lindsell, SC 192, box 2. folder: A Christian Defense for Free Enterprise Correspondence and First Draft, 1980, WCA.

23. David T. Beito and Marcus M. Witcher, "New Deal Witch Hunt: The Buchanan Committee Investigation of the Committee for Constitutional Government," *Independent Review* 21, no. 1 (2016): 47–71.

24. Harold Lindsell, *Free Enterprise: A Judeo-Christian Defense* (Wheaton, IL: Tyndale House, 1982), 9.

25. Lindsell, *Free Enterprise*, 70–72.

26. Ed McAteer was a devout evangelical and member of Bellevue Baptist Church where Adrian Rogers preached. He represents members of the conservative Protestant community who were not leaders at the pulpit, but took it upon themselves to get involved in the religious right.

27. Howard Phillips to Jerry Falwell, February 27, 1979, Paul M. Weyrich, collection number 10138, box 15, folder 20: Christians in Politics 1978–1979, American Heritage Center, University of Wyoming (hereafter AHC).

28. Allan J. Mayer, John J. Lindsay, Howard Fineman, Stryker McGuire, Jonathan Kirsch, and Michael Reese, "A Tide of Born-Again Politics," *Newsweek*, September 15, 1980, 28–32, 36.

29. Helen Parmley and Sam Attlesey, "Crusade Defends Holy Land," *Dallas Morning News*, August 24, 1980, 35A. Marley, however, lists the number at 2,000. David John Marley, *Pat Robertson: An American Life* (New York: Rowman & Littlefield, 2007), 68.

30. Pat Robertson, "National Affairs Speech," National Affairs Briefing, Dallas, TX, 22, August 1980, author's personal collection.

31. Rushdoony, *Law and Society*, 311.

32. Rushdoony, *Law and Society*, 322.

33. Rushdoony, *Law and Society*, 312, 313.

34. Martin, *With God on Our Side*, 217.

35. Reagan, Republican National Convention Acceptance Speech.

36. Pat Robertson, *Pat Robertson's Perspective*, June/July 1980, 2, CBN Info File, Pat's Perspective 1977–1982, 1 of 2, RULSPCA.

37. Robertson, "Prayer Calendar Partners," *The Flame*, September 1980 (?), Flame (Fall 1973–1981), RULSPCA.

38. Lindsey Williams, *There Is No True Energy Crisis: An Eye-Witness Account Report by* (1980), 3, pamphlet private collection.

39. Williams, *There Is No True Energy Crisis*, 5, 6.

40. Williams, *There Is No True Energy Crisis*, 17.

41. Williams, *There Is No True Energy Crisis*, 18.

42. Williams, *There Is No True Energy Crisis*, 30.

43. "Ferne" is a pseudonym given to a woman who donated a collection of her reading material to a fundamentalist Baptist church in western Massachusetts. This church is also where the author collected a variety of educational material left over from the church's Christian school, which operated during the 1970s and 1980s. Ferne's collection consisted of two boxes of loose books dating principally from 1978 to the early 1990s.

44. Greg Laurie, *Occupy till I Come: How to Spiritually Survive the Last Days* (Eugene, OR: Harvest House, 1982), 12, private collection.

45. Laurie, *Occupy till I Come*, 22.

46. Laurie, *Occupy till I Come*, 96.

47. Jerry Falwell, "America Back to God," 1976, 10, Falwell Ministries, Record group 3, sub-group 4, box 2, unit 7: OTGH# 386, LUA.

48. Jerry Falwell, untitled sermon, 1980, 10, 11, Falwell Ministries, record group 3, sub-group 4, box 2, unit 8: OTGH# 396, LUA.

49. The short tenures of secretaries of the interior was pointed out by Watt in an interview with the author conducted on April 21, 2014, as well as in political scientist R. McGreggor Cawley's book *Federal Land, Western Anger: The Sagebrush Rebellion and Environmental Politics*, (Lawrence: University of Kansas Press, 1993).

50. James Watt, untitled draft, October 6, 1982, 6, James G. Watt Papers, acc. #7667, box 9, folder 2, Secretary of the Interior—Christian Religious Stand of Watt 1982, AHC.

51. Glenn Scherer, "Christian-Right Views Are Swaying Politicians and Threatening the Environment," *Grist*, October 28, 2004, http://grist.org/article/scherer-christian/. After the article was published, *Grist* corrected the original point regarding Watt's comments to Congress.

52. Liberty University Archives, Communications Department, Asset ID: 222746, Tape No: F1-AOP-001.mov, Tape Name PAW Fund Raiser/Norman Lear Pilot, Sermon Title: DUB from ¾. On front screen "People for the American Way, Washington Media," 10-4-82. This video is hosted by Burt Lancaster. He warned that the religious right mixed faith with politics and urged people to stand up to them. To vilify the religious right, they show how school boards are censoring teachers.

53. James Watt, "I Was a Candidate," *Voice*, July–August, 1965, 9, 10, James G. Watt Papers, accession #7667, box 1, folder 2 Biographical Material 1962–1980, AHC.

54. James Watt, interview by author, Arizona, April 21, 2014.

55. Nixon quickly responded to the environmental movement marked by the Earth Day 1970 observance by establishing the Environmental Protection Agency and passing landmark environmental bills including the Clean Air and Water Act.

56. James Watt, "The Challenge of the Lake Erie Basin," speech delivered at John Carroll University, March 24, 1970, 2, James Watt Collection, accession #7667, box 2, folder 3, Correspondence, April–July 1970, AHC.

57. When Falwell died in 2007, the same catafalque that was used for Reagan was rushed to Lynchburg, Virginia, for Falwell. In Falwell's newsletter, *Falwell Confidential*, he wrote a piece on August 16, 2002, entitled "Ronald Reagan, My Political Hero." During the 1980s, Falwell remained a supporter of Reagan even though other conservatives such as Weyrich became upset that the president was not conservative enough.

58. James Watt, interview by author, Arizona, April 21, 2014. Mark Hatfield was a devout evangelical but one who leaned much more toward those in the community considered moderate or liberal. Hatfield wrote very pro-environmental articles for Christian publications and should be identified with those who later embraced Ron Sider's Evangelical Environmental Network.

59. Letter from James Watt to Mr. B. Demar Hooper, November 10, 1981, James G. Watt Papers, acc. #7667, box 3, folder 10, Correspondence July–Dec.1981. AHC.

60. Jerry Falwell, Tape Name: Dr. Jerry Falwell on CNN, Recorded Date: 12-03-1984, asset ID: 262190, tape no: F1-ANS-019.mov, tape series: News CNN, Communications Department, Liberty University. This is one of several times Falwell spoke out on Watt's behalf when the secretary of the interior was accused making of anti-Semitic remarks in a 1982 letter warning that opposition to Watt's energy program by Jewish liberals would weaken US support for Israel. Falwell, when asked what he thought on the matter, outwardly defended Watt by saying that he read the letter in question himself and found nothing wrong with it. Falwell, an ardent state of Israel advocate, had no problem defending Watt in this situation. The larger fight with the environmental movement proved something Falwell did not address at the time.

61. Jerry Falwell, Tape Name: Talking Right & Living Right—Proverbs 15:1–33, recorded date: 07-25-1982, asset ID: 255863, tape no: F1-POT-0515.mov, tape series program, Old Time Gospel Hour, 43:17:24, Communications Department, Liberty University.

62. Harry M. Covert Jr., "Reagan's Dynamic Interior Secretary Watt: U.S. Resources Plentiful," *Moral Majority Report*, April 5, 1983, 4.

63. Jerry Falwell, tape name: Sandi Patti Concert reel 2 of 2, rec. date 04-03-1983, asset ID: 222719, tape no: F1-AMV-PT002.mov, tape series MV—Sandi Patti, 14:18:08: 28, Department of Communication, Liberty University.

64. James Watt, tape name: LBC Graduation 1983—James Watt Line (reel 2 of 2), rec date: 05-09-1983, asset ID: 223671, tape no: F1-LHF-026.mov, tape series: LU Historical Footage, Department of Communication Liberty University.

65. Watt, untitled draft, October 6, 1982, 1–3.

66. *A Manifesto for the Christian Church Declaration and Covenant*, Paul M. Weyrich, collection number 10138, box 15, folder 22 Coalition on Revival 1984–1987, AHC

67. E. Calvin Beisner and Daryl S. Borgquist, eds., *The Christian World View of Economics*, (Mountain View, CA: The Coalition on Revival, 1986), 15, in Paul M. Weyrich, collection number 10138, box 15, folder 22 Coalition on Revival 1984–1987, AHC.

68. William S. Pinkston Jr., *Biology for Christian Schools* (Greenville, SC: Bob Jones University Press, 1980), 552. Pinkston concluded, "Although a Christian should not be an 'ecology nut,' screaming for the protection of the environment to the exclusion of its wise use, a Christian must not personally practice nor permit governments to practice unwise environmental management." This is being a "good steward. . . . After all, not only money and abilities are given to us by the Lord, but also the physical world is in our charge. Using it and the biological community wisely is part of our responsibility" (556–57).

69. Jerry Combee, Laurel Hicks, and Mike Lowman, *The Modern Age: The History of the World in Christian Perspective, Vol. II* (Pensacola, FL: A Beka Book Publication, 1981), 390.

70. Combee, Hicks, and Lowman, *The Modern Age*, 507.

71. Nan Gilbert, "Land That I Love," in *Widening Horizons: The Modern McGuffey Readers*, ed. Ullin Whitney Leavell, Mary Louise Friebele, and Tracie Cushman (Pensacola, FL: A Beka Book Publication, 1981), 269–73.

72. Glen Chamber and Gene Fisher, *United States History for Christian Schools* (Greenville, SC: Bob Jones University Press, 1982), 585, 586.

73. Chamber and Fisher, *United States History for Christian Schools*, 608.

74. Chamber and Fisher, *United States History for Christian Schools*.

75. William S. Pinkston Jr., *Life Science for Christian Schools* (Greenville, SC: Bob Jones University Press 1984), 370–75.

76. Russell Kirk, *Economics: Work and Prosperity* (Pensacola, FL: A Beka Book Publication, 1989), 305.

77. Kirk, *Economics Work and Prosperity*, 308.

78. Kirk, *Economics Work and Prosperity*, 358–59.

79. Ronald Reagan, "Election Eve Address: A Vision for America," November 3, 1980, Ronald Reagan Presidential Library & Museum, https://www.reaganlibrary.gov/11-3-80.

80. Sierra Club Conservation Campaign, 1987–1988, National Conservation Campaigns, Americans For Robertson (AFR) Environment, box: 2 # 2 Environment Folders, RULSCA.

81. "Acid Rain Background Memorandum," AFR, RULSCA.

82. Richard L. Lawson to Pat Robertson, February 11, 1988, with attachment dated November 18,1987, and co-signed by Alexander B. Trowbridge, President National Association of Manufacturers; Thomas R. Kuh, Exec. Vice Pres. Edison Electric Institute; John A. Knebel, President American Mining Congress; John A. Anderson, Exec. Director Electricity Consumers Resource Council; Richard L. Lawson, President National Coal Association; R. Milton Deaner, President American Iron and Steel Institute; Joseph Farrell, President American Waterways Operators; William B. Marx, President Council of Industrial Boiler Owners, AFR Environment, box: 2 # 2 Environment Folders, RUA.

83. James Hofford, email to author, June 30, 2014.

84. Jim Hofford to Ms. Connie Snapp, December 21, 1988, with attachment, "Press Release," 1, AFR Environment, box: 2 # 2 Environment Folders. RUA.

85. Hofford, "Press Release," 2.

86. Hofford, "Press Release," 3.

87. Jim Hofford, "An Environmental Statement for Pat Robertson," 1988, 3, AFR Environment, box: 2 # 2 Environment Folders. RUA.

88. Hofford, "An Environmental Statement," 4.

89. Hofford, "An Environmental Statement," 5.

90. James Hofford, email to author, June 30, 2014.

91. Pat Robertson, "A Presidential Bid Ended," 1988 Republican National Convention, New Orleans, August 16, 1988, http://www.patrobertson.com/Speeches/PresidentialBidEnded.asp.

92. John E. Silvius, chapter 5, "Christian Stewardship of the Environment," quoted in James M. Grier, John E. Silvius, Irene B. Alyn, Lois K. Baker., *A Life of Integrity: Right Choices* (Schaumburg, IL: Regular Baptist Press, 1991), 43, private collection.

5. The Struggle between Christian Environmental Stewardship and Anti-Environmentalism in the Religious Right

1. Camp Hydaway is located about a mile and a half from the campus. Set up like a classic 1950s summer camp, Hydaway possesses well-kept lawns, a sandy beach on a lake, and a student center that looks more like a cozy lodge. While the students have

access to canoes, kayaks, and even a waterslide, they can also enjoy hikes on nearby trails.

2. Jerry Falwell, Asset ID: 223191, tape no.: F1-CMS-0094, tape name: JF A Year-End Inventory, rec date: 4-22-1990, tape series: Messages at TRBC–Sunday Morning at TRBC, Communications Department, Liberty University.

3. Sarah Lyall, "Earth Day 1990; Music and, Oh Yes, Earth Day in Park," *New York Times*, April 23, 1990, http://www.nytimes.com/1990/04/23/us/earth-day-1990-music-and-oh-yes-earth-day-in-park.html.

4. Robertson M. Parham, "Earth Care," *Commentary*, January 16, 1990, Robert M. Parham, "The Bible Speaks on Caring for the Earth," *Commentary*, March 26, 1990, Robert M. Parham, "What Can Southern Baptists Do to Be Earth Keepers?," *Commentary*, March 26, 1990, AR 138-2, box 117, folder 16 Environment: Southern Baptists, Southern Baptist Historical Library & Archives (hereafter SBHLA).

5. *Citizens of all Creation*, Soil & Water Stewardship Week, April 29–May 6, 1990, AR 138-2, box 156, folder 12 Environment: Soil and Water Stewardship Week 1998–1992, SBHLA.

6. Kelly Capers, "Home Mission Board Begins Recycling Program," *Baptist Press*, September 28, 1990, AR 138-2, box 117, folder 16 Environment: Southern Baptists, SBHLA.

7. Joel Snider, "Celebration of Creation," *Crievewood Family Update* 17, no. 16 (April 18, 1990), AR 138-2, box 117, folder 16 Environment: Southern Baptists, SBHA.

8. Lissa Atkins and Kelly Simmons, "Rockingham Country Residents Get into the Earth Day Spirit—Area Cities, Towns Sponsor Cleanups," *News & Record*, Greensboro, NC, April 20, 1990, R1.

9. Rene T. Bradley, "Southwide's Senior Value Books, Nature," June 3, 1990, *Palm Beach Post*, June 3, 1990, 5F.

10. Virgil Adams. "Plant Gardening Seeds in Young Minds," *Atlanta Journal-Constitution*, April 22, 1990, R/2.

11. Pastor George Mason, "Spirit and Stuff," *Wilshire Pulpit*, April 22, 1990, 2, AR 138-2, box 117, folder 16 Environment: Southern Baptists, SBHA.

12. Mason, "Spirit and Stuff."

13. Mason, "Spirit and Stuff."

14. Pat Robertson, *The New Millennium: 10 Trends that Will Impact You and Your Family by the Year 2000* (Dallas: World Publishing, 1990), 209.

15. Robertson, *The New Millennium*, 226

16. Robertson, *The New Millennium*, 225–26.

17. Robertson, *The New Millennium*, 227.

18. Robertson, *The New Millennium*, 238.

19. The only possible exception to this statement is Robertson's and Bob Slosser's 1982 book *The Secret Kingdom*, in which he explains that there is both a physical and an invisible world. By only living in the physical, he argues, humans are limiting themselves. If they look to God, all their needs can be met. This ideology indeed upsets the basic logic behind Christian environmental stewardship, not to mention the secular environmental movement. However, the incongruity did not stop Robertson. The idea that God can take from the invisible/infinite world and give to the physical was not an absolute promise. Robertson was largely banking on the idea that such possibilities give hope to people who need help, and he never made the argument that humans in the

physical world could use resources without a thought of tomorrow. Later in the 1990s, Robertson returned to his self-help through faith themes and acknowledged that help from God is not a guarantee for everyone. He almost comes across as saying that God is a personal friend of his and that God has come through on various important occasions. Overall, his point was that God may help those who believe, but Robertson cannot promise anything.

20. See David John Marley, *Pat Robertson: An American Life* (New York: Rowman & Littlefield Publishers, Inc, 2007); David Edwin Harrel, *Pat Robertson: A Life and Legacy* (Grand Rapids, MI: William B. Eerdmans, 2010).

21. Pat Robertson, *The New Millennium*, one page after the dedication: "My profound appreciation goes to Dr. James Black whose indefatigable labor, warm good nature, and vast book publishing experience is responsible for the structure of this work."

22. Position Paper, "Stewardship: All for God's Glory," National Association of Evangelicals SC-113, box 72, folder 14: 48th Annual Convention, Phoenix 1990., Archives of Wheaton College.

23. Edwin R. Squires, "Good News Bad News Re: Our Environment," *United Evangelical Action*, May–June 1990, 5.

24. "Taylor Announces New Environmental Center," *United Evangelical Action*, May–June 1990.

25. "Earth Day 1990 Solutions," *United Evangelical Action*, May–June 1990, 10.

26. Billy A. Melvin, "One Perspective on the Environment," *United Evangelical Action*, May–June 1990, 18.

27. Richard Land, interview by author, September 19, 2017.

28. Richard D. Land, "The Southern Baptist Convention, 1979–1993: What Happened and Why?" *Baptist History and Heritage*, 28, no. 4 (October 1993): 10.

29. Like religious right supporters, Land was a friend of the Republican Party. For example, after interviewing for the position for the CLC, Land was sure the hiring committee would choose another candidate and told his wife they would need to move to Washington, DC, because George W. Bush had previously offered Land a job for helping his father secure southern Baptist votes during the 1988 election. After returning home from the interview, however, he received a call from the committee asking him to return. Land then called his friend and conservative evangelical Paige Patterson and asked him what to do. Patterson told him to return immediately and volunteered to babysit Land's children if that was an issue. Richard Land, telephone interview by author, September 19, 2017.

30. Michael G. Strawser, Matthew Hawkins, and Joe C. Martin, "Persuasive Ambassadors: The Southern Baptist Commitment to Religious Freedom for All," in *The Rhetoric of Religious Freedom in the United States*, ed. Eric C. Miller (Lanham, MD: Lexington Books, 2018), 40. Additionally, during the 1990s, Land developed a working relationship with Jerry Falwell, who led his church to become a member of the Southern Baptist Convention. Land was also a close friend of Paige Patterson, who is considered one of the leading figures in the Southern Baptist Convention and is known for pushing political and theological conservatives into leadership positions.

What Strawser, Hawkins, and Martin allude to in this section is known as the conservative "takeover" of the SBC, which first gained traction with the election of Pastor Adrian Rogers in 1979. The conservative wing of the SBC managed to win each subsequent presidential election. The "takeover" did not mean that the moderates went away; they complained bitterly about the situation and felt they were a minority and treated as second-class citizens. They responded by lamenting the change and tried countering by publishing their own arguments in hopes of bolstering their numbers by persuasion. Nevertheless, the conservative SBC presidents made changes within the institution by, in a certain sense, purging the ranks—especially taking aim at the seminaries in order to replace professors who did not adhere to an inerrant interpretation of the Bible. Controversy reigned. People called for peace, others reminisced about the "good old days" when things were better. However, by the early 1990s, the "purge" had taken a toll on the officers within the SBC, and Land's securing the position of executive director of the CLC signified that even this organization, traditionally run by evangelical moderates, was now in the hands of the conservative faction.

31. Ms. Billie Thomas to Richard Land, March 6, 1990, Richard Land Papers, AR 933, box 143, folder 1 Environment, SBHLA.

32. Thomas to Land.

33. Thomas to Land.

34. Richard Land to Ms. Billie Thomas, March 23, 1990, Richard Land Papers, AR 933, box 143, folder 1 Environment, SBHLA.

35. On December 3, 1990, Land wrote to William Reilly at the Environmental Protection Agency to invite him to speak on the environmental issue at the upcoming CLC annual seminar in March of 1991. Land included several pages of *Light* magazine featuring information about the seminar to give Reilly an "idea of where the Christian Life Commission is 'coming from.'" Richard Land to Mr. William Reilly, December 3, 1990. Southern Baptist Convention Christian Life Commission/Ethics and Religious Liberty Commission Seminar Proceedings Collection, AR 138-6, box 13, folder 1 Christians and the Environment—Correspondence—Aug ust1989–March 1991, SBHLA.

36. Richard Land, "Think about It!" *Light*, April–June 1990, Southern Baptist Convention Christian Life Commission/Ethics and Religious Liberty Commission Seminar Proceedings Collection, AR 138-6, box 13, folder 1 Christians and the Environment—Correspondence—August1989–March 1991, SBHLA.

37. Land, "Think about It!"

38. Richard D. Land to Reverend Dennis Wright, February 6, 1991, Southern Baptist Convention Christian Life Commission/Ethics and Religious Liberty Commission Seminar Proceedings Collection, AR 138-6, box 13, folder 1 Christians and the Environment—Correspondence—August1989–March 1991, SBHLA.

39. Richard Land to Joel C. Gregory, December 6, 1990, Southern Baptist Convention Christian Life Commission/Ethics and Religious Liberty Commission Seminar Proceedings Collection, AR 138-6, box 13, folder 1 Christians and the Environment—Correspondence—August1989–March 1991, SBHLA.

40. Richard D. Land to Dr. Jerry Vines, February 18, 1991, Southern Baptist Convention Christian Life Commission/Ethics and Religious Liberty Commission Seminar Proceedings Collection, AR 138-6, box 13, folder 1 Christians and the Environment—Correspondence—August 1989–March 1991, SBHLA.

41. Richard D. Land and Louis Moore, eds., *The Earth Is the Lord's: Christians and the Environment* (Nashville, TN: Broadman Press, 1992), back cover.

42. Fact sheets, the Christian Life Commission, SBC, Christian Life Commission/Ethics and Religious Liberty Commission Publications and Promotional Material Collection AR 140, box 8, folder 16 Environment, 1981–1995, SBHLA.

43. "Environmental Facts," the Christian Life Commission, SBC, Christian Life Commission/Ethics and Religious Liberty Commission Publications and Promotional Material Collection AR 140, box 8, folder 16 Environment, 1981–1995, SBHLA.

44. ENDANGERED EARTH, the Christian Life Commission, SBC, Christian Life Commission/Ethics and Religious Liberty Commission Publications and Promotional Material Collection AR 140, box 8, folder 16 Environment, 1981–1995, SBHLA.

45. Richard D. Land "Overview: Beliefs and Behaviors," in *The Earth Is the Lord's*, ed. Richard D. Land and Louis A. Moore (Nashville, Tennessee: Broadman Press), 19.

46. Richard D. Land "Overview: Beliefs and Behaviors," in *The Earth Is the Lord's*, ed. Richard D. Land and Louis A. Moore (Nashville, Tennessee: Broadman Press), 20, 21.

47. Richard Land, interview by author, September 19, 2017.

48. Hilary Sills to the Honorable Tom DeLay, May 21, 1992, Paul M. Weyrich Collection, acc #: 10138, box 22, folder 2 Rio Earth Summit, American Heritage Center, University of Wyoming, Laramie, Wyoming.

49. Sills to DeLay. The letter further states: "To help business and conservatives combat the inevitable, I strongly agree on the need for an information clearinghouse to provide the free market environmentalist arguments. Certainly, with expenditures at over $1 billion a year on the world climate research, the U.S. has a story to tell, yet receives little or no credit for this effort at home or abroad. This figure does not include private sector research."

50. Philip C. Clarke, "Hyping Environmental Scare Stories," *Cadillac Evening News*, May 21, 1992, Paul M. Weyrich Collection acc #: 10138, box 22, folder 2 Rio Earth Summit, AHC.

51. Liane Galina to Richard B. Dingman, Executive Vice President of the Free Congress Foundation, facsimile for bill, Dixy Lee Ray's stay at the Copacabana Palace, May 19, 1992, Paul M. Weyrich Collection acc #: 10138, box 22, folder 2 Rio Earth Summit, AHC.

52. Paul M. Weyrich to Fred Smith, June 11, 1992, Paul M. Weyrich Collection acc #: 10138, box 22, folder 2 Rio Earth Summit, AHC.

53. Paul M. Weyrich to Richard L. Lawson, June 15, 1992, Paul M. Weyrich Collection acc #: 10138, box 22, folder 2 Rio Earth Summit, AHC.

54. "Don't Abandon Wetlands," *USA Today*, December 12, 1991, and Stuart Hardy, "Use Sense with Wetlands," *USA Today*, December 12, 1991, Inventory of the Christian Life Commission Resource Files, AR 138-2, box 117, folder 21 Environment—Wetlands, SBHLA.

55. "Manage Wild Game Wisely," *USA Today*, January 13, 1993, and Christine Jackson, "Don't Kill Wild Animals," *USA Today*, January 13, 1993, Inventory of the Christian Life Commission Resource Files, AR 138-2, box 156, folder 6 Environment—Endangered Species, 1991–2000, SBHLA.

56. Frank Edward Allen, "Seen and Heard: Schoolchildren Learn Ecology by Doing—To Alleged Polluters," *Wall Street Journal*, April 30, 1992, Inventory of the Christian Life Commission Resource Files, AR 138-2, box 156.1, folder 2 Environment—1988–1992, SBHLA.

57. Ronald L. Cooper, "The Greenhouse Effect and Pre-Flood Days," *Impact*, May 1993, I, Hall-Hoag Collection 1079, 76.62, Brown University Archives (hereafter BUA).

58. Cooper, "The Greenhouse Effect," iii. Cited from Sherwood B. Idso, "Carbon Dioxide Can Revitalize the Planet," OPEC Bulletin, March 1992, pp. 22–27.

59. Dale Jamieson, *Reason in a Dark Time* (New York: Oxford University Press), 81, 82.

60. Henry M. Morris, "Pantheistic Evolution," *Impact*, December 1992, i–ii, Hall-Hoag Collection 1079, 76.62, BUA.

61. Peter J. Leithart, *The Green Movement: It's False Claims and Religious Agenda* (Ft. Lauderdale, FL: Coral Ridge Ministries, 1992), 19–21 on DDT, 36–37 on climate change. Leithart made sure to highlight Dixy Lee Ray's credentials before discussing her views on climate change as a natural phenomenon: "Dixy Lee Ray, former governor of Washington and chair of the Atomic Energy Commission, says" (36), Christian Life Commission Ethics & Religious Liberty Commission Resource Files AR 138-2, box 156, folder 8 Environment: Ethics, 1988–1992, SBHLA.

62. Laurel Hicks, Delores Shimmin, Gregory Rickard, Ed Rickard, Julie Rickard, Barbara Porcher, and Cindy Froman, *Science: Order & Reality*, 2nd ed. (Pensacola, FL: A Beka Books, 1993), 20.

63. Hicks, *Science*.

64. Hicks, *Science*.

65. Hicks, *Science*, 166.

66. Hicks, *Science*, 167

67. Hicks, *Science*.

68. Hicks, *Science*, 166.

69. Hicks, *Science*, 167.

70. Hicks, *Science*, 470.

71. Hicks, *Science*.

72. Hicks, *Science*.

73. Jerry Falwell, tape name: JF We Keep Changing the Subject II Corinthians 4:3–5, rec. date: May 31, 1992, asset ID: 223386, tape no: F1-CMS-0298.mov, Tape Series Messages at TRBC—Sunday Morning at TRBC, Department of Communications, Liberty University.

74. Falwell, "We Keep Changing the Subject."

75. Kenneth D. Wald, Dennis E. Owen, and Samuel S. Hill Jr, "Churches and Political Communities," *American Political Science Review* 82, no. 2 (1988): 545.

76. Chuck Asayo, *The Paper*, January 1994, The Paper, Jan '93—'96, box #2, Regent University Library—Special Collections & Archives.

77. Chuck Asayo, *The Paper*, February 1993, The Paper, Jan '93—'96, box #2, Regent University Library—Special Collections & Archives.

78. Edwin Feulner, "Compulsive Environmentalism—Only on Weekends" *The Paper*, September 1993, 5. The Paper, Jan '93—'96, box #2, RUA.

79. Feulner, 5.

80. Randall J. Barnett, "More than Just Global Warming: One-Worlders May Be Pushing Politics with disaster" *Focus*, Summer 1990, 21, Focus Magazine Singles, RUA.

6. The National Association of Evangelicals Turns against the Environment

1. Lamar E. Cooper Sr., "How a Local Church Can Begin a Recycling Program," in *The Earth Is the Lord's*, ed. Richard D. Land and Louis A. Moore (Nashville, TN: Broadman Press, 1992), 200–1.

2. Lamar E. Cooper Sr., "Environmental Danger: Chicken Little or little chicken?" 1, inventory of the Richard Land Papers AR 933, box 143, folder 1 Environment, 1990–1992, SBHLA.

3. Cooper, "Environmental Danger," 2.

4. "Religious Leaders and Scientists Issue First-Ever Joint Declaration on Environment Meet with Congressional Leaders, Urge Bold Action by Administration," inventory of the Richard Land Papers, AR 933, box 143, folder 1 Environment, 1990–1992, SBHLA.

5. Cooper, "Environmental Danger," 2.

6. Laura Session Stepp, "Denominations Find Common Ground in Saving the Earth," *Washington Post*, May 23, 1992.

7. Emily W. Elmone to Richard Land, June 2, 1992, inventory of the Richard Land Papers, AR 933, box 143, folder 1 Environment, 1990–1992, SBHLA.

8. "Earth Day: The Greatest Sham on Earth," *New American*, March 26, 1990, inventory of the Richard Land Papers, AR 933, box 143, folder 1 Environment, 1990–1992, SBHLA.

9. Robert W. Lee, "Six 'Crises' All Leading to World Government," *New American*, November 20, 1989, inventory of the Richard Land Papers, AR 933, box 143, folder 1 Environment, 1990–1992, SBHLA.

10. *New American*, June 1, 1992, inventory of the Richard Land Papers AR 933, box 143, folder 1 Environment, 1990–1992, SBHLA.

11. "About CFACT," https://www.cfact.org/about/ (accessed November 3, 2019).

12. Robert Dugan Jr. to Jerry Falwell, June 17, 1985, National Association of Evangelicals, SC-113, box 144, folder 5 J. Falwell 1983–1987, Archives of Wheaton College (hereafter AWC).

13. Robert Dugan Jr. to Ronald Sider, March 3, 1993, NAE, SC-113, box 51, folder 13 EEN/Environment (2 of 2) 1993–1995, AWC.

14. Robert Dugan Jr., "Theme Yields Statement on Environment," *NAE Washington Insight*, April, 1990, 1, NAE, SC-113, box 61, folder 3 Insight 1990–1997, AWC.

15. Wesley Granberg-Michaelson to Robert Dugan, August 12, 1988, NAE, SC-113, box 29, folder 12 Environment 1997, AWC.

16. Donald Hodel, "Economic Ecology," *World Vision*, December 1992–January 1993, 7, NAE, SC-113, box 51, folder 13 EEN/Environment (2 of 2), 1993–1995, AWC.

17. Dixy Lee Ray to Dear Fellow American, received on October 28, 1992, 3, NAE, SC-113, box 51, folder 13 EEN/Environment (2 of 2), 1993–1995, AWC.

18. David A. Noebel, "From the President's Desk," *Summit Journal*, September 1993, 4, NAE, SC-113, box 51, folder 12 EEN/Environment (1 of 2), 1993–1995, AWC.

19. E. Calvin Beisner to Dugan and Cizik, October 25, 1993, NAE, SC-113, box 51, folder 12 EEN/Environment (1 of 2), 1993–1995, AWC.

20. Beisner to Dugan and Cizik.

21. Robert Dugan to Ron Sider, October 28, 1993, NAE, SC-113, box 51, folder 13 EEN/Environment (2 of 2), 1993–1995, AWC.

22. E. Calvin Beisner, "Are God's Resources Finite?: A Group of Christian Leaders Claim They Are, but Does the Claim Square with the Evidence?" *World*, November 27, 1993, 10.

23. Allen Johnson to Tom Strode, October 13, 1993, NAE, SC-113, box 51, folder 12 EEN/Environment (1 of 2), 1993–1995, AWC.

24. E. Calvin Beisner to Dugan and Cizik, October 25, 1993, 7. NAE, SC-113, box 51, folder 12 EEN/Environment (1 of 2), 1993–1995, AWC.

25. Richard Land, interview by author, September 19, 2017.

26. "Is Global Warming a Threat to the World Environment?" *Light*, November 24, 1993, 4.

27. Handwritten note on letter from Frederick W. Krueger to Robert Dugan, November 24, 1993, NAE, SC-113, box 51, folder 12 EEN/Environment (1 of 2), 1993–1995, AWC.

28. Stephen Budiansky, "Doomsday Myths," *U.S. News & World Report*, December 13, 1993, 81–88.

29. Robert Dugan to Billy Melvin, December 23, 1993. NAE, SC-113, box 51, folder 12 EEN/Environment (1 of 2), 1993–1995, AWC.

30. Robert Dugan to Ron Sider, November 15, 1993, NAE, SC-113, box 51, folder 12 EEN/Environment (1 of 2), 1993–1995, AWC.

7. "It Could Have Taken a Very Different Path"

1. Note and article, "A Biblical View of Ecology" newsletter published by Intercessors for America, 1990, Richard Land Papers, AR 933, box 143, folder 1 Environment. SBHLA.

2. Jerry Falwell, tape name: "JF the Last Memorial Day," rec. date 05-29-1994, asset ID 253662, tape series: Messages at TRBC—Sunday Morning at RBC, Communications Department, Liberty University.

3. Marla Cone and Melissa Healy, "Scientists to Catalog America's Ecosystems," *Register-Guard*, Eugene, Oregon, October 3, 1993, NAE, SC-113, box 29, folder 12 Environment 1997, Archives of Wheaton College (hereafter AWC).

4. Mark Tooley, "Gore's God," *Crisis*, October 1996, 25.

5. David Gonzalez, "Religions Are Putting Faith in Environmentalism," *New York Times*, November 6, 1994, 34.

6. Michael J. Paquette, "Religions Take 'Earth Day' Leap into Environmental Theology," *Washington Post*, April 16, 1994.

7. "Biblical Roots," Evangelical Environmental Network, 1994, 3, NAE, SC-113, box 51, folder 12 EEN/Environment (1 of 2), 1993–1995, WCA.

8. Tooley, "Gore's God," 23.

9. Samantha Smith, "Pagan Howl-Le-Lu-Ia Chorus," *Metro Voice*, June 1996, 53.

10. Ron Sider to Ms. Diane Knippers, July 9, 1997, NAE, SC-113, box 29, folder 12 Environment 1997, WCA.

11. "'Noah Congregation' or Trojan Horse?," associated with letter Edwin A. Olson to Robert Dugan, April 10, 1996, NAE, SC-113, box 29, folder 12 Environment 1997, WCA.

12. Jerry Falwell, tape name: "Where the Battle Rages," rec date: 12-01-1996, asset ID: 254242, tape no: FB-CMS-0146, tape series: Messages at TRBC—Sunday Morning at TRBC, Department of Communications, Liberty University.

13. Richard Land and Louis Moore, *The Earth Is the Lord's: Christians and the Environment* (Nashville, TN: Broadman Press, 1992), 23.

14. Michael J. Paquette, "Religious Group Seeks 'Greening' of Evangelicals," *Long Beach Press-Telegram*, April 16, 1994.

15. Noble Sprayberry, "Environmentalists Find Allies in Church," *Chattanooga Times*, April 18, 1996.

16. Carlyle Murphy, "More Congregations Caring for Creation: Americans of All Faiths Are Looking at Environmental Issues from a Spiritual Perspective," *Waterloo Region Record*, February 7, 1998; Carlyle Murphy, "Creation's Caretakers: More Americans See Conservation as Religious Mandate," *Fort Worth Star-Telegram*, February 8, 1998.

17. Adelle M. Banks, "Ecological Concerns Drive Groups," *Press-Register*, April 17, 1999.

18. Larry Witham, "Alliance Shuns Nature Worship," *Washington Times*, April 18, 2000.

19. "A Faith Community Commitment to the Environment and Our Children's Future," 2000, Richard Land Papers, AR 933, box 143, folder 2 Environment—"A Faith Community Commitment to the Environment," April 2000, Southern Baptist Historical Library & Archives.

20. "A Faith Community Commitment": "For example, the ALAR scare caused millions of moms to stop giving apples and apple juice to their children. This politically motivated scare was not based on sound science. It had negative health effects on the nation's youth and it caused massive economic dislocation in the apple industry."

21. Laurel Hicks et al., *Science: Order & Reality*, 2nd ed. (Pensacola, FL: A Beka Books, 1993): 471.

22. Keith Graham, *Biology: God's Living Creation* (Pensacola, FL: A Beka Books, 1986): 513.

23. Jean Spitsbergen, Heather Fulfer, and Brian Ashbaugh, *Biology: God's Living Creation* (Pensacola, FL: A Beka Book, 1997), 216.

24. Spitsbergen, Fulfer, and Ashbaugh, *Biology*, 234.

25. Spitsbergen, Fulfer, and Ashbaugh, *Biology*.

26. Spitsbergen, Fulfer, and Ashbaugh, *Biology*.

27. CNN, tape name: *Inside Politics*, rec. date 11-20-2002, asset ID: 250127, Communications Department, Liberty University.

28. CNN, *Inside Politics*. The Kyoto Treaty was a follow up agreement to the 1992 Earth Summit. Participants hoped to find agreement regarding lowing greenhouse gasses and therefore combat climate change.

29. CNN, *Inside Politics*.

30. "Seminary Student's Climate Change Project Is Not SBC's," *Baptist Press*, March 10, 2008, http://www.bpnews.net/27582/seminary-students-climate-change-project-is-not-sbcs.

31. "Seminary Student's Climate Change Project"; and Richard Land, interview by author, by telephone, September 19, 2017.

32. Rabbi Eric Yoffie and Jerry Falwell, JF, "Ten Steps in Developing Your Faith," rec. date: 04-26-2006, asset ID: 256578, tape number FB-LCH-261, Tape Series: LU Chapel/Convocation, Department of Communications, Liberty University.

33. Jerry Falwell, "Climate Initiative Is a Bad Idea," *Falwell Confidential*, February 10, 2006, 1, FAL 2: Falwell Publications, *Falwell Confidential* Part 1, FAL 2:1 box 1, series 2, folder 9, *Falwell Confidential*, 2006, Liberty University Archives and Special Collections (hereafter LUA).

34. Falwell, "Climate Initiative," 2.

35. Jerry Falwell, "Evangelicals and Global Warming," *Falwell Confidential*, November 17, 2006, FAL 2: Falwell Publications, *Falwell Confidential* Part 1, FAL 2:1 box 1, series 2, folder 9, *Falwell Confidential*, 2006, LUA.

36. Falwell "Evangelicals and Global Warming," 1, 2.

37. Jerry Falwell, "Spend Sunday at Thomas Road Baptist Church," email, February 21, 2007, FAL 2: Falwell Publications, *Falwell Confidential* Part 1, FAL 2:1 box 1, series 2, folder 10, *Falwell Confidential*, January–May 2007, LUA.

38. Jerry Falwell, "Preaching Out Against 'Global Warming' Panic," *Falwell Confidential*, February 23, 2007, FAL 2: Falwell Publications, *Falwell Confidential* Part 1, FAL 2:1 box 1, series 2, folder 10, *Falwell Confidential*, January–May 2007, LUA.

39. Falwell, "Preaching Out Against 'Global Warming,'" 2.

40. Jerry Falwell, tape name: Live From Liberty opens: Jerry Falwell Standups, rec. date: 02-15-2007, asset ID: 262654, tape no: FB-LFL-FF0029.mo., tape series: Live from Liberty Footage, Department of Communication, Liberty University.

41. Jerry Falwell, tape name: JF "The Myth of Global Warming," rec. date: 02-25-2007, asset ID: 255421, tape no: FB-CMS-0791.mov, tape series: Messages at TRBC—Sunday Morning at TRBC, Department of Communication, Liberty University.

42. Jerry Falwell, "Jesse Helms Comes to Liberty," *Falwell Confidential*, October 7, 2004, FAL 2: Falwell Publications, *Falwell Confidential* Part 1, FAL 2:1 box 1, series 2, folder 6, *Falwell Confidential*, 2004, LUA.

43. http://trbc.org/new/sermons.php?url=20070225_11AM.html (accessed January 20, 2011).

44. Jerry Falwell Jr. and Glenn Beck, tape name: JF JR on Glenn Beck, rec. date: 05-18-2010, asset ID: 344696, time: 1:07:50:15, Department of Communication, Liberty University.

45. Falwell Jr. and Beck.

46. Lord Christopher Monckton, tape name: Convo., rec. date: 03-10-2010, asset ID: 347139, Department of Communications, Liberty University.

47. Monckton, Convo.

48. Elmer Towns, tape name: Elmer Towns—Questions about Jesus' Return, rec. date: 02-20-2011, asset ID: 276045, tape no: F-PBC-00067.mov, tape series: TRBC—Pastor's Bible Class, Department of Communications, Liberty University.

49. Dr. Ergun Caner, tape name: Dr. Ergun Caner: Scratch & Sniff Spirituality: "The Old Lies of the New Age," rec. date: 07-06-2008, asset ID: 255505, tape number FB-CMS-0935, time: 59:47:10, Department of Communication, Liberty University.

50. R. Terrance Egolf and Rachel Santopietro, *Earth Science*, 4th ed. (Greenville, SC: BJU Press, 2012), 520.

51. Katherine Hayhoe and Andrew Farley, *A Climate for Change: Global Warming Facts for Faith-Based Decisions*, (New York: FaithWords, 2009), 128.

52. "Seminary Student's Climate Change Project."

53. Adelle M. Banks, "Southern Baptist Leader Richard Land Announces Retirement," *Sojourners*, August 2, 2012. https://sojo.net/articles/southern-baptist-leader-richard-land-announces-retirement.

Conclusion

1. Arlie Russell, *Strangers In Their Own Land: Anger and Mourning on the American Right* (New York and London: The New Press), 179.

2. E. Calvin Beisner, "A Challenge to Evangelical Climate Scientist Katharine Hayhoe," Cornwall Alliance, February 4, 2020. https://cornwallalliance.org/2020/02/a-challenge-to-evangelical-climate-scientist-katharine-hayhoe/. The "Kardashian Index" is understood as someone being famous without any substantive reason.

3. "Important Issues in the 2020 Election," Pew Research Center, August 13, 2020, https://www.pewresearch.org/politics/2020/08/13/important-issues-in-the-2020-election/.

BIBLIOGRAPHY

Adams, Virgil. "Plant Gardening Seeds in Young Minds," *Atlanta Journal-Constitution*, April 22, 1990, R/2.

Allitt, Patrick. *Religion in America since 1945: A History*. New York: Columbia University Press, 2003.

Ammerman, Nancy. *Baptist Battles: Social Change and Religious Conflict in the Southern Baptist Convention*. New Brunswick, NJ: Rutgers University Press, 1990.

Anderson, Benedict. *Imagined Communities: Reflections on the Origin and Spread of Nationalism*. New York: Verso, 1991.

Anderson, Hans Christian, "The Flax." In *Foot Prints: The Christian Reading Series*, edited by Laurel Hicks and Mike Davis, 64–68. Pensacola, FL: A Beka Books, 1980.

"Another TACT Finalist: Youth Lives Busy, Useful Life," *Dallas Morning News*, April 3, 1971, 14A.

Aronowitz, Stanley. *How Class Works: Power and Social Movement*. New Haven, CT: Yale University Press, 2003.

Atkins, Lissa, and Kelly Simmons. "Rockingham Country Residents Get into the Earth Day Spirit—Area Cities, Towns Sponsor Cleanups," *News & Record*, Greensboro, NC, April 20, 1990, R1.

Askew, Thomas, and Richard Pierard. *The American Church Experience: A Concise History*. Grand Rapids, MI: Baker House Books, 2004.

Bailey, Caroline Sherwin. "The First Fight." In *Flags Unfurled*, edited by Laurel Hicks. Pensacola, FL: A Beka Book Publications, 1974.

Balmer, Randall. *Thy Kingdom Come: How the Religious Right Distorts the Faith and Threatens America, An Evangelical's Lament*. New York: Basic Books, 2006.

——. *Mine Eyes Have Seen the Glory: A Journey into the Evangelical Subculture in America*, 4th ed. New York: Oxford, 2006.

Banks, Adelle M. "Ecological Concerns Drive Groups," *Press-Register*, April 17, 1999.

Beale, David O. *In Pursuit of Purity: American Fundamentalism since 1850*. Greenville, SC: Unusual Publications, 1986.

Beito, David T. and Marcus M. Witcher, "New Deal Witch Hunt: The Buchanan Committee Investigation of the Committee for Constitutional Government," *Independent Review* 21, no. 1 (2016): 47–71.

Benson, Bruce Ellis, and Peter G. Heltzel, eds. *Evangelicals and Empire: Christian Alternatives to the Political Status Quo*. Grand Rapids, MI: Brazos Press, 2008.

Berkeley, Kathleen. *The Women's Liberation Movement in America*. Westport, CT: Greenwood Press, 1999.

Blaker, Kimberly. *The Fundamentals of Extremism: The Christian Right in America*. Boston: New Boston Books, 2003.

Bloesch, Donald G. *The Invaded Church*. Waco, TX: Word Books, 1975.

Boyer, Paul. *When Time Shall Be No More: Prophecy Belief in American Culture*. Cambridge, MA: Belknap Press, 1992.

Bradley, Rene T. "Southwide's Senior Value Books, Nature," *Palm Beach Post*, June 3, 1990.

Brasher, Brenda E. *Encyclopedia of Fundamentalism*. New York: Routledge, 2001.

Bromley, David G., and Anson Shupe, eds., *New Christian Politics*. Macon, GA: Mercer University Press, 1984.

Brown, Ruth Murray. *A History of the Religious Right: For a "Christian America."* Amherst, MA: Prometheus Books, 2002.

Bruce, Steven. *The Rise and Fall of the New Christian Right: Conservative Politics in America, 1978–1988*. Oxford: Oxford University Press, 1988.

Brown, Steven Preston. *Trumping Religion: The New Christian Right, the Free Speech Clause, and the Courts*. Tuscaloosa: University of Alabama Press, 2002.

Budiansky, Stephen. "Doomsday Myths," *U.S. News & World Report*, December 13, 1993, 81–88.

Campbell, David E., ed. *A Matter of Faith: Religion in the 2004 Presidential Election*. Washington, DC: Brookings Institution Press, 2007.

Carmody, John. *Theology for the 1980s*. Philadelphia: Westminster Press, 1980.

Carpenter, Joel A. *Revive Us Again: The Reawakening of American Fundamentalism*. New York: Oxford University Press, 1997.

Carson, Rachel. *Silent Spring*. Boston: Houghton Mifflin, 1962.

Cawley, R. McGreggor. *Federal Land, Western Anger: The Sagebrush Rebellion and Environmental Politics*. Lawrence: University of Kansas Press, 1993.

Chamber, Glen, and Gene Fisher, *United States History for Christian Schools*. Greenville, SC: Bob Jones University Press, 1982.

Combee, Jerry, Laurel Hicks, and Mike Lowman, *The Modern Age: The History of the World in Christian Perspective, Vol. II*. Pensacola, FL: A Beka Book Publication, 1981.

Cooper Sr., Lamar E. "How a Local Church Can Begin a Recycling Program." In *The Earth Is the Lord's*, edited by Richard D. Land and Louis A. Moore. Nashville, TN: Broadman Press, 1992.

Covert Jr., Harry M. "Reagan's Dynamic Interior Secretary Watt: U.S. Resources Plentiful," *Moral Majority Report*, April 5, 1983, 4.

Cromartie, Michael, ed. *No Longer Exiles: The Religious New Right in American Politics*. Washington, DC: Ethics and Public Policy Center, 1993.

Cronon, William. *Changes in the Land: Indians, Colonists, and the Ecology of New England*. New York: Hill and Wang, 1983.

Cronon, William, ed. *Uncommon Ground: Rethinking the Human Place in Nature*. New York: W. W. Norton, 1995.

——. "The Trouble with Wilderness; or, Getting Back to the Wrong Nature." In William Cronon, ed., Uncommon Ground: Rethinking the Human Place in Nature, edited by William Cronon, 69–90. New York: W. W. Norton &Co., 1995.

Cumbey, Constance E. *The Hidden Dangers of the Rainbow. The New Age Movement and Our Coming Age of Barbarism*. Shreveport, LA: Huntington House, 1983.

De Bell, Garrett, ed. *The Environmental Handbook: Prepared for the First National Environmental Teach-In*. New York: Ballantine Books/Friends of the Earth Book, 1970.

Demause, Lloyd. *Reagan's America*. New York: Creative Roots, 1984.

Devine, Robert S. *Bush versus the Environment*. New York: Anchor, 2004.

DeWitt, Calvin B. "The Scientist and the Shepherd: The Emergence of Evangelical Environmentalism." In *The Oxford Handbook of Religion and Ecology*, edited by Roger Gottlieb, 568–87. Oxford: Oxford University Press, 2006.

Dochuk, Darren. *From Bible Belt to Sun Belt: Plain-Folk Religion, Grassroots Politics, and the Rise of Evangelical Conservatism*. New York: W. W. Norton, 2011.

——. *Anointed with Oil: How Christianity and Crude Made Modern America*. New York: Basic Books, 2019.

Dunlap, Tomas R. *DDT: Scientists, Citizens, and Public Policy*. Princeton, NJ: Princeton University Press, 1981.

——. *Faith In Nature: Environmentalism as Religious Quest*. Seattle: University of Washington Press, 2004.

Dunn, Charles W. *Religion in American Politics*. Washington, DC.: Congressional Quarterly Press, 1989.

"Earth Day 1990 Solutions," *United Evangelical Action* (May–June 1990): 10.

Eckberg, Douglas Lee, and T. Jean Blocker. "Varieties of Religious Involvement and Environmental Concerns: Testing the Lynn White Thesis." *Journal for the Scientific Study of Religion* 28, no. 4 (1989): 509–17.

Egolf, R. Terrance, and Rachel Santopietro, *Earth Science*, 4th ed. Greenville, SC: BJU Press, 2012.

Eley, Geoff, and Ronald Grigor Suny, eds., *Becoming National: A Reader*. Oxford: Oxford University Press, 1996.

Ellingson, Stephen. *To Care for Creation: The Emergence of Religious Environmental Movement*. Chicago: University of Chicago Press, 2016.

Ellwood, Robert S. *1950: Crossroads of American Religious Life*. Louisville, KY: Westminster John Knox, 2000.

Emerson, Michael O., and Christian Smith. *Divided by Faith: Evangelical Religion and the Problem of Race in America*. Oxford: Oxford University Press, 2000.

"Energy Crisis: Bleakness or Blessing? *Christianity Today*, December 21, 1973, 33, 34.

Erickson, Paul D. *Reagan Speaks: The Making of an American Myth*. New York: New York University Press, 1985.

Evans, John H., and Justin Feng, "Conservative Protestantism and Skepticism of Scientists Studying Climate Change," *Climatic Change* 121. no. 4. (December 2013): 595–608.

Everett, Arthur. "Earth Day Sweeps County: Students, and Aged Join in Demonstration," *Dallas Morning News*, April 23, 1970, 1.

Fackre, Gabriel. *The Religious Right and the Christian Faith*. Grand Rapids, MI: William B. Eerdmans Publishing, 1982.

Falwell, Jerry. *How You Can Help Clean Up America*. Lynchburg, VA: Liberty Publishing, 1978.

——. *America Can Be Saved*. Murfreesboro, TN: Sword of the Lord Publishers, 1979.

——. *Dr. Jerry Falwell Teaches Bible Prophecy*. Lynchburg, VA: Old Time Gospel Hour, 1979.

——. *Listen, America!* Garden City, NJ: Doubleday, 1980.

——. *Dr. Jerry Falwell Teaches Bible Creation.* Lynchburg, VA: Old Time Gospel Hour, 1983.

——. *Falwell: An Autobiography.* Lynchburg, VA: Liberty House Publishers, 1997.

Falwell, Jerry, Ed Dobson, and Ed Hindson, eds. *The Fundamentalist Phenomenon: The Resurgence of Conservative Christianity.* Garden City, NJ: Doubleday, 1981.

Falwell, Macel, and Melanie Hemry. *Jerry Falwell: His Life and Legacy.* New York: Howard Books, 2008.

Finch, Philip. *God, Guts, and Guns.* New York: Seaview/Putnam, 1983.

"The Fly and the Moth." In *Foot Prints: The Christian Reading Series,* edited by Laurel Hicks and Mike Davis, 62–63. Pensacola, FL: A Beka Books, 1980.

Foreman, Dave. *Confessions of an Eco-Warrior.* New York: Crown, 1991.

Fowler, Robert Booth. *The Greening of Protestant Thought.* Chapel Hill: University of North Carolina Press, 1995.

Gallagher, Sally K. *Evangelical Identity & Gendered Family Life.* New Brunswick, NJ: Rutgers University Press, 2003.

Gallup, George, Jr. *The UnChurched American—10 Years Later.* Princeton, NJ: Princeton Religion Research Center, 1988.

Gallup, George, Jr., and Sarah Jones. *100 Questions and Answers: Religion in America.* Princeton, NJ: Princeton Religion Research Center: Hermitage Press, 1989.

Gallup, George H. *The Gallup Poll: Public Opinion 1972–1977.* Wilmington, DE: Scholarly Resources, 1978.

——. *The Gallup Poll: Public Opinion 1979.* Wilmington, DE: Scholarly Resources, 1980.

——. *The Gallup Poll: Public Opinion 1980.* Wilmington, DE: Scholarly Resources, 1981.

Gilbert, Nan. "Land That I Love." In *Widening Horizons: The Modern McGuffey Readers,* edited by Ullin Whitney Leavell, Mary Louise Friebele, and Tracie Cushman, 269–73. Pensacola, FL: A Beka Book Publication, 1981.

——. "Land That I Love." In *Widening Horizons: The Modern McGuffey Readers,* edited by Ullin Whitney Leavell, Mary Louise Friebele, and Tracie Cushman. Pensacola, FL: A Beka Book Publication, 1986.

Gilkey, Langdon. *Creationism on Trial: Evolution and God at Little Rock.* Minneapolis, MN: Winston Press, 1985.

Girgus, Sam B., ed. *The American Self: Myth, Ideology, and Popular Culture.* Albuquerque: University of New Mexico Press, 1981.

Gjelten, Tom. "2020 Faith Vote Reflects 2016 Patterns," National Public Radio, November 8, 2020. https://www.npr.org/2020/11/08/932263516/2020-faith-vote-reflects-2016-patterns (accessed, July 15, 2021).

Gonzalez, David. "Religions Are Putting Faith in Environmentalism," *New York Times,* November 6, 1994, 34.

Gottlieb, Robert. *Forcing the Spring: The Transformation of the American Environmental Movement.* Washington, DC: Island Press, 1993.

Gottlieb, Roger. *A Greener Faith: Religious Environmentalism and Our Planet's Future.* Oxford: Oxford University Press, 2006.

Gottlieb, Roger S., ed. *This Sacred Earth: Religion, Nature, Environment.* New York: Routledge, 1996.

Graham, Billy. *Just As I Am: The Autobiography of Billy Graham*. San Francisco: HarperCollins, 1997.

Graham, Billy. "The Generation Gap." *Hour of Decision*, pamphlets, WCBGCA, 1972.

Graham, Keith. *Biology: God's Living Creation*. Pensacola, FL: A Beka Books, 1986.

Green, John, Lyman Kellstedt, and Corwin Smidt. *Religion and the Culture Wars: Dispatches from the Front*. Lanham, MD: Rowman & Littlefield, 1996.

Green, John C., Mark J. Rozell, and Clyde Wilcox, eds. *The Christian Right in American Politics: Marching to the Millennium*. Washington DC: Georgetown University Press, 2003.

Guth, James L., John C. Green, Lyman A. Kellstedt, and Corin E. Smidt. "Faith and the Environment: Religious Beliefs and Attitudes on Environmental Policy." *American Journal of Political Science* 39, no. 2 (1995): 364–82.

Guth, James L., John C. Green, Corwin E. Smidt, Lyman A. Kellstedt, and Margaret M. Poloma. *The Bully Pulpit: The Politics of Protestant Clergy*. Lawrence: University Press of Kansas, 1997.

Hadden, Jeffrey K., and Anson Shupe. *Televangelism: Power & Politics on God's Frontier*. New York: Henry Holt, 1988.

Hamilton, Michael, ed. *This Little Planet*. New York: Charles Scribner's Sons, 1970.

Hankins, Barry. *Francis Schaeffer and the Shaping of Evangelical America*. Grand Rapids, MI: Eerdmans, 2008.

Hangen, Tona J. *Redeeming the Dial: Radio, Religion and Popular Culture in America*. Chapel Hill: University of North Carolina Press, 2002.

Hardin, Garrett. "The Tragedy of the Commons." In *The Environmental Handbook: Prepared for the First National Teach-In*, edited by Garrett De Bell, 31–50. New York: Ballantine Books, 1970.

Harding, Susan Friend. *The Book of Jerry Falwell: Fundamentalist Language and Politics*. Princeton, NJ: Princeton University Press, 2000.

Harrel, David Edwin. *Pat Robertson: A Life and Legacy*. Grand Rapids, MI: William B. Eerdmans, 2010.

Hart, D. G. *That Old-Time Religion in Modern America: Evangelical Protestantism in the Twentieth Century*. Chicago: Dee Publishing, 2002.

Hayes, Carlton J. H. *Nationalism: A Religion*. New York: Macmillan, 1960.

Hays, Samuel P. *Beauty, Health, and Permanence: Environmental Politics in the United States, 1955–1985*. Cambridge: Cambridge University Press, 1987.

——. *A History of Environmental Politics since 1945*. Pittsburgh, PA: University of Pittsburg Press, 2000.

Hayes, Kenneth. "Baptist Leaders Speak Out on Pollution Problems," *California Southern Baptist*, January 7, 1971.

Hayhoe, Katherine and Andrew Farley, *A Climate for Change: Global Warming Facts for Faith-Based Decisions*. New York: FaithWords, 2009.

Hefley, James. "Christians and the Pollution Crisis," *Moody Monthly* 71, no. 9 (1970): 21.

Helvarg, David. *The War against the Greens: The "Wise-Use" Movement, the New Right, and Anti-Environmental Violence*. San Francisco: Sierra Club Books, 1994.

Hendershot, Heather. *Shaking the World for Jesus: Media and Conservative Evangelical Culture*. Chicago: University of Chicago Press, 2004.

Herbert, T. Walter. *Faith-Based War: From 9/11 to Catastrophic Success in Iraq*. London: Equinox, 2009.

Hemans, Felicia. "The Landing of the Pilgrim Fathers." In *Of America Vol. II*, edited by Beverly Rainey, 63. Pensacola, FL: A Beka Book.

Hicks, Laurel, Delores Shimmin, Gregory Rickard, Ed Rickard, Julie Rickard, Barbara Porcher, and Cindy Froman. *Science: Order & Reality*, 2nd ed. Pensacola, FL: A Beka Books, 1993.

Hicks, Laurel, ed., *Liberty Tree*. Pensacola, FL: A Beka Book, 1974.

Hicks, Laurel, and Mike Davis, ed. *Foot Prints: The Christian Reading Series*. Pensacola, FL: A Beka Books, 1980.

Houston, James M. "The Environmental Movement: Five Causes of Confusion," In *Christianity Today* (September 15, 1972): 8–10.

Hobsbawm, E. J. *Nations and Nationalism Since 1780: Programme, Myth, Reality*. Cambridge: Cambridge University Press, 1990.

Hochschild, Arlie Russell. *Strangers in Their Own Land: Anger and Mourning in the American Right*. New York: New Press, 2016.

Horowitz, Daniel. *Jimmy Carter and the Energy Crisis of the 1970s: The "Crisis of Confidence" Speech of July 15, 1979: A Brief History*. Boston: Bedford/St. Martin's, 2005.

Houck, Davis W., Amos Kiewe, and Robert E. Denton, eds. *Advisor, Actor, Ideologue, Politician: The Public Speeches of Ronald Reagan*. Westport, CT: Greenwood Press, 1993.

Hunter, James Davison. *Culture Wars: The Struggle to Define America*. New York: Basic Books, 1991.

Ingersoll, Julie J. *Building God's Kingdom: Inside the World of Christian Reconstruction*. New York: Oxford University Press, 2015.

"Important Issues in the 2020 Election," Pew Research Center, August 13, 2020.

"Is Global Warming a Threat to the World Environment?" NAE, SC-113, box 51, folder 12 EEN/Environment (1 of 2), 1993–1995, Archives of Wheaton College., November 24, 1993.

Jamieson, Dale. *Reason in a Dark Time*. New York: Oxford University Press, 2014.

Jewett, Robert. *Mission and Menace: Four Centuries of American Religious Zeal*. Minneapolis, MN: Fortress Press, 2008.

Johnson, Alex. "Jerry Falwell Jr. Asked to Lead Trump Higher Education Task Force," NBC News, January 31, 2017. http://www.nbcnews.com/news/us -news/jerry-falwell-jr-asked-lead-trump-education-task-force-n715116 (accessed July 15, 2021).

Jorstad, Erling. *Evangelicals in the White House: The Cultural Maturation of Born Again Christianity 1960–1981*. New York: Edwin Mellen Press, 1981.

Kearns, Laurel. "Cooking the Truth: Faith, Science, the Market, and Global Warming." In *Ecospirit: Religions and Philosophies for the Earth*, edited by Laurel Kearns and Catherine Keller, 97–124. New York: Fordham University Press, 2007.

Kellstedt, Lyman A., John C. Green, James L. Guth, and Corwin E. Smidt. "Has Godot Finally Arrived? Religion and Realignment." *Public Perspective* 6 (1995): 18–22.

Kengor, Paul. *God and Ronald Reagan: A Spiritual Life*. New York: Regan Books, 2004.

Kent, Stephen A. *From Slogans to Mantras: Social Protest and Religious Conversion in the Late Vietnam War Era*. Syracuse, NY: University of Syracuse Press, 2001.

Kinch Jr., Sam Jr. "Steelman Doesn't Look Republican," *Dallas Morning News*, October 24, 1976, 12A.

Kintz, Linda. *Between Jesus and the Market: The Emotions That Matter in Right-Wing America*. Durham, NC: Duke University Press, 1997.

Kirk, Russell. *Economics: Work and Prosperity*. Pensacola, FL: A Beka Book Publication, 1989.

Kline, Benjamin. *First along the River: A Brief History of the U.S. Environmental Movement*. San Francisco: Acada Books, 1997.

Kohn, Hans. *The Idea of Nationalism: A Study in Its Origins and Background*. New York: Macmillan, 1944.

Koop, C. Everett, and Francis A. Schaeffer. *Whatever Happened to the Human Race?* Westchester, NY: Crossway Books, 1979.

Kosek, Joseph Kip. *Acts of Conscience: Christian Nonviolence and Modern American Democracy*. New York: Columbia University Press, 2009.

Laats, Adam. "Forging a Fundamentalist 'One Best System': Struggles Over Curriculum and Educational Philosophy for Christian Day Schools, 1970–1989," *History of Education Quarterly* 50, no. 1 (Feb. 2010): 55–83.

Lahr, Angela M. *Millennial Dreams and Apocalyptic Nightmares: The Cold War Origins of Political Evangelicalism*. Oxford: Oxford University Press, 2007.

Land, Richard D. "The Southern Baptist Convention, 1979–1993: What Happened and Why?" *Baptist History and Heritage*, 28, no. 4. (October 1993): 3–13.

Land, Richard D. and Louis Moore, eds., *The Earth Is the Lord's: Christians and the Environment*. Nashville, TN: Broadman Press, 1992.

Lappe, Frances Moore. *Diet for a Small Planet*. New York: Ballantine Books, 1971.

Larsen, David. "God's Gardeners: American Protestant Evangelicals Confront Environmentalism, 1967–2000." PhD diss., University of Chicago, 2001.

Layman, Geoffrey. *The Great Divide: Religious and Cultural Conflict in American Party Politics*. New York: Columbia University Press, 2001.

Laurie, Greg. *Occupy till I Come: How to Spiritually Survive the Last Days*. Eugene, OR: Harvest House, 1982.

Leege, David C., and Lyman A. Kellstedt, eds. *Rediscovering the Religious Factor in American Politics*. New York: M. E. Sharpe, 1993.

Leitch, Addison H. "Without Natural Affection," *Christianity Today*, May 11, 1973, 50.

Leithart, Peter J. *The Green Movement: It's False Claims and Religious Agenda*. Ft. Lauderdale, FL: Coral Ridge Ministries, 1992. 19–21

Lienesch, Michael. *Redeeming America: Piety & Politics in the New Christian Right*. Chapel Hill: University of North Carolina Press, 1993.

Lindsay, Michael. *Faith in the Halls of Power: How Evangelicals Joined the Evangelical Elite*. Oxford: Oxford University Press. 2007.

——. "Evangelicals in the Power Elite: Elite Cohesion Advancing a Movement." *American Sociological Review* 73, no. 1 (2008): 60–82.

Lindsell, Harold. *The Battle for the Bible*. Grand Rapids, MI: Zondervan. 1976.

——. *Free Enterprise: A Judeo-Christian Defense*. Wheaton, IL: Tyndale House, 1982.

——. "Suicide Ahead?," *United Evangelical Action* 29, no. 1 (1970): 13–17.

——. "De-Polluting Ecology Theology," *Christianity Today*, May 8, 1970.

——. "Waste as a Wrong," *Christianity Today* 19, April 11, 1975, 26.

——. "The Lord's Day and Natural Resources," *Christianity Today* 20, no 16 (1976): 816–20.

Lindsey, Hal, and C. C. Carlson. *The Late Great Planet Earth*. Grand Rapids, MI: Zondervan, 1970.

Lippy, Charles. *Being Religious American Style*. Westport, CT: Greenwood Press, 1994.

Lipset, Seymour Martin, and Earl Raad. "The Election and the Evangelicals." *Commentary* 71 (March 1981): 25–31.

Livingstone, David, D. G. Hart, and Mark Noll, eds. *Evangelicals in Historical Perspective*. Oxford: Oxford University Press. 1999.

Lyall, Sarah. "Earth Day 1990; Music and, Oh Yes, Earth Day in Park," *New York Times*, April 23, 1990. http://www.nytimes.com/1990/04/23/us/earth-day-1990-music-and-oh-yes-earth-day-in-park.html (accessed Feb. 2016).

Mackabee, Stephen T. "A Question of Authority: Religion and Cultural Conflict in the 2004 Election." *Political Behavior* 29, no. 2 (2007): 221–48.

Marcus, Eric. *Making Gay History: The Half-Century Fight for Lesbian and Gay Equal Rights*. New York: Perennial, 2002.

Marine, Gene, and Judith Van Allen. Food *Pollution: The Violation of Our Inner Ecology*. New York: Hold, Rinehart & Winston, 1972.

Marsden, George M. *Reforming Fundamentalism: Fuller Seminary and the New Evangelicalism*. Grand Rapids, MI: W. B. Eerdmans, 1987.

——. *Understanding Fundamentalism and Evangelicalism*. Grand Rapids, MI: W. B. Eerdmans, 1991.

Marsden, George M., ed. *Evangelicalism and Modern America*. Grand Rapids, MI: W. B. Eerdmans, 1984.

Marsden, George M., Mark A. Noll, and Nathan Hatch. *The Search for Christian America*. Westchester, NY: Crossway Books, 1983.

Marley, David John. *Pat Robertson: An American Life*. New York: Rowman & Littlefield, 2007.

Martin, William. *With God on Our Side: The Rise of the Religious Right in America*, 2nd ed. New York: Broadway Books, 1996.

Marshall, Peter and David Manuel, *The Light And the Glory: Did God Have a Plan for America?* Grand Rapids, MI: Fleming H. Revell, 1977.

Martocci, Laura. *Bullying: The Social Destruction of Self*. Philadelphia: Temple University Press, 2015.

Mayer, Allan J., John J. Lindsay, Howard Fineman, Stryker McGuire, Jonathan Kirsch, and Michael Reese, "A Tide of Born-Again Politics," *Newsweek*, September 15, 1980, 28–32, 36.

Mayer, William G., ed. *The Swing Voter in American Politics*. Washington, DC.: Brookings Institution Press, 2008.

McCammack, Brian. "Hot Damned America: Evangelicalism and the Climate Change Policy Debate" *American Quarterly* 59, no. 3 (2007): 645–68.

McCarraher, Eugene. *Christian Critics: Religion and the Impasse in Modern American Social Thought*. Ithaca, NY: Cornell University Press, 2000.

McCright, Aaron M. "Challenging Global Warming as a Social Problem: An Analysis of the Conservative Movement's Counter-Claims." *Social Problems* 47, no. 4 (2000): 499–522.

McIntire, Carl. "Ecology Anti-Christian," *Christian Beacon*, June 17, 1971, 1–2.

McVenn, Gertrude E. "Catching the Colt." In *Foot Prints: The Christian Reading Series*," edited by Laurel Hicks and Mike Davis, 78–79. Pensacola, FL: 1980.

McVicar, Michael J. *Christian Reconstruction: R. J. Rushdoony and American Religious Conservatism*. Chapel Hill: University of North Carolina Press, 2015.

Melvin, Billy A. "One Perspective on the Environment." *United Evangelical Action* (May–June 1990): 18.

Merk, Frederick, and Lois Bannister Merk. *Manifest Destiny and Mission in American History*. Cambridge, MA: Harvard University Press, 1995.

Merchant, Carolyn. *Death and Nature: Women, Ecology, and the Scientific Revolution*. San Francisco: Harper & Row, 1980.

Merrill, Karen R., ed. *The Oil Crisis of 1973–1974: A Brief History with Documents*. Boston: Bedford/St. Martin's, 2007.

Miller, Donald. *Reinventing American Protestantism: Christianity and the New Millennium*. Berkeley: University of California Press, 1997.

Miller, Timothy. *The 60s Communes: Hippies and Beyond*. Syracuse, NY: University of Syracuse Press, 1999.

Moore, Walter B. "Harris County's Cleanup," *Dallas Morning News*, January 14, 1971, 2.

Moore, Judy Hull and Stan Shimmin. *Exploring God's World*, edited by Laurel Hicks Pensacola, FL: A Beka Books, 1976.

Moreton, Bethany. *To Serve God and Wal-Mart: The Making of Christian Free Enterprise*. Cambridge, MA: Harvard University Press, 2009.

Murphy, Carlyle. "More Congregations Caring for Creation: Americans of All Faiths Are Looking at Environmental Issues from a Spiritual Perspective," *Waterloo Region Record*, February 7, 1998. B8.

Murphy, Carlyle. "Creation's Caretakers: More Americans See Conservation as Religious Mandate," *Fort Worth Star-Telegram*, February 8, 1998. 12.

Murray, Keith. "Suggestions Toward an Ecological Platform." In *The Environmental Handbook: Prepared for the First National Environmental Teach-In*, edited by Garrett De Bell, 317–335. New York: Ballantine Books, 1970.

Nash, Roderick. *The Rights of Nature: A History of Environmental Ethics*. Madison: University of Wisconsin Press, 1989.

Neuhaus, Richard John. *The Naked Public Square: Religion and Democracy in America*. Grand Rapids, MI: William B. Eerdmans, 1984.

Neuhaus, Richard John, and Michael Cromartie. *Piety & Politics: Evangelicals and Fundamentalists Confront the World*. Washington, DC: Ethics and Public Policy Center, 1987.

Newman, Mark. *Getting Right with God: Southern Baptists and Desegregation, 1945–1995*. Tuscaloosa: University of Alabama Press, 2001.

Nixon, Richard, "The Energy Emergency." In *The Oil Crisis of 1973–1974: A Brief History with Documents*, edited by Karen R. Merrill, 66–71. Boston: Bedford/St. Martin's, 2007.

Nixon, Richard, "Address to the Nation About Policies to Deal With the Energy Shortages," November 7, 1973. https://www.presidency.ucsb.edu/documents/address-the-nation-about-policies-deal-with-the-energy-shortages (accessed July 27, 2021).

Noll, Mark A. *Religion and American Politics: From the Colonial Period to the 1980s*. New York: Oxford University Press, 1990.

Numbers, Ronald C. *The Creationists*. New York: Knopf, 1992.

Oppenheimer, Mark. *Knocking on Heaven's Door: American Religion in the Age of Counterculture*. New Haven, CT: Yale University Press, 2003.

Paquette, Michael J. "Religious Group Seeks 'Greening' of Evangelicals," *Long Beach Press-Telegram*, April 16, 1994, A14.

Paquette, Michael J. "Religions Take 'Earth Day' Leap into Environmental Theology," *Washington Post*, April 16, 1994.

Peattie, Margaret Rhodes. "Dangers of Pioneer Life." In *Flags Unfurled*, edited by Laurel Hicks, 66–84. Pensacola, FL: A Beka Book, 1974.

Pinkston Jr., William S. *Biology for Christian Schools*. Greenville, SC: Bob Jones University Press, 1980.

Pinkston Jr. William S. *Life Science for Christian Schools*. Greenville, SC: Bob Jones University Press. 1984.

Pogue, Neall W. "The Religious Right's Compassionate Steward and Conservationist: The Lost Environmental Philosophies of Pat Robertson, 1977–1989," *Environmental Ethics*, 38, no. 4 (2016): 483–97.

Porterfield, Amanda. *The Transformation of American Religion: The Story of a Late-Twentieth Century Awakening*. New York: Oxford University Press, 2001.

Pride, Mary. *The Way Home (Beyond Feminism—Back to Sanity)*. Westchester, IL: Crossway Books, 1985.

The Princeton Religion and Research Center and the Gallup Organization, Inc., *The Unchurched American: Study Conducted for the Religious Coalition to Study Backgrounds, Values and Interests of Unchurched Americans*. Princeton, NJ: Princeton Religion Research Center, 1978.

"The Proud Oak Tree." In *Foot Prints: The Christian Reading Series*, edited by Laurel Hicks and Mike Davis, 61–62. Pensacola, FL: A Beka Books, 1980.

Putnam, Robert D. *Bowling Alone: Collapse and Revival of American Community*. New York: Simon & Schuster, 2000.

Quebedeaux, Richard. *The Worldly Evangelicals*. San Francisco: Harper & Row, 1978.

Rainey, Beverly, ed. *Of America Vol. II*. Pensacola, FL: A Beka Book, 1975.

Reagan, Ronald, Alfred A. Balitzer, and Gerald M. Bonetto. *A Time for Choosing: The Speeches of Ronald Reagan 1961–1982*. Chicago: Regnery Gateway, 1983.

Ricci, David M. *Why Conservatives Tell Stories and Liberals Don't: Rhetoric, Faith, and Vision on the American Right*. Boulder, CO: Paradigm Publishers. 2011.

Robbins, Jeffery W., and Neal Magee, eds. *The Sleeping Giant Has Awoken: The New Politics of Religion in the United States*. New York: Continuum, 2008.

Robertson, Pat. *Answers to 200 of Life's Most Probing Questions*. New York: Thomas Nelson Publishers, 1984.

——. *The New Millennium: 10 Trends that Will Impact You and Your Family by the Year 2000*. Dallas: World Publishing, 1990.

——. *The New World Order*. Dallas: World Publishing, 1991.

——. *The Turning Tide*. Dallas: World Publishing, 1993.

——. *Bring It On: Tough Questions. Candid Answers*. Nashville, TN: W. Publishing Group, 2003.

Robertson, Pat, and Bob Slosser. *The Secret Kingdom: A Promise of Hope and Freedom in a World of Turmoil*. Nashville, TN: Thomas Nelson, 1982.

Rome, Adam. *The Genius of Earth Day: How a 1970 Teach-In Unexpectedly Made the First Green Generation*. New York: Hill and Wang, 2013.

Rose, Susan D. *Keeping Them Out of the Hands of Satan*. New York: Routledge, 1988.

Rosenbaum, Walter A., ed. *Environmental Politics and Policy*, 7th ed. Washington DC: Congressional Quarterly Press, 2008.

Rothenberg, Stuart, and Frank Newport. *The Evangelical Voter: Religion and Politics in America*. Washington DC: Free Congress Research & Education Foundation, 1984.

Rowell, Andrew. *Green Backlash: Global Subversion of the Environmental Movement*. New York: Routledge, 1996.

Rozell, Mark J., and Gleaves Whitney, eds. *Religion and Bush Presidency*. New York: Palgrave Macmillan, 2007.

Ruether, Rosemary Radford. "Religious Ecofeminism: Healing the Ecological Crisis." In *The Oxford Handbook of Religion and Ecology*, edited by Roger Gottlieb, 362–75. Oxford: Oxford University Press, 2006.

Rudd, Robert. "Pesticides and the Living Landscape." In *DDT, Silent Spring and the Rise of Environmentalism*, edited by Thomas R. Dunlap, 75–79. Seattle: University of Washington Press, 2008.

Russell, Arlie. *Strangers in Their Own Land: Anger and Mourning on the American Right*. New York and London: The New Press.

Rushdoony, Rousas John. *The Institutes of Biblical Law*. Nutley, NJ: Craig Press, 1973.

——. *Law and Society: Volume II of the Institutes of Biblical Law*. Vallecito, CA: Ross House Books, 1982.

Saad, Lydia. "Americans Believe Religion Is Losing Clout," Gallup, December 23, 2008, http://www.gallup.com/poll/113533/Americans-Believe-Religion-Losing-Clout.aspx (accessed July 15, 2021).

Schaeffer, Francis A. *Pollution and the Death of Man: The Christian View of Ecology*. Wheaton, IL: Tyndale House Publishers, 1970.

——. *How Should We Then Live?: The Rise and Decline of Western Thought and Culture*. Old Tappan, NJ: Fleming H. Revell Company, 1976.

——. *Escape from Reason*. Westchester, IL: Crossway Books, 1968.

Schaeffer, Franky. *Crazy for God*. Cambridge, MA: Da Capo Press, 2007.Schellenberger, Michael, and Ted Nordhaus. "The Death of Environmentalism: Global Warming Politics in a Post-Environmental World." *Geopolitics, History and International Relations* 1, no. 1 (2009): 121–63.

Scherer, Glenn. "Christian-Right Views Are Swaying Politicians and Threatening the Environment," *Grist*, October 28, 2004. http://grist.org/article/scherer-christian/ (accessed July 27, 2021).

Scott, Lindy, ed. *Christians: The Care of Creation, and Global Climate Change*. Eugene, OR: Pickwick Publications, 2008.

Scully, Matthew. *Dominion: The Power of Man, the Suffering of Animals, and the Call to Mercy*. New York: St. Martin's Press, 2002.

"Seminary Student's Climate Change Project Is Not SBC's," *Baptist Press*, March 10, 2008. http://www.bpnews.net/27582/seminary-students-climate-change-project-is-not-sbcs (accessed July 27, 2021).

Sherkat, Darren E., and Christopher G. Ellison. "Structuring the Religion-Environment Connection: Identifying Religious Influences on Environmental Concern and Activism." *Journal for the Scientific Study of Religion* 46, no. 1 (2007): 71–85.

Short, Brant C. *Ronald Reagan and the Public Lands: America's Conservation Debate, 1979–1984*. College Station: Texas A&M University Press, 1989.

Silvius, John E. "Christian Stewardship of the Environment." In *A Life of Integrity: Right Choices*, edited by James M. Grier, John E. Silvius, Irene B. Alyn, Lois K. Baker. Schaumburg, IL: Regular Baptist Press, 1991.

Skinner, Kiron K., Annelise Anderson, and Martin Anderson, eds. *Reagan: A Life in Letters*. New York: Free Press, 2003.

Slotkin, Richard. *The Fatal Environment: The Myth of the Frontier in the Age of Industrialization*. New York: Harper Perennial, 1994.

Smidt, Corwin E., Kevin R. den Dulk, James M. Penning, Stephen V. Monsma, and Douglas L. Koopman. *Pews, Prayers, and Participation: Religion and Civic Responsibility in America*. Washington, DC: Georgetown University Press, 2008.

Smidt, Corwin E., and James M. Penning, eds. *Sojourners in the Wilderness: The Christian Right in Comparative Perspective*. New York: Rowman & Littlefield, 1997.

Smith, Christian. *American Evangelicalism: Embattled and Thriving*. Chicago: University of Chicago Press, 1998.

———. *Christian America? What Evangelicals Really Want*. Berkeley: University of California Press, 2000.

Smith, Christian, and Michael O. Emerson. *Passing the Plate: Why American Christians Don't Give Away More Money*. Oxford: Oxford University Press, 2008.

Smith, Oran P. *The Rise of Baptist Republicanism*. New York: New York University Press. 1997.

Smith, Samantha. "Pagan Howl-Le-Lu-Ia Chorus," *Metro Voice*, June 1996, 53.

Steinberg, Ted. *Down to Earth: Nature's Role in American History*. Oxford: Oxford University Press, 2002.

Stepp, Laura Session. "Denominations Find Common Ground in Saving the Earth," *Washington Post*, May 23, 1992.

Stevenson, Burton Egbert, ed. *American History in Verse*. Greenville, SC: BJU Press, 1975.

Strawser, Michael G., Matthew Hawkins, and Joe C. Martin, "Persuasive Ambassadors: The Southern Baptist Commitment to Religious Freedom for All." In *The Rhetoric of Religious Freedom in the United States*, edited by Eric C. Miller. Lanham, MD: Lexington Books, 2018.

Spitsbergen, Jean, Heather Fulfer, and Brian Ashbaugh. *Biology: God's Living Creation*. Pensacola, FL: A Beka Book, 1997.

Sprayberry, Noble. "Environmentalists Find Allies in Church," *Chattanooga Times*, April 18, 1996. A1.

Squires, Edwin R. "Good News Bad News Re: Our Environment," *United Evangelical Action* (May–June 1990): 5.

Stoll, Mark. *Protestantism, Capitalism, and Nature in America*. Albuquerque: University of New Mexico Press, 1997.

———. *Inherit the Holy Mountain: Religion and the Rise of American Environmentalism*. New York: Oxford University Press, 2017.

Stricklin, David. *A Genealogy of Dissent: Southern Baptist Protest in the Twentieth Century*. Lexington: University Press of Kentucky, 1999.

"Students in Texas to Note 'Earth Day,'" *Dallas Morning News*, April 14, 1970, 13.

Sutton, Matthew Avery. *Jerry Falwell and the Rise of the Religious Right: A Brief History with Documents*. Boston: Bedford, 2013.

———. *American Apocalypse: A History of Modern Evangelicalism*. Cambridge: Belknap Press of Harvard University Press, 2014.

"Taylor Announces New Environmental Center," *United Evangelical Action* (May–June 1990).

Tipton, Steven M. *Getting Saved from the Sixties: Moral Meaning in Conversion and Cultural Change*. Berkeley: University of California Press, 1982.

Tooley, Mark, "Gore's God," *Crisis* (October 1996): 25.

Thrapp, Dan L. "Christian Leaders Join Ecology Drive," *Los Angeles Times*, April 20, 1970, D12.

Thomson, Fred P. untitled editorial, *United Evangelical Action* (Fall 1970): 35.

Turner, John G. *Bill Bright and Campus Crusade for Christ: The Renewal of Evangelicalism in Postwar America*. Chapel Hill: University of North Carolina Press, 2008.

Vecchione, Judith. "Awakenings," *Eyes on the Prize*, interview of Amzie Moore, Public Broadcasting Service, 1986.

Veldman, Robin Globus. *The Gospel of Climate Skepticism: Why Evangelical Christians Oppose Action on Climate Change*. Oakland: University of California Press, 2019.

Vig, Norman J., and Michael E. Kraft. *Environmental Policy in the 1980s: Reagan's New Agenda*. Washington, DC: Congressional Quarterly Press, 1984.

Vig, Norman J., and Michael E. Kraft, eds. *Environmental Policy: New Directions for the Twenty-First Century*, 4th ed. Washington DC: Congressional Quarterly Press, 2000.

Vileisis, Ann. *Kitchen Literacy: How We Lost Knowledge of Where Food Comes From and Why We Need to Get It Back*. Washington DC: Island Press/Shearwater Books, 2006

Wagner, Melinda Bollar. *God's Schools: Choice and Compromise in American Society*. New Brunswick, NJ: Rutgers University Press, 1990.

Wald, Kenneth D., and Allison Calhoun-Brown. *Religion and Politics in the United States*, 6th ed. Washington, DC: Rowman & Littlefield, 2011.

Wald, Owen Hill, Dennis E. Owen, and Samuel S. Hill Jr. "Churches as Political Communities." *American Political Science Review* 82, no. 2 (1988): 531–48.

Walking, Alberta, and Mary R. Parkman, "Pioneers." In *Flags Unfurled*, edited by Laurel Hicks, 58–63. Pensacola, Florida: A Beka Book.

Weber, Timothy. *Living in the Shadow of the Second Coming*. Grand Rapids, MI: Academy Books, 1983.

"Wheeler Opposes Tax Hikes," *Dallas Morning News*, April 22, 1972, 11A.

White, Lynn, Jr. "The Historical Roots of Our Ecologic Crisis." *Science* n.s. 155, no. 3767 (1967): 1203–1207.

White, Richard. "Are You an Environmentalist or Do You Work for a Living?" In *Uncommon Ground: Rethinking the Human Place in Nature*, edited by William Cronon. New York: W. W. Norton.

Widman, Ron. "When You've Seen One Beer Can You've Seen Them All," *Eternity* 21, no. 5 (May 1970): 13, 14, 32.

Wilcox, Clyde. *God's Warriors: The Christian Right in Twentieth-Century America*. Baltimore, MD: Johns Hopkins University Press, 1992.

Williams, Emmett L. and George Mulfinger. *Physical Science for Christian School*. Greenville, SC: Bob Jones University Press, 1974.

Williams, Lindsey. *There Is No True Energy Crisis: An Eye-Witness Account Report*, pamphlet, 3, private collection, 1980.

Wilkinson, Katharine K. *Between God & Green: How Evangelicals Are Cultivating a Middle Ground on Climate Change*. New York: Oxford University Press, 2012.

Wilkinson, Loren, ed. *Earth Keeping: Christian Stewardship of Natural Resources*, Grand Rapids, MI: William B. Eerdmans, 1980.

Wilson, J. Matthew. *From Pews to Polling Places: Faith and Politics in the American Religious Mosaic*. Washington, DC: Georgetown University Press, 2007.

Wirt, Sherwood Eliot. "The Defilement of the Earth." In Sherwood *The Social Conscience of the Evangelical*, Eliot Wirt. New York: Harper & Row, 1968.

Witham, Larry. "Alliance Shuns Nature Worship," *Washington Times*, April 18, 2000.

Worster, Donald. *A Passion for Nature: The Life of John Muir*. Oxford: Oxford University Press, 2008.

Wright, Richard T. "Responsibility for the Ecological Crisis." *Bio Science* 20, no. 15 (1970): 851–53.

Wuthnow, Robert. *The Restructuring of American Religion: Society and Faith since World War II*. Princeton, NJ: Princeton University Press, 1988.

Zicklin, Gilbert. *Countercultural Communes: A Sociological Perspective*. Westport, CT: Greenwood Press, 1983.

INDEX

Page numbers with *italics* indicate illustrative material. Titles of written works will most easily be located under the author's name.